THE
SOUL &
SPIRIT
OF
TEA

Wild tea cultivar, Taiwan 2011. Photograph © Scott Chamberlin Hoyt.

THE
SOUL &
SPIRIT
OF
TEA

21 TEA-INSPIRED ESSAYS
FOR THE EARLY
TWENTY-FIRST CENTURY

Edited by Phil Cousineau & Scott Chamberlin Hoyt
with a foreword by James Norwood Pratt

Talking Leaves Press
New York City
2013

Talking Leaves Press
A Division of Tea Dragon Films
70A Greenwich Avenue
New York, NY 10011
www.teadragonfilms.com
info@teadragonfilms.com

"Top 20 Tea Definitions" reprinted with permission from *James Norwood Pratt's Tea
Dictionary* (Preliminary Edition) Produced & Published by: Devan Shah & Ravi
Sutodiya for Tea Society.

Cover design by Deborah Dutton.
Typeset in Weiser.

ISBN: 978-0-981-75534-2

Library of Congress Control Number: 2013945198

First Printing: Fall 2013

Printed in Canada

CONTENTS

Part I
THE FLAVOR OF TEA

Part II
THE SPIRIT OF TEA

Part III
THE FUTURE OF TEA

APPENDICES

Foreword

ENLIGHTENED SATISFACTION

James Norwood Pratt

Tea is the leaf of awareness. Like Zen, it is a direct transmission outside any scriptures that can bring a moment's peace and quiet, and this is tea's one reason for existing: we like the way it makes us feel. Tea provides a chance to pause, reflect and connect. Taken in solitude it helps us re-connect with our real self: tea gives the spirit an adjustment, as it were, which restores normal, healthy functioning. Shared with others, tea softens the heart at the same time it loosens the tongue: we talk easily and speak from the heart. Tea connects us in a community of spirit. Community is not simply where you live. It is also all about who you are and where your heart is. Children become adults and the old ones leave us but this ancient and now world-wide community has persisted over five thousand years and offers us harmony at any time we wish. Nothing has contributed more to human happiness and enjoyment of friendship, leisure, sociability and conversation than tea. It is the most benign form of hedonism and has become humanity's favorite habit.

James Norwood Pratt
San Francisco
Summer Solstice 2013

Preface

GOOD TEA, GOOD TIME

Scott Chamberlin Hoyt

I like to imagine *The Soul & Spirit of Tea* as a time capsule—a collection of stories drawn from a variety of perspectives, from history to direct personal experience (of experts and neophytes alike), to current cultural phenomena and scientific research. Of course, there are tea-legends that stem from direct transmission of the numinous kind—which to varying degrees, is occurring around and within us, all of the time. So in one sense, this is time capsule, of the timeless kind.

Twenty years ago, it seemed impossible to find good tea, even as I was spending the majority of my time in New York City. Then teas seemed to become even worse. The diversified consumer products (and failing pharmaceutical) company that I had helped break ground for at the age of 5 years old, was sending me back to the factory in New Jersey, after a long time away. I would have been completely tea-less, except for the fact that my office was only a 20 minute drive from the University town of Princeton. It was there that I discovered oolong teas from Taiwan. Paul Shu who with his wife Way Ming, had a ready supply of these wonderful teas—teas that made the difference between same-old tea, and good to excellent tea.

I learned only a few facts about tea, but nonetheless, the steady stream of tea that I was imbibing, increased and inspired my curiosity about Taiwanese high mountain teas. Over 7 years of visiting his shop, Paul would always seem reluctant to say much about where exactly he bought them, or even much about the tea growers themselves. He'd just ply me with tea, so that even the "back country" developments and mini-parks on the way home to the Jersey shore, seemed illumined at times. And so I began to realize increasingly, the utter and complete waste of resources involved in making synthetic mood altering single-entity drugs that always seemed to be accompanied by adverse side effects. (I knew that, from reading the literature of course!) And I learned first-hand, how the incredible peace and the serene nature of plant infusions, like that of TEA or camellia sinensis, the cultivar, the single plant species, gradually modified over thousands of years, and R&D'ed with tens of millions of human trials—could alter my life's course, and re-open my soul and my spirit, to a more vital reality.

Over the years of enjoying good tea, I have been fortunate to seek out and build meaningful relationships with like minded tea-people, people who adore and feel gratitude every day, for the Way(s) in which tea has enabled all of us, to appreciate the subtle; the living-in-the-moments, of tea.

There are perhaps, hundreds of books written about tea in the Chinese language, and unless you are a scholar of many ancient Chinese characters, we will never learn what they say. Even books like the I Ching are nearly impossible to decipher correctly, unless you are a scholar, well-versed in the old characters. You need not be anything more than a tea lover, to appreciate the essays in this collection. You need not wait to find out what is in this time capsule, 100 years from now.

I urge you to take all the time you need, to make time your friend, and savor these essays over many pots of tea. You will find that life is thriving elsewhere, certainly well-beyond the bounds of the Internet—and you will discover hitherto unknown aspects of tea, no longer hidden from plain sight.

Scott Chamberlin Hoyt
Danville, Vermont
Full Thunder Moon 2013

THE SOUL & SPIRIT OF TEA

Introduction

THE SPIRALING FORCE OF TEA

Phil Cousineau

"Find yourself a cup; the teapot is behind you.
Now tell me hundreds of things."

—SAKI

One somnolent summer day, in August 2012, I was researching the
origins of the word tea while drinking a memorable cup of Pu-erh
at Roy Fong's Imperial Tea Court in San Francisco. After an hour of
reading the devilishly fine print, I needed a break. Searching through
my road-burnished leather satchel, I found a copy of the current
Smithsonian magazine and riffled through its pages. A headline
caught my attention, an announcement of a momentous discovery
in its archives:

> "The Only Footage of Mark Twain in Existence:
> Silent Film Footage taken of Mark Twain
> at his estate in 1909."

You could have knocked me over with a tea leaf. It scarcely
seemed possible that my boyhood literary hero had been captured
on film, in 1909, the year before his death at seventy-three, and no

one had known about it for over a century. But it was the description of the footage that really made my eyes bulge with surprise: "Mark Twain Drinking Tea with his Daughters."

The synchronicity brought a smile to my face.

Quickly, I found a link to the Smithsonian website, swerved back to my laptop, and typed it in. Moments later, I was looking at a video view box that featured an old-fashioned black title card inscribed with white words:

Thomas Edison's title card from his short film on Mark Twain, 1909.

I was prepared for the reference to Twain's given name, Samuel Clemens, which I learned as a boy from my father when we read *Huckleberry Finn* out loud together, but I was totally unprepared for the film credit. Photographed by Thomas Edison? Who would've guessed?

While I wondered about the curious collaboration, the title card dissolved into the opening shot. It was none other than Mr. Clemens himself, appearing like an apparition in the doorway of Stormfield, his "charmingly quiet" estate in Hartfield, Connecticut. Strange bands of twisting white light flowed around him, as if Edison had filmed him through some kind of newfangled ectoplasmic lens, or during an eruption of the aurora borealis. Underscoring its age, the grainy footage crackled and flickered, unsurprising considering the one hundred-plus years of deterioration it had endured. Still, the rapscallion author looked triumphant, standing like a sentinel in his trademark white suit, defiantly tugging at his ever-present cigar, shifting his weight from side to side, looking uncomfortable about the very idea of being filmed. After a lifetime of seeing only static images of him in photographs, it was unnerving to see him, well, *move*, which is to say come to life (which has always been the secret strength of movies).

After several restless seconds, Twain strode up the gravel path of his garden toward the camera (probably one of Edison's original Kinetoscopes)—and suddenly vanished. A split second later he magically reappeared in full stride around the far corner of the house and scurried across the gravel path, as if in a hurry to take tea with his daughters. Passing by the camera, he blew a puff of smoke from his cigar and vanished again. Then another filmcard appeared and once again the scene shifted, this time to the terrace of his estate, where "The Father of American Literature," as William Faulkner described him, was sitting with his two daughters in high-backed rattan chairs around a rectangular table with a samovar-like teapot set in the center.

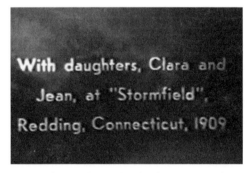

With daughters, Clara and Jean, at "Stormfield", Redding, Connecticut, 1909

Thomas Edison's last title card, which mentions his daughters.

The sudden film cuts were fascinating because they reminded me of how editing in the movies can seem to suspend time and space. One minute we're here, the next minute we're there, as if in a dream. Watching Twain drink tea with his daughters transported me a hundred years and three thousand miles. It was 1909 and I was there, sitting at a table with them, marveling at how Edison had persuaded the famously frenetic Twain to slow down long enough to be filmed.

All it took was time and tea.

Consider the marvel of what is captured here.

The proud father beamed like the Pharos lighthouse as he dropped two teaspoons of sugar into his teacup, crooked his elbow and took a sip. His daughters drank gracefully from their own cups, followed again by their father, who muttered a few silent words. A butler in black waistcoat approached and offered a floppy sun hat to Clara. She plopped it on her head and smiled at her sister Jean. Twain took two more sips. A sly smile appeared on his face.

What I would give to know what he was saying. Small talk was unheard of where Mark Twain was concerned. Was he complaining about how everybody complains about the weather but nobody does anything about it? Was he gently reminding them about their mother, Olivia, who had died five years before, about how much she enjoyed taking time for tea every afternoon?

Mark Twain, and daughters Clara and Jean, Stormfield House, 1909.

Ultimately, it doesn't matter as much what they were talking about as much as the fact that they were taking time and making space for tea, which in turn provides the freedom for leisurely talk, laughter, and pleasure.

After watching the film clip the first time, an old thought of D. T. Suzuki's came to mind. Writing in his classic *Zen and Japanese Culture* he said, "Who would then deny that when I am sipping tea in my tearoom I am swallowing the whole universe with it and that this very moment of my lifting the bowl to my lips is eternity itself transcending time and space?"

THE SOUL & SPIRIT OF TEA

After their third cup of tea, Twain and his daughters stood and walked away, as if at the silent command of their director, and vanished into the steam of time.

THE SIMPLEXITY OF TEA—OR SIMPLEXITEA

Only one hundred and forty-seven seconds, less than two minutes of film footage, have elapsed. Yet it feels far longer, as if the filmstrip has been stretched like amusement park taffy. Nothing, but everything, has happened. It is an elegant example of what scientists call *simplexity*, the process by which the simplest of actions achieve the most complex results. *Simplexity* is also the goal of this anthology, a simple celebration of the complex forces that writhe within tea plants, which in turn help stir the life within us.

The fascination with the surging life force is a very old one. The Welsh poet Dylan Thomas described it as "The force that through the green fuse drives the flower. . . ." The French philosopher Henri Bergson called it the *élan vital;* Martin Luther King, Jr., the soul force; the ancient Latins, the *genius loci*. Years ago, a wise old Comanche Indian, Buster Parker (Quanah Parker's grandson), described it to me as *something holy moving through the world*. So mysterious is it that when the British astronomer Sir Arthur Eddington was asked to describe the animating power in the universe he said, "Something Unknown is doing we don't know what."

For many years, I have thought of it as the oscillating force, the alternately rising and falling energy that has been described for millennia, in countless cultures from New Guinea to New Mexico, as *spirit and soul*. And depending on the quality of the time we take, the space we make, the mood we are in, and the type of tea we choose to drink, the serpentining energy in tea will rise and fall within us.

A Refreshing View of Tea

To explore the phenomenon of the spiraling energy in tea, we have enlisted the work of twenty-one contributors to "tell [us] a hundred things," as the short story maven Saki suggested we do around the teapot. Among those sitting around our tea table are tea scholars, scientists, filmmakers, journalists, a musician, an architect, a monk and a Taoist priest, two tea estate owners, and the grandson of one of the most famous tea drinkers of the twentieth century. Not unlike Wallace Stevens' "Thirteen Ways of Looking at a Blackbird," this book revels in the many ways we can regard tea, as "the news that stays the news." These essays can be read consecutively, or savored one at a time, like samples of tea from exotically painted canisters in your favorite tea shop.

For instance, the scholar and poet James Norwood Pratt describes the spirit of tea as inextricably connected with the spirit of the times in America, which is seeing a major cultural shift in tea consumption, which he says forebodes a "happier, healthier" society. For him, the force within tea is due to its "liquid sunshine," which is a gift to the world, a transmission of peace and pleasure.

The scholar Aaron Fisher writes about tea as a medicine in the indigenous sense, an "adaptogenic" plant that has the power to heal whatever needs healing. He reminds us that the ancients described tea as the true meeting place of Heaven, Earth and Man. Fisher poetically cites the plant's two streams of energy: "Teas, like Pu-erh, are grounding, connecting us to the spirit of the mountains and earth; but a fine Oolong is uplifting, freeing us from the daily coils we orbit to roam the drunken clouds."

The Taoist scholar Sat Hon reminds us that alchemy is one of the oldest metaphors for tea, since it is "a metaphor for resurrection, while tea is the living manifestation of rejuvenation itself. As the tea-leaf is rejuvenated from its shriveled state back to its full vigor with scalding water, so does the alchemist who returns from a death-like state by a jolt of awakened consciousness."

The British journalist Sarah Murray paints a Turnesque portrait of the great age of tea clippers as an entry point to better understand the "immutable bond" that water has with tea. Her essay echoes the view of the old Japanese tea masters, that "the quality of a brew is largely determined by the nature of the water used to make it." Her piece is a tocsin call to remind us that "without pure, clean water there is no tea."

The English architect Jonathan Winpenny beautifully articulates the importance of sacred time and space, citing his grandmother's advice, "Simmer down then . . . Time must stand still for high tea." His essay is a call for us to create "a corner of the world to call your own." Douglas George Kanentiio, an Iroquois journalist, uses a Cinemascope-like lens to depict life in the Canadian logging camps, where native workers made their own teas out of local roots and often survived while other workers perished. "All plants have their own reality," he writes, "their own duties and powers. Each is not only unique but is given the gift of life and must be respected if its full potential is to be realized." An unusual perspective is provided by Zen scholar J. L. Walker, who discovers the role of the archetypal fool in the world of tea. "To evoke a recognition of the essential wholeness of Heaven, Earth, and Humanity is the function of the fool in the teapot." She also reminds us of the intertwining relationship between meditation, tea, and enlightenment, concluding, "Tea also cannot be described in words, but only tasted directly right here and now."

The Indian tea plantation owner and scholar Rajah Banerjee's essay is an exercise in offering positive solutions to the unfortunate trend of losing fertile tea ground to the plague of pesticides. "When asked why we take the time and trouble to promote biodynamic tea farming I like to say that it awakens both the farmer and the consumer to the realization that the agricultural practices are determined by the earth's evolution." Another unusual perspective is offered by the singer-songwriter Jen Ahlstrom. Her interest in tea is in its influence on creativity. "I believe that tea can provide a space, a channel for this inspiration to pass through," partly she concludes, because tea and creativity both share the wonder of providing "A lifetime compressed into one moment."

Dr. Selena Ahmed is a scientist studying human-environment interactions with a special focus on sustainable agro-ecosystems. Her essay looks at "terroir," the taste of the place," which is the result of spirit of land infusing spirit of tea. In its optimal state it can produce the sensory delight of a great tea, such as Pu-erh, but can be jeopardized by influences like climate change. "Since my very first interviews in Yunnan in 2006," she writes, "farmers have been reporting that the climate has changed and impacted their tea agro-ecosystems." The reason it is important to protect our ancestral tea lands, she reminds us, is because "Each cup of tea is a unique experience. To be remembered but never experienced again."

THE WISDOM OF TEA

Years ago, I hiked the Samaria Gorge, in Crete, with a local guide named Nikos Maskaleris. One night we indulged in a number of different drinks, ranging from Mythos beer to Ouzo, coffee to a wonderful local tea. When I asked him how he knew when to drink what, he said, "Oh, you're talking about *phyllosophia*, the wisdom of plants." He smiled like Anthony Quinn in *Zorba the Greek*, and said, "Just trust your heart. It knows what you need."

Years later, in 2012, I found myself back in Crete where I was leading one of my annual mythological study tours. On the day we visited the nearly four-thousand-year-old Palace of Knossus our local guide, George Spiradakis, asked if we would like to take our afternoon picnic in the nearby private gardens of the man who discovered the site, in 1900, Sir Arthur Evans. Casually, he added that we could use the same Roman marble table where the famous English archaeologist took his afternoon tea. For three years, he said, Evans excavated the vast ruins, and over the next five years sat at his Roman tea table day after day transcribing and trying to decipher the thousands of mysterious clay tablets he had unearthed there. The tranquility of the garden and comfort of his favorite tea allowed him to "pause, and reflect and connect," as James Norwood Pratt describes the myriad benefits of tea. After Evans published his findings he was besieged with visitors from all over the world who were eager to meet him and explore the site. After giving them a tour of the ancient palace he invited them to share a cuppa tea at his beloved Roman table, which he found to be the most amenable place on Crete to discuss the wonders of the lost world of the Minoans.

I thought of Nikos, George, and Arthur Evans recently while reading *The Man Within My Head*, Pico Iyer's marvel-marbled book about novelist Graham Greene. There he describes a strange but wonderful custom for travelers arriving in Bolivia. The first thing they do is imbibe the local coca tea, *mate de coca*, to help them adjust to the thin atmosphere. Without that little adjustment, Iyer writes, it can take forever to get used to the new world you have just entered.

As a self-proclaimed scavenger after metaphors, I see this traveler's tale as emblematic of what human beings have done for at least the last five thousand years. Thirsty and exhausted souls from the Inuits in the Arctic to the Indians of Brazil, Paraguay and Uruguay have enjoyed various forms of tea to help them adjust to changes in their environment, alter their moods, or simply wake up their senses. As Norwood Pratt insists, this is a special gift that nature has provided for us. And for that, as the Iroquois journalist Douglas George describes his own people's use of tea, we should be grateful. "Each person was free to take a cup of tea," he writes, "stand before the people and give verbal thanks for its healing properties." The essays that follow all share that sentiment in common. We, too, are free to take a cup of tea and free to give thanks for its healing forces, and free as well to pass on the good news of this wondrous plant.

Incidentally, that day at the Imperial Tea Court, I discovered that the root of our English word tea is a tangled but fascinating tale. The tea scholar Victor H. Mair traces it back to the Chinese (Amoy dialect) *t'e*, which in Mandarin is *ch'a*, both of which were spread across the world first by caravans to Tibet and India, and then by Dutch and English ships to the European continent. Eventually, the leaf and the word were carried to the Americas, where it was discovered by the bard Leonard Cohen, who expressed the sentiments of millions of us when he sang, "I was blessed with a passion for tea."

Phil Cousineau
San Francisco
Spring 2013

Big Island Tea owners Eliah Halpenny and Cam Muir stand in the shade of the native forest they are re-establishing around their tea garden.

Part I

THE FLAVOR OF TEA

Chapter 1

THE WATER IN YOUR TEACUP

Sarah Murray

It was the nineteenth-century equivalent of a photo finish. On September 6, 1866, three magnificent vessels surged forward on the same tide and docked in London to the roar of waiting crowds. The ships, *Serica*, *Ariel*, and *Taeping*, had arrived within minutes of each other. And while in most races the time separating contestants at the finish line is measured in seconds, the arrival of three sailing ships on the same day—let alone within the same hour—was remarkable.

These vessels, which had set off from the other side of the world some three months earlier, were contenders in the annual Tea Race, a 16,000-mile contest running from Foochow (today's Fuzhou) in southeastern China back to England. But this was no ordinary race event. It was an event the British public followed with all the excitement of a Super Bowl, with huge bets placed on the vessels and cash prizes for victorious captains. Nor were the contestants ordinary cargo carriers. These were crack sailing ships, daring feats of marine engineering representing the very latest in seaborne technology. With vast billowing sails gathering its gusts, the wind was the gas in their tanks. But speeding the passage of these nineteenth-century speed machines was yet another powerful, free and natural force: Water.

Water has an immutable bond with tea, from the boiling liquid needed to infuse its leaves, to the moisture sucked up from the soil by tea bushes clinging to a hillside plantation, to the soft rains that nourish the plants as they grow. In India, water is right there in the phrase "chai pani," which means "tea water" and has also come to refer to a tip (a little extra cast with which to pick up a snack, or even a cuppa'). When it comes to the brewing, it's said that the quality of water and its mineral content has a significant effect on tea's taste. In ancient China, the belief was that tea made using spring water from high up in the mountains resulted in the best infusion (with water from wells making the worst). Japanese tea masters also assert that the quality of a brew is largely determined by the nature of the water used to make it.

For nineteenth-century tea clipper captains, the relationship with water was a logistical one, expressed through their skills as navigators and their ability to harness the ocean currents to steer their vessels home as fast as possible, and clipping as much off the average three-month sailing time as they could. Velocity was of the essence. At the time, it was thought that the freshest and earliest-picked leaves created the best brew. So reaching home ahead of the pack brought not only public acclaim but also monetary rewards in the form of the premium that could be charged on each pound of the "first flush," or newest teas, of the season—with the price rising if the leaves arrived in one of the Tea Race's winning vessels.

First, however, the tea clippers had to undertake a long and arduous voyage. They generally headed down through the South China Sea towards the Sunda Strait and into the Indian Ocean. From there, they rounded the Cape of Good Hope, on Africa's southern tip, and sailed across the Atlantic Ocean, through the Doldrums, past the Cape Verde islands and up the English Channel through the Thames to London. It was dangerous, too. Piracy was rampant out on the ocean. And if they escaped the clutches of waterborne criminals, sailors faced monsoons and severe storms. Yet, for the captains and their crews, the perils made the arrival home that much sweeter, particularly when greeted by enraptured crowds waiting eagerly on the docks.

Thanks to the genius of the Scottish shipbuilders who designed and constructed the tea clippers, captains had at their disposal the world's fastest cargo vessels. Their composite construction combined the strength of an iron frame with sleek wooden hulls sheathed in copper. With knife-like edges, the hulls sliced through waves, while robust sterns countered the effects of large swells in the fiercest of squalls. Traveling at about seventeen knots (equivalent to more than twenty miles per hour), they achieved a speed that's extraordinary even by today's standards. While modern yachts have surpassed them in speed, no commercial vessels have since outdone them. Meanwhile, above water, all was a flourish of sails and seaborne swagger. Billowing clouds of white fabric not only gave the tea clippers the glamour that would inspire countless paintings, but also the ability to continue sailing with only the tiniest breath of wind, allowing them to "ghost" gracefully along the ocean even in the calmest of conditions.

Today, the millions of tons of tea that are traded globally by multinational companies every year still travel on water. But instead of the graceful creatures that "clipped" along the ocean's surface in the nineteenth-century, tea is moved across the high seas inside twenty-foot metal shipping containers carried by vast industrial vessels, the biggest of which could accommodate an ice hockey rink, an American football field, and a basketball court. These cargo-carrying giants are low-slung crafts with several warehouses-worth of goods piled high on their decks.

The brain behind container shipping was a North Carolina truck driver born in 1913. Worried about the competition from ships to his trucking business, Malcom McLean came up with the idea of simply driving loaded trailers onto vessels—his own vessels. As his ideas developed, he realized that a far more efficient use of space would be to do away with the wheels of the trailers and simply use the trailer bodies. Enter the shipping container.

On April 26, 1956 he put his idea into practice. That day, what one reporter described as an "old bucket of bolts" set sail from the port of Newark, New Jersey, and headed down the East Coast for Houston, Texas. The vessel, a converted Second World War tanker, was a curious-looking craft, but with its reinforced deck carrying fifty-eight metal boxes, Malcom McLean's *Ideal-X* became the first-ever scheduled container ship service.

His invention was to end break-bulk shipping, a laborious system whereby each piece of cargo had to be separately loaded, packed, arranged, and unloaded—a practice that had altered little in centuries. In the process, it changed the way chests of tea were handled. In the old clipper days, expert Chinese stevedores had stowed tea chests in the ship's hold individually, placing each carefully onto bamboo matting to protect them from damp. Today, once loaded into a shipping container, consignments of tea can simply be lifted by cranes on and off ships, in one quick and easy movement.

The container helped transform not only the tea trade but also the world economy. It's a revolution that has escaped our attention. Few people notice containers or think about what's inside them. But more than 90 percent of global trade travels in these robust metal boxes. Almost everything we touch today has at some point been in a shipping container, and more than two hundred million of them move across the oceans each year, many containing the world's supplies of tea. Yet the voyage of cured leaves across the ocean is only part of the drink's connection with water.

One of the most important moments in the relationship between tea and water occurs in the home. The flow of boiling water onto the leaves is what, after all, produces a cup of tea. Some of us even use hot water to warm the pot before starting to make the tea. And pouring water onto cured leaves is a serious business—an act that in some places, with the help of Zen Buddhism, has evolved into an elaborate ceremony lasting several hours.

In nineteenth-century Britain, brewing tea even acquired seductive potential. In a scene from Mary Elizabeth Braddon's sensational 1862 novel *Lady Audley's Secret*, Lucy Audley, the heroine, offers her husband's dashing nephew, Robert Audley, a cup of tea. Braddon wrote:

> Surely a pretty woman never looks prettier than when making tea. The most feminine and most domestic of all occupations imparts a magic harmony to her every movement, a witchery to her every glance. The floating mists from the boiling liquid in which she infuses the soothing herbs, whose secrets are known to her alone, envelop her in a cloud of scented vapor, through which she seems a social fairy, weaving potent spells with Gunpowder and Bohea.

However, long before any "floating mists" of boiling water can be harnessed in the making of a cup of tea, the leaves of the *Camellia sinensis* plant must be cured. And at this stage in tea's lifecycle, water is the very last thing that producers want near their valuable commodity. For as anyone versed in the standard method of production knows, water is not part of the processing of tea. In fact, the process focuses on removing moisture, not adding it. After harvesting, the leaves are laid out in the open until they become limp. They are then spread out on metal trays in a factory where warm air removes all moisture from them. By the time the rolling and firing processes are complete, tea is just about the driest product you can get.

So where does tea consume most water? It starts back on the tea estate, where the bushes require constant supplies of water to flourish. In fact, it takes a total of thirty-five liters of water to produce a single cup of tea, according to the United Nations Food and Agriculture Organization. The FAO's calculations assess what's known as the "embedded" or "virtual" water in products—in tea's case, that's the total volume required to turn tea from a tiny seedling to a healthy bush and then to its final form, as a steaming cup of perfumed liquid.

Of course, as an agricultural commodity, tea is not alone in tapping heavily into the world's reserves of water. Agriculture accounts for more than 70 percent of global water consumption, and in developing countries, which are responsible for growing much of the world's tea, this rises to more than 90 percent. (By contrast, industry uses only about 23 percent of global water supplies.) When it comes to embedded or virtual water, countries that export water-intensive products are effectively exporting their water supply. Meanwhile, the global population is continuing to expand, and as developing countries become wealthier, their citizens are acquiring an appetite for water-intensive foods, particularly meat (a single beef steak takes an astonishing 7,000 liters of water to produce). Many estimate that food demand will increase by 70 percent to 90 percent by 2050, leading to a doubling in the amount of water needed to feed the world.

But back to our tea—35 liters certainly sounds like a lot of water for a single cup. And it is. Yet when you consider other drinks, tea's water footprint looks relatively light. By contrast, coffee requires 140 liters of embedded water to produce one cup, with wine not far behind it at 120 liters a glass. Beer is a somewhat more modest water consumer at 75 liters per glass, but orange juice beats the lot, taking some 170 liters to produce one glass. Compared to these thirsty drinks, tea starts to look like a more sustainable product in its water consumption. Moreover, tea plantations are often rain fed, not usually requiring the industrial irrigation systems needed to raise many agricultural commodities.

Nevertheless, tea does take its toll on the world's water supplies. Like all crops, the chemical fertilizers that are used in industrial cultivation can run off into the surrounding soil, polluting groundwater, lakes and rivers. Since tea is often grown on steep slopes, the force of gravity increases this effect. And while tea production requires little use of herbicides, the plant is susceptible to soil-borne fungal diseases and parasitic worms, which means that farmers often use nematicide (a type of chemical pesticide) on their tea estates.

In its ocean-borne journeys, tea also has a hand in water pollution. Those modern cargo vessels may be highly efficient forms of transport, but they use water as a ballast to stabilize the vessel—water that is later emptied into harbors or coastal waters. What this means is that what's collected on one side of the world—containing everything from marine-borne plants and fish to small invertebrates, bacteria and the eggs and larvae of various species—can find itself washing up against entirely foreign shores. Once there, these alien species may reproduce and start to compete for resources with their native marine neighbors or, worse still, wipe them out altogether, threatening the ecological health of the world's oceans.

Even tea's packaging may have an impact on water. That plastic wrapping around the box may help keep the contents fresh, but if it doesn't get dumped in landfill, it could end up in the ocean as part of the Great Pacific Garbage Patch, a vast mass of marine trash twice the size of Texas. This floating collection of discarded man-made material consists mainly of plastics, which do not break down but instead turn into plastic particulate, or polymer fragments. These gradually become smaller and smaller, but they never disappear, remaining suspended forever at the upper levels of the ocean.

This is all very worrying, for when it comes to water consumption, the challenge the world faces is not only excess consumption but also the contamination of its precious supplies, whether fresh or salt water. And if it's not being polluted, water is a resource that's becoming increasingly scarce. In Africa, fourteen countries are already experiencing water stress, according to the WWF, with another eleven expected to face this challenge by 2025. Some studies estimate that, if no efficiency improvements are made to the way we use water, by 2030 one third of the planet's population (mainly people in developing countries) will be living in parts of the world where there is less than half of the water volumes they need to survive and prosper.

Companies, governments, global institutions and non-profit organizations are starting to think about this. Some are taking action. The International Maritime Organization has, for example, developed guidelines for preventing the spread of unwanted organisms through the discharge of shipping ballast water. On tea estates, organizations such as the Rainforest Alliance are helping farmers make more efficient use of water in agriculture.

Small modifications can have a big impact. Water harvesting and drainage systems can increase water conservation, while creating stone bunds, or barriers—particularly the sloped grounds of many tea plantations—helps prevent the run-off of pesticides and other chemicals into neighboring water systems. Fostering biodiversity around tea plantings helps reduce the need for those chemicals in the first place by increasing natural pest and disease control. And when irrigation is needed, drip systems consume less water than sprinklers, helping increase the "crop per drop."

Such changes cannot come soon enough. For with no action, the consequences are dire. More of the world's population could be deprived of the water needed to remain clean and healthy. Water prices could rise sharply. Production of staple foods could slow to dangerously low levels. Rivers, lakes and reservoirs—many already threatened—could dry up. As riots in countries from Algeria to India have demonstrated, chronic water shortages can lead to civil unrest. And where water flows across borders, pressure on supplies can even spark wars.

So what about the future of tea drinking? Tea consumption has come a long way since the eighteenth and early nineteenth centuries. Back then, tea was a precious commodity that was affordable only to rich individuals and families, who kept their supplies locked up in beautifully crafted wood tea caddies decorated with intricate veneers or ivory inlays. Today, tea is the second most popular drink in the world after water. Shipped across the world in vast quantities and packaged in cardboard and plastic, we take it for granted. Yet without pure, clean water there is no tea. So unless more is done to preserve global water supplies, this fragrant drink could one day regain its place among the world's rarer luxuries.

Sarah Murray is a specialist writer on environmental sustainability and author of *Moveable Feasts—From Ancient Rome to the 21st Century, the Incredible Journeys of the Food We Eat.*

Chapter 2

RIDING THE BLACK DRAGON
THE DAO OF OOLONG TEA

Aaron Fisher

From the plains below, the silvery peaks were lost, wandering above the clouds. Far above, past where even the most adventurous dragons soared, the gardens of Mount Peng Lai glistened in the morning sun. And wallowing in a remote pond of blue lilies, the great golden water tortoise Jing sat in the mud, gloomy and forlorn, his once radiant form a dulled bronze. Occasionally, the mists below would part and for the briefest moment he would look down to the earthly realms below and shine golden rays of joy on the pond, illuminating all the waters around him and cascading dapples of gloss on the blue lilies that surrounded him. The old tortoise was nostalgic watching the humans far below Heaven. He remembered the times when the children of Heaven visited him and rode on his back, and he would have long chats with the Jade Emperor himself, his oldest and dearest friend. But no one had visited him in the last eon, including the Emperor (presumably because he was busy with more important matters of court).

On one such dreary day, the old turtle finally made up his mind that he would pay a visit to court, in hopes that the august emperor would remember their friendship. He took a long time walking ever so slowly to the palace, feeling uplifted by his quest. After a short wait, he was admitted to the court.

"My dear friend, Jing!" The Jade emperor exclaimed, extending his hands in an offering of welcome.

"Your highness," he replied, bowing low.

"What has brought my old friend from his lily pond to court on this fine day?"

"Your holiness, in honor of my long service to your majesty and all the joys we shared together in the gardens, I have a small request to ask of you." The old turtle spoke slowly and eloquently, impressing the court with his manners.

"Why anything, my friend. Ask what you will and it shall be granted," the emperor said.

Shining more brightly, the old turtle asked: "I wish to be reborn on earth as a tea tree, your majesty."

Extremely surprised, the Jade emperor stroked his long beard. No one had ever requested permission to leave Mount Peng Lai.

"Why in all the Heavens would you wish to be incarnated as a tree?" he asked.

"For a long time now I have watched the lands below. I have seen the great reverence the people show to tea trees, and I long to be loved and relished as they are. In that way, my spirit will be amongst the people and in their lives. For all the ages, my children will also be worshipped and cared for. I will become a legend and shine golden once more."

Impressed with the old turtle's sentiments, the Jade Emperor granted his wish. And soon thereafter a beautiful tea bush was discovered on Mount Wuyi, with the brightest crown the people had ever seen. They say that each morning, its leaves would glow with an otherworldly halo, and that those who drank its Empyrean nectar would be transported to the gardens of Heaven on the back of a black dragon.

THE WAY OF TEA

Before we climb out onto the thick branch of Oolong on the great Tea tree, we might first take in the garden and soil—the *terroir*—that surrounds Her. Knowing about where this ancient tree has sprouted, as well as the size and shape of Her glorious trunk, will give us some perspective and appreciation for the growth and girth that holds out the branch called Oolong. She's an ancient tree, and there is so much more than we can say about Her here, but hopefully we'll find the inspiration to continue studying the sutras She's written in the veins of each of Her leaves. A life spent searching for and learning Her ways would not be wasted. In surveying the landscape where Tea was born, honor demands that we first pay homage to the Great Nature Tea sprung out of, for in the vast tome of Tea, man would only come into the last few pages of the story. The first million years or so, those old trees sat in the virgin forest, perhaps meditating on their future greatness in humanity. This vast well of Nature—trees covered in nascent dew—is the real origin and heritage of Cha Dao. Beyond a deep bow, however, there isn't much we can say about those forested eons, as no human words intruded upon those pristine landscapes, so any hope we have of glimpsing them will come through the drinking.

PALEOLITHIC TEA

In remote Yunnan, birthplace of all tea, three-thousand-year-old cave paintings have been discovered. They depict people gathering and processing tea, suggesting just how far back into antediluvian mists mankind's relationship to the Leaf extends. Amongst the paintings, we also find several images portraying people worshipping the old tea trees, laying fruit and flowers, incense and prayers beneath the Leaf they so revered. Nowadays, we often forget this reverence, belittling it with sentiments about how tea was once "medicine to Chinese people," which is true. But that's only part of the story.

When we say that tea is medicine, we are returning it to its place amongst the heritage of our human story and all the light its pages are gilded with. It isn't "medicine" in the modern sense of the word, as a substance that heals a particular illness, but rather in the way that a Native American would use the word: as that which connects us to Mother Earth and all life in harmony. This means anything that brings alignment and health to body, mind or spirit, all of which not only aid in our connection to Nature but also result from it.

This is, in fact, the paragon of all our individual and collective woes, for as we've moved towards grander states of awareness, we've also cultivated a greater and greater respect for harmony with Nature and an understanding of how far we've strayed from congruous life-ways. As such, tea is indeed a great healer, uniting us body, mind and soul with the forest trees, and through them the Earth: water, wind and mountain, as well as what's beyond our small planet, through the sun, moon and starshine they gather into their leaves.

The spirit of Tea is, therefore, an aspect of the Mother spirit of our Earth. Within these very leaves we can find connection to the mountain and water at their source, as well as the cosmic bodies they photosynthesized into our physical world. And all of this wants to be human, as that is what the Earth does—it peoples! Fortunately, it also teas . . .

We humans all too often forget that we grew out of this Earth as much as the trees; and in drinking tea the weather finds its way into our body, mind and soul, allowing us to feel spring or winter in an incredibly intimate way. We are, of course, animated by what we consume: the essence of the tea we drink quickly vanishes, diffusing into our own spirit until we are seeing with Tea's eyes. For that reason, I often paint pictures of a steaming bowl of tea without a drinker and add some calligraphy that says: "Tea drinks Man." Her spirit truly brings us back into alignment with our own nature, and thus in harmony with all the cosmos. As the sage once said: "Man follows the Earth, the Earth follows the Universe, the Universe follows the Dao, and the Dao follows only itself." And there are many hoary tales that suggest the way Tea's spirit has sought out its own destiny in mankind.

They say that the great emperor Shen Nong was meditating in the forest when a tea leaf fell into his boiling water. After a sip, he exclaimed: "This is the greatest of all medicinal herbs!" Shen Nong, which means "Divine Farmer", is said to have reigned for a thousand years, though what he really represents is the collective wisdom of pre-civilized, aboriginal China and the birth of civilization—apparent in the fact that he is attributed with teaching the people to farm, boil water, harvest medicinal herbs, etc. The legend of tea's origin in his old pot (*ding*) is, like most myths, fertile with meanings and shifts in perspective that we can, borrowing on his name, "harvest" fruitfully even today.

The most obvious and important aspect of Shen Nong's story is that the tea sought him out. In our tradition we have a saying: "As the man seeks the Leaf, the Leaf seeks the man." It is good life wisdom as well. The myth is showing us that tea wanted to be human, that it was calling out for his attention. Tea is one of the plant kingdom's calls to us, speaking sutras of our origins in Nature: it was designed to be human. And we have receptors for it—body, mind and soul. If you've ever drunk a living tea, and felt the way it connects to you, then you know what I mean. Some would say that tea and man co-evolved these thousands of years, and that the receptors are there because of our ancestors' relationship to the Leaf, which might explain why some people have a greater affinity for tea—more of their ancestors drank it. However, I am a hopeless romantic. I like to think that our receptors for tea were there long before Shen Nong took that first sip, and that we were like estranged lovers fated to meet. It seems only natural, as we also grew out of this Earth.

TEA AS MEDICINE

The other aspect of this old legend I'd like to explore (I leave the rest to you) is that Shen Nong called tea the greatest of all medicinal herbs. And he was an expert in the field, discovering, categorizing and teaching herbal science to the Chinese people. Tea's healing powers are related to the fact that it is "adaptogenic", which means that it has the power to heal whatever needs healing. Most herbs and medicines are medicine when used to treat a particular illness, and poison otherwise.

Tea, however, adapts to the needs of the drinker, not just physically, but spiritually and psychologically as well. When you have problems, drink tea; when there aren't any problems, drink tea! Tea, like the liquid that carries its essence, gets into the cracks of life. It flows where it is needed, aiding in most physical healing. It also has a way of encouraging whatever intention we set for our tea session: whether celebratory, as a way of making peace or binding marriage, or as a way of promoting deeper and more still meditation. The spirits of this world sing so many songs to us, but none so long lasting or as pronouncedly healing as tea.

Since the first sip that human beings enjoyed several thousands of years ago, tea has fully immersed itself in its human journey. It has been the currency of nations, brought peace, founded empires, and spread to every continent. It has been offered in marriages and funerals, and even today spans the entire spectrum of human experience, fueling everything from greed and materialism to the highest of spiritual states. It is the second most consumed beverage on the planet, after water. It also extends deep into our history, with thousands of years of heritage and culture. And when you add to its already voluminous story the books about the people who made any one of its thousands of wares—like the generations of Japanese who have carved bamboo whisks for example—tea's story becomes vast indeed.

There is timelessness in tea. Her sutras are scribed in the deeper, nonverbal veins of a leaf and communicated directly to our bodies. As we turn away from Her majestic trunk towards human refinement, let us not forget just how deeply into the Earth and beyond Her words reach, remembering—each of us—to turn as much or more to the guidance in Her healing liquor as we do to the exploration of Her limbs, specifically Oolong tea . . .

THE DAO OF OOLONG TEA

Oolong tea, the "Black Dragon," is the pinnacle of all tea production. It is the Leaf taken to its most human form, sophisticated and refined to create a work of art way beyond what Tea's simple leaves could give on their own. It is a testament to the reasoning behind putting the radical for "man (人)" in the center of the Chinese word for "tea (茶)." No longer the simple leaves tossed into a bowl, or boiled in a side-handled pot, when Tea reaches this limb of Her vast tree, we find ourselves in the elegant courts of old, with winged roofs and nearby waterfalls as the backdrop for all the finery of silk and top-knots held up with ornately carved woods.

There is a common misconception promulgated by tea authors and vendors that all tea is a single species, *Camellia sinensis*, and that the differences in teas are all to do with processing. This is in part true, but also rather misleading. There are two main kinds of tea trees, small and large leaf. The large leaf varietals are the original trees, blossoming in Southwestern Yunnan, where the jungles are vibrant and the waters cascade down from the great Himalayas to the West. These trees have a single trunk and deep roots. As tea traveled East and North, whether naturally or propagated by man, it evolved to the colder climates, forming smaller bush-like plants with many small trunks and roots that expand outwards. The leaves also got smaller and smaller as tea migrated North, until they reached frosty Japan where the leaves are so diminutive that they look like threads or needles when they are dried.

This evolution happened rapidly, for tea is a sexual plant, and its seeds therefore produce unique plants each and every time they are planted. Of course we can use cuttings, clipped branches that clone the original, to propagate varietals we like, and that is what is usually done these days. However, most tea plants long ago were completely unique, ensuring that some of them would adapt to the new environs they found themselves in. And as tea evolved, so did the processing.

The cell walls of plants are thick, and so boiling was the only way to get at the liquor deep inside the leaves that were first plucked by man. But over time, She taught us how to process and dry the leaves in ways that would uncover their inner secrets. Consequently, the different methods of processing tea co-evolved in response to the different varietals in different regions. In other words, the farmers and master processors were listening. And that is why it is confusing to say that Oolong tea is merely a kind of processing, for it developed in response to certain varietals in the province of Fujian. While one might process tea from other regions like Oolong—and many are doing this—the results will never be the same as when an Oolong varietal is matched with expert processing.

This skill of listening and harnessing the inherent nature of a tea bush is everything Oolong tea is about. In Chinese, this is called "Gongfu", which means "mastery". It means doing something in the Way (Dao) that is in harmony with its inherent nature. The best art is always done this way: the master asks not what she wants from the medium, but what it wants from her. Michelangelo often said that his amazing sculptures were already in the stone, and he but removed the superfluous material around them. Watching a master make Oolong inspires one with the same passion.

It's five a.m. on Mount Wuyi, birthplace of Oolong, and the pickers have all assembled in the courtyard waiting for the master. He casually strolls downstairs, looking around at the mountains his grandfather's grandfather made tea in, when they carried stones several kilometers to build the majestic terraces that guard the old trees. He goes up to the hill and sits for some time, surveying the weather. Finally, he decides there'll be no picking today. The next morning, this age-old scene repeats itself, only the master decides that today is the day, sending the pickers off to gather the tea. Later, the leaves will be masterfully processed by hand in the traditional way: withered indoors and out, carefully monitored at every step. A charcoal brazier might be placed in one corner when the master magically recognizes the higher humidity there simply by walking through the

THE SOUL & SPIRIT OF TEA

room. Next the tea is periodically shaken, dancing around a bamboo tray to bruise the edges red. Though this looks easy, it takes years of practice. Then it is pan-fried to arrest the oxidation and rolled to break down the cell walls.

Finally, the tea is roasted over charcoal with great care. These masters only have one harvest a year, and their whole income is based on it. There are more steps in this process than any other kind of tea, and each requires a greater precision and mastery to produce a fine Oolong. They rarely sleep during the tea season, instead spending their days walking amongst the trees and supervising the picking of the leaves, which wither in the afternoon and are then processed throughout the evening and night.

Farmers carried thousands of heavy stones across kilometers to build the dreamlike terraces here, which draw the eye up the cliffs, past the old tea bushes to the waterfalls and lush green ecology, then on to the amazing purple of an evening sky. Each stone was hand-carried, weighing several kilos, to its final resting place, where it has gathered moss these hundreds of years; and each one has a story. And then the trees themselves have been painstakingly cared for, some old grandfathers themselves from the time the garden was built, looking down from their porches at their descendants below. *Shui Jing Gui*, Golden Water Tortoise, is among them, even today. The skill and mastery that goes into the processing of each leaf, refining the plucked leaves into the golden liquor they will one day be, is awe-inspiring.

All of this effort, time, energy and heritage shine from the leaves before us. And it is our job to brew them with as much reverence and refinement as they were cared for, plucked and processed. In doing so, we also continue this tradition of Gongfu tea. As with Gongfu production, Gongfu preparation is about brewing the tea the way it wants to be brewed. It is a practice of grace and beauty, honing ourselves as much as the tea. For it is through us that the leaves will find their culmination, and we are here at their behest. Perhaps we're reminded of the old Chinese story in which a student asks the master how to brush the perfect scroll of calligraphy, and the master casually replies: "Perfect yourself and paint naturally."

In fine Oolong tea we find the gauge of our progress, for it responds to the brewer like no other tea; what teaware we use to imbibe it, which water and from where, how we pour the liquor, in what direction and from how high—are all very relevant in taking the music to its crescendo, fulfilling the potential in our tea that began with the stones carried up into those cliffs three hundred years ago.

It will take us a lifetime to master this, for it is in all that we do. More than any teaware or methodology, the spirit of the one brewing is what most influences the tea. And if we're to make great tea, we must first learn to be great people. A man of tea (*Chajin*) is preparing tea throughout the day, for he knows that what he eats affects his tea: how he walks and breathes, how he treats others—all affect his tea. If we are to make a refined liquor, we must also refine ourselves.

In this way, tea ennobles man. It uplifts us and teaches us peace and calm association with one another, also connecting us to the Nature it arose out of. With tea, we are the people we were always meant to be: in harmony with Nature and one another. They say that in finding the Dao of a thing, you find the Great, Eternal Dao. The best a man can do is to master something, and in doing so master himself. If one succeeds, one will have found the magical place where human action meets the cosmic, in line with all that is.

There was once a famous martial artist who came to have tea with my master. The man carried an energy that betrayed his power and skill in all his movements, from the way he walked to the way he sat down on the bench. My master brewed a fine old Wuyi Cliff Tea for him. As we sat for an hour or so, the martial artist was uplifted, carried aloft from under old Lu Tong's armpits. When his spirit finally found its way back to his mortal coil, his eyes were pacified and his body soft, his previous alertness and skill defeated by a cool tranquility he could but surrender to. With a sly grin, my master leaned over the table and said: "You see, my Gongfu is greater than yours!"

From the unique evolution that crafted these bushes to the centuries of processing skill honed to Her form, dancer following dancer in step. . . . From the Leaf to our tea space and all the decades of practice, so much energy and poetry have manifested in this cup. And if we've succeeded at all, its fragrance will allude to these notes: melodies overlaying rhythm in intricacy that delves deep down into subtleties not ordinarily available to the mortal man; the aromas and flavors layered over one another like a string section; the Qi in our bodies keeping rhythm, while the spirit of this old Black Dragon summons us aloft with the wind instruments. Is it, then, a surprise that we wax poetic in Her presence?

There is nothing like the magic when all the elements of a fine Oolong tea come together. It is transportive. We feel somehow lifted from our terrestrial cages to soar amongst the bottom reaches of Mount Peng Lai on the back of this "Black Dragon" we've captured, not daring to enter the true sanctum above. We understand now why the ancients said of tea that it was the true meeting place of Heaven, Earth and Man. Other teas, like Pu-erh, are grounding, connecting us to the spirit of the mountains and earth; but a fine Oolong is uplifting, freeing us from the daily coils we orbit to roam the drunken clouds. Like the dragon (*long* 龍) that is its namesake, we too muster poetry and inspiration from the water we boil and spring into the air, unfettered at last.

To brew such tea with mastery concludes the symphony of tea, trumpets blaring from Nature to a refined Oolong processed and prepared to perfection by mastered hands. And within our souls, such tea does sing: of poetry and grace, of times where people flew with dragons rather than in metal planes. It tells us of the cloudwalkers up past the mists of Wuyi, where the dragons roam with our now-drunk spirits. In the tea space, we find the peace our civilization was founded on, our art and our spirit. And that old tortoise shines, from his perch amongst those cliffs, his Heavenly joy once again so radiantly renewed.

Aaron Fisher (Wu Wei Hai, "Wu De") is the Senior Managing Editor of all English Publications at Wushing Publications, Ltd., a contributor to the magazine *The Art of Tea*, and co-founder and editor-in-chief of the online magazine *The Leaf* (www.the-leaf.org).

Chapter 3

THE TERROIR OF PU-ERH TEA AND HUMAN WELLBEING

Selena Ahmed

What growing factors contribute to our final experience when we drink a cup of tea? This is the terroir of tea, or the taste of place. Terroir involves the complex interactions of environmental and cultural factors that shape agricultural products. This French word derives from terre, or land. It is one of my favorite words because it emphasizes the crucial role of human-environment interactions in imparting distinct sensory characteristics and health properties to our food, beverages and botanicals. The concept of terroir highlights links between environmental and human wellbeing by relating that what is good for the land is also good for us.

Tea (Camellia sinensis; Theaceae) is a wonderfully diverse product. Over 1,700 years of human management has interacted with natural selection in topographically varied areas and resulted in an explosion of tastes and aromas. Here, we take a journey to indigenous agro-forests in the motherland of the tea plant, Yunnan Province of southwestern China, to explore the terroir that gives us diverse sensory delight during pu-erh tea drinking. We get to the root of place in communities where I have been conducting socioecological research on tea since 2006 to understand the role of environmental and cultural variation for overall tea quality. Get ready for muddy paths. The journey into the terroir of pu-erh tea is rich with complex interactions.

DEFENDING TERROIR

We pass a dusty frontier town along the national highway in the China-Burma borderlands towards the heart of tea country. Taking a left turn off the highway onto an unpaved road, my favorite tea mountain sits in all its magnificence directly in front of us. Rice paddies vibrant with Dai harvesters in brilliant hues stretch across the landscape on either side of us as we make our ascent. Three months ago this road was flurried with local farmers bringing tea to market and entrepreneurs eager to buy fresh spring tea at source to ensure legitimacy of terroir labels. That was the dry season. Now in August, towards the end of the East Asian Monsoon, no cars have passed these roads for three weeks, and very few cars have made the journey for the past two months. It is not worth the risk of the mud capturing your vehicle and a 15,000 RMB vehicle repair charge for the type of damage wreaked by roads carved by heavy rains.

As a researcher with an agenda, I make the journey year after year during the monsoons by foot or vehicle. The well-trodden 1996 Jeep driven by Mr. Liu that we have hired for the occasion is now king of the road. We need not worry about vehicles approaching in the opposite direction side-scraping us towards the edge of steep roadsides. During the monsoons, it is the roads themselves that twist and turn us, throwing us sideways, no matter how Mr. Liu steers. His driving is not to be disregarded. He has been driving on these roads since many years before the first entrepreneurs declared these mountains the ultimate tea destination, as well as many years before most local farmers acquired licenses to drive vehicles purchased from pu-erh tea wealth.

Along our ascent, we stop at a watering hole that is a central gathering location in an Akha village, so that we can request to borrow a shovel in case we find ourselves stuck in mud. An Akha man returns some minutes later with a hand-carved shovel made from local hardwood and passes it to Mr. Liu, then resumes filling up his bucket and walks away. Mr. Liu calls after him to question where he should return the shovel and the man tells us to place it near the watering hole on the way down. This is the code of these tea mountains—to help a traveler, no questions asked.

News of our vehicle's movement up the mountain rapidly carries from village to village, as family and friends alert each other by mobile phone that the roads are now passable. By the time we near our destination village, an SUV fashioned with extensive detailing is driving out towards the lowlands. We later learn that this SUV only returns to the village after an unsuccessful attempt out. The rains are a gentle reminder and check and balance that the climate is in control, no matter the rapid rate of development spurred by China's pu-erh tea market. The monsoons remind local farmers to hold on to subsistence ways of life and not rely 100% on a cash economy.

As the village of Bujalpuxveeq appears in the distance, I am warmed by a familiarity that makes me smile. I envision the spiritual gates made of bamboo and rattan that guard this village from intruders and negative energy. Traditional Akha village gates have hand-carved male and female figurines at each side of the gate which are replaced each year. As my eagerness to drink a cup of tea with my local hosts escalates, we meet an armed checkpoint. Two men dressed in army fatigues and belted with machetes surround the car and peer through the windows. In the highland hinterlands of the China-Burma border, one's imagination can run wild of our encounter.

This is not a military checkpoint and these are not militants. These are local Akha tea farmers. They are checking our vehicle for outside tea and defending their terroir. Tea from the agro-forests of Bujalpuxveeq fetches some of the highest prices in the world. Akha farmers are proud of their ancestral tea systems; they are intricately linked to their cultural heritage, livelihoods and wellbeing. Local Akha governance prohibits tea from outside the village to enter in order to prevent false labeling of terroir. Without official product regulation, well over a hundred times the amount of tea falsely labeled from this village floods the market, compared to what is actually produced.

In a nearby village with equally prized terroir as that of Bujalpuxveeq, it was not too long ago that several households purchased low quality tea from the lowlands and mixed and sold it with their tea. Knowledge of this product falsification by tea businessmen resulted in a drop in the tea prices and a serious hit to livelihoods for the entire village that is still trying to redeem itself from this terroir labeling mishap. To prevent a similar situation, local farmers in Bujalpuxveeq have taken to defend their prized terroir to the extent they can at the village level, through fines and social ostracism for product falsification at site. A few local farmers that violated these regulations were forced to treat the community to a buffalo sacrifice, paid fines upwards of $10,000 USD, and were subjected to social ostracism from community gatherings.

What about Bujalpuxveeq's terroir and resulting tea have earned it this attention among the most sought-after pu-erh? A visit to Abo's home and tea agro-forests will enlighten us. But first, lets back up with some background on pu-erh tea in Yunnan.

WHAT IS PU-ERH?

The classification of pu-erh is muddied, which well suits the earthy taste characteristics of this tea. On the basis of existing taxonomic evidence, I support that pu-erh botanically refers to processed leaves and buds of the broad-leaf variety of the tea plant, Camellia sinensis var. assamica (L.) O. Kuntze, in the Theaceae, or tea, family. However, some scientists contend that pu-erh is a species of its very own. This may be the case but is not clear given existing genetic and morphological evidence, including a scientific article that I co-authored on DNA barcoding of tea samples for Nature Publishing Group's Scientific Reports (Stoeckle et al. 2011). In this article, Mark Stoeckle, Damon Little and a team of budding scientists, Catherine Gamble, Rohan Kirpekar and Grace Young, the latter three of whom were high school students at the time, sequenced samples of reference pu-erh leaf material from Yunnan that was classified by botanists at Kunming Institute of Botany. Findings from this study showed that this pu-erh leaf material was not genetically distinct from reference samples of the assamica variety but was genetically distinct from the sinensis variety. As additional genetic work unfolds to support or refute the hypothesis that pu-erh is a species of its own, I will stick to the claim that pu-erh is sourced from the very same species and variety as black teas of the large-leaf variety of the tea plant.

The Pu, an ancestral people of the Mon-Khemer language family who are related to the Bulang, Wa and De'ang socio-linguistic groups of Yunnan, are regarded as the first cultivators of the tea plant (Huang 2005) in agro-ecosystems that date back over 1,700 years (Xiao and Li 2002). Geographically, pu-erh production primarily occurs in Yunnan Province of southwestern China, the ancestral home of the Pu. Pu-erh production also occurs to a lesser extent in the neighboring provinces of Sichuan, Guangxi and Guizhou. I accept the extended geographic classification that pu-erh can be produced in habitats in countries that I view as the "tea belt," which likely encompass the center of origin of the tea plant. The tea belt stretches from southwestern China into Burma, India, Laos, Cambodia, and Vietnam. Tea is a multicultural citizen and has become a global citizen uniting cultures.

Pu-erh can be processed as a loose or pressed green tea or a post-fermented black tea. Processing of loose green pu-erh starts with withering and pan-frying leaves to remove moisture content and deactivate enzymes, such as polyphenol oxidase, that oxidize tea's antioxidant compounds and contribute to its taste and health properties. Leaves are then rolled either by hand or, increasingly, by mechanical grinders in order to break down the plant cell walls for further preservation. Finally, leaves are spread out on mats under the sun to dry and capture the "taste of the sun" (tai yang wei). The incomplete deactivation of enzymes for pu-erh compared to green tea, coupled with sun drying, results in a distinct oxidizing process and a smooth taste with age. Dried green pu-erh leaves can be steamed and compressed into various shapes in bamboo or stone molds. Historically, pressed green pu-erh was a main commodity on the caravan trade routes now collectively known as Tea-Horse Road (Chama Dao) or Southern Silk Road, the oldest tea trade route in the world. It was also one of the highest trade routes of the ancient world, which photographer Michael Freeman captured so beautifully in our three-kilo book, *Tea Horse Road: China's Ancient Trade Route to Tibet*. Along its journey of hundreds and thousands of kilometers, tea oxidized and fermented as it interacted with moisture and temperature fluctuations, and its flavor transformed to a smooth earthiness. Today, producers and connoisseurs try to recapture the flavor of this ancient trade route by storing green pu-erh in clay jars, bamboo baskets, caves, and underground pits. Alternatively, the characteristics of aged pu-erh can be artificially imparted by heap fermenting loose green pu-erh after the rolling process using a microbial food-processing technology (*hou fa jiao*, "post-fermentation," "cooking," or "ripening") of inoculating leaves with select microorganisms and controlling temperatures and moisture content.

TEA ECOLOGY AND CO-EVOLUTION

Tea is an elegant plant. It is especially elegant in its native habitat and form. The tea plant stands tall as a woody plant species up to twenty meters tall in evergreen broad-leaved forests rich with biodiversity in all its glory. Lu Yu's *Chajing* ("Tea Canon") of the 7th century, which many regard as the first monograph on tea resources, opens with a statement emphasizing the large stance of the tea plant in its native habitat: "Tea comes from an extraordinary tree of the South" and continues, "whose girth is one that requires two men to embrace it". The native habitat of tea plants in southern Yunnan is tropical and sub-tropical forest that has been recognized as a global hotspot of biodiversity, the Indo-Burma hotspot of biodiversity. Yunnan's variable landforms and microclimates seek to fuel this biodiversity and are an essential component of the terroir of pu-erh tea.

Along with biological diversity, cultural diversity influences Yunnan's biodiversity and contributes to the terroir of pu-erh tea. Yunnan Province is home to at least twenty-six socio-linguistic groups that have been involved in either tea production or consumption for centuries. These cultural groups have produced and consumed pu-erh for its health and stimulant properties as well as for its cultural and ritual values. The diverse human-environment interactions where pu-erh is sourced in Yunnan result in a botanical product that is highly heterogeneous in terms of sensory and health attributes.

Scientists have uncovered fossil evidence suggesting that tea plants evolved from two Magnolia species including Magnolia latifolia and Magnolia miocenica in forests of southwest Yunnan (He 1997). The original tea variety was thus probably the assamica variety that grows in southwestern Yunnan and differentiated into the sinensis variety above 25 degrees north in the Yunnan-Guizhou Plateau (Ming 1992). At present, both varieties are found across tea-growing regions, and hybridization occurs where these varieties overlap, resulting in hundreds of cultivars.

Genetic diversity of pu-erh results from hybridization among cultivars, as well as through exchange with other species that are closely related to the tea plant in the taxonomic section Thea of Camellia. There are a total of twelve species in section Thea that are all referred to as "wild tea," or that which is other than the commercial tea plant, Camellia sinensis. A process known as introgression, which is essentially genetic exchange, occurs among these tea relatives due to natural and horticultural processes. The process of introgression from wild tea germplasm can benefit cultivated tea by providing the genetic base for greater resilience to environmental change, as well as for human preferences such as increased yield, disease and drought resistance. The tea plant and its ten wild relatives are distributed in the Yunnan-Guizhou Plateau, with Yunnan as the center of diversity of tea resources (Ming, 1992; Ming and Zhang, 1996; Chang and Bartholomew, 1984; Ming, 2000; Long et al., 2003).

I have observed farmers directly harvesting wild tea species instead of cultivated Camellia sinensis due to accessibility, personal taste preferences and select medicinal properties. Other times I have observed farmers collecting seeds of wild tea species from forests surrounding their communities and introducing these into their tea-gardens. This allows these farmers to exploit a wide range of unique phytogenic characteristics. For example, Akha farmers that I interviewed for an article that I co-authored in the interdisciplinary journal *Ecology and Society* shared that they introduce wild tea seeds into their gardens and manage tea germplasm on the basis of their preference of leaves with large area, plucking shoot weight and color, as well as medicinal, stimulant, and sensory attributes. When I brought some of these tea samples from forests and cultivated tea gardens into the lab for phytochemical analysis, I confirmed that human selection has indeed influenced the phytochemical composition of tea and its resulting properties.

PU-ERH TEA AND HUMAN WELLBEING

Similar to that of green tea, the health benefits of green pu-erh derive from polyphenolic catechins and the stimulating properties derived from caffeine. Catechins and caffeine are secondary metabolites that plants produce as defense compounds against predators, pathogens, oxidative stress, and protection from other environmental variables. Rooted and unable to move when attacked or under stressful environmental conditions, plants have evolved these defense compounds as protection. Some of these secondary metabolites such as catechins just so happen to be beneficial to humans that consume them. Given that secondary metabolites are defense compounds, their concentrations vary widely with environmental conditions. The more stressed a plant, the more secondary metabolites it is likely to produce.

Aged green pu-erh and post-fermented black pu-erh have additional health claims unique to fermented foods and beverages. Microorganisms in aged and black pu-erh create fermentation-derived compounds known as statins. Historically, pu-erh was primarily used as a medicine that was harvested from forests and eventually co-evolved with humans into a beverage product cultivated in agricultural ecosystems. Pu-erh tea is valued in traditional ethnomedical systems of Yunnan's diverse socio-linguistic groups for its ability to strengthen the immune system, improve circulation, balance the body's hot and cold levels, detoxify blood, treat rheumatism and stones, remedy headaches, clear skin conditions, promote oral hygiene, treat stomach conditions, and reduce swelling and soft tissue. It is further valued for its nutritional value, including providing essential nutrients, aiding in digestion, and regulating weight. Pu-erh is also valued for its role in mental wellbeing, because it invigorates the mind and relieves stress (Ahmed et al., 2010).

We now turn our attention back to the prized terroir of my favorite tea production village to better understand what makes two cups of tea processed and prepared in the exact same way taste different.

REFLECTIONS ON TERROIR

We are greeted by Abo's glowing eyes as we enter his home. This is the face that welcomed me to these tea mountains over six years ago, a face that comforted me in a land unknown to me, and has since welcomed me back with the warmest sense of home. Abo places the black kettle on the kitchen hearth that is characteristic of the area. The Akha always have a fire burning, no matter how warm the ambient temperature. It is their source for heating water, transforming raw foods to cooked foods, and processing and preparing tea. Abo walks over the rattan mats where pu-erh tea harvested the previous day has been drying overnight. He grabs a small handful of tea and throws it into the black kettle directly on the fire. Without any measurement, a perfect brew. That is knowledge and experience.

We bring our tea, in white enamel cups imprinted with the "double happiness" marriage symbol (standard ware from the Cultural Revolution era) to the veranda. It's the golden hour for light and for admiring the cultivated agro-forests around the village. As always, I am transported to Abo's oldest tea agro-forest as soon as the steam from the infusion warms my face. The very same tea prepared from water in the lowlands several kilometers away does not induce this experience, and drinking this tea when I am home in the U.S.A. is even farther away. Here, tea plants flourish as trees three to nine meters tall in a semi-cultivated, semi-forested environment. Some are dripping with orchids like jewels in radiant yellows and surreal blues. Mist and fog in the early harvest hours nurture these trees and accompany a morning orchestra of birdcalls. A rich canopy provides a perfect balance of sun and shade for tea plants from above, and deep black topsoil feeds these plants from below with a mineral content that seems ideal. The slope, too, is considered just right: not too steep or too flat for perfect drainage. The high altitude just under 1,800 meters provides ample oxidative stress for tea plants to produce defensive secondary metabolites, which are ultimately what gives tea its medicinal and flavor attributes. The dry spring and autumn seasons concentrate tea flavors, and the rains dilute flavor. The western exposure of the slope and accompanying hours of direct sunlight ensures balanced development of growth and flavor compounds.

At the ecological, species, and genetic levels, these tea gardens are packed with diversity. Abo cultivates over ten tea cultivars in his oldest tea agro-forest that is half a hectare in size. It is not only tea in these agro-forests, but dozens of other woody tree species that local farmers rely upon for food, medicine, fiber, and timber. The structure, function and biodiversity of this agro-forest mimics a forest environment in many ways and provides many similar ecological services. The dense forest cover around the agro-forest further acts as a buffer from pests and disease, as well as from winds that can dry out the flavor profiles of tea plants. Thus, there is no need for the application of herbicides, pesticides and fertilizers for beautiful tea-leaves that will embrace you with high-octane flavor. In fact, farmers sometimes intentionally allow certain caterpillar species to infest their tea systems for amplification of particular flavor compounds. These agro-forests are much more on target with "sustainable agriculture" than simply "organic".

THE SOUL & SPIRIT OF TEA

Local Akha value their old tea trees as ancestral gifts. In many cases, local farmers are cognizant of the ancestor who planted each tree and discern various taste and medicinal attributes for each plant. Some of the most respected of the tea trees are considered relatives themselves. There is a lot of love and respect for these tea systems.

All of these elements and their interactions are part of the terroir, a key indicator of tea quality. Remove an element, and the system is changed. Your sensory experience and health benefits derived from tea drinking are changed.

In an article that I recently published in Conservation Letters with collaborators at the New York Botanical Garden, City University of New York, Minzu University of China and University of Florida, we show that tea quality from the terroir of such agro-forests has higher secondary metabolite content and variation than from the terroir of tea grown in forests, mixed crop fields, and monoculture terrace plantations. Thus, humans that drink tea from these agro-forests procure higher health benefits implicated in tea consumption. Why may tea agro-forests have the highest amounts of secondary metabolites? My hypothesis is that tea in monoculture terrace plantations are pampered with pesticides, herbicides and fertilizers and thus do not have the ecological cue to produce secondary defense compounds. On the other extreme, forest populations have higher plant species richness and thus more host species for pests. In addition, forests have greater ecological services such as soil fertility compared to agro-forests, and thus tea plants in these systems are less stressed out.

What does all of this mean in the context of climate change, the multiplier of all risk? This is the question that I am currently addressing with collaborators at University of Florida, Tufts University and Minzu University. What we do know is that each cup of tea from diverse terroir is a unique experience, to be remembered but never experienced again.

Selena Ahmed, PhD, is an Assistant Professor in Sustainable Food Systems at Montana State University. Her
research expertise is in the ethnography, ecology, and phytochemical quality of tea agro-forests of Yunnan, China.
She is currently focusing on how climate change impacts
the medicinal and sensory quality of botanicals and socio-
economic responses. Selena has widely published on tea,
including a co-authored large-format book with photographer Michael Freeman, *Tea Horse Road: China's Ancient Trade
Route to Tibet*, along with over a dozen scientific papers. This
work builds on her training on health (NIH TEACRS Post-
doctoral Fellowship at Tufts University), biology and plant
sciences (PhD from the City University of New York and
the New York Botanical Garden), anthropology and ethno-
botany (MSc from the University of Kent at Canterbury,
UK), and economics (BA from Barnard College). Selena
loves carrying out field research, training students, and engaging in educational outreach.

Chapter 4

THE MYSTERY OF TASTE BUDS

Jason Walker

Taste is a tricky word to pin down. The base mechanics of taste refer simply to the stimulation of the gustatory calyculi—commonly known as taste buds. The debate goes on as to how many "tastes" the tongue can register, and the intensity to which different people can perceive those tastes. Sweet, sour, salty, and bitter tastes are generally accepted. Along with number of tastes to detect, there is the question of the intensity and duration with which tastes can be detected. To further complicate matters, we live among both normal and super-tasters who possess varying concentrations of taste buds on their tongue surfaces.

But the mouth's sensations offer more than what the taste buds can capture. And so taste has also come to mean a combination of taste and smell. "Taste" gets wrapped up with flavor and aroma, but flavor and aroma relate most often to the sensations of the nose. Food and drink deliver aromas through the front of the nose as well as entering the nasal cavity via the back of the mouth. Chewing and other mouth movements help move aromatic compounds from the mouth, up the throat, and into the back of the nose. Eating a favorite aromatic food when a stuffy nose weakens sense of smell leaves one to remark that foods don't "taste" the same when suffering from a head cold. Few would argue against the close connection between taste and smell.

Even so, nose and taste buds cannot detect all that is going on. The mouth feels texture. Teas exhibit a splendid diversity of textures that create "mouth-feel." Some teas are creamy, with a coating like milk or melted butter. Some create a cooling sensation like menthol. Others are harshly dry. Still others have a fruit-like, tart acidity that causes the mouth to water. There are even others with a subtle astringency I can only describe as like having your tongue slipped inside a silk stocking. "Palate" or "taste" can often be used to encapsulate smell, taste and texture. But even these terms fail to encompass all that tea has to offer.

A sublime tea has an exceeding number of desirable components. Certainly taste, aroma, and texture are part of that experience, but wonderful teas offer rewarding aftertastes as well. In fact, some tea cultures emphasize the importance of aftertaste over other components. Even using the word "taste" in "aftertaste" is somewhat misleading. Good aftertaste often involves a sweetness that can echo in the mouth after the tea is swallowed. With higher-grade teas, the sweet aftertaste is accompanied by one or more flavor and taste sensations. A syrup-like coating may also be present in the aftertaste of the finest teas. Other times the aftertaste is jammy or sticky. Some tea masters remark that the further down the throat this coating can be felt, the better the tea. The effects of aftertaste may also register as a thickness, increased sensitivity of the tongue surface, or heaviness. Different teas "sit" differently on the stomach. Some give your belly an empty, rumbly feeling. Aftertaste, therefore, can be a combination of tastes and textures.

Tasting a tea is now understood as a multi-sensory unfolding of changing experience. The taste you experience at the beginning of a sip may not be the same as you finish that same sip. A taste experience is a book with many chapters. In addition, different cultures "taste" teas in different ways. Tasting traditions from China and Taiwan seek to experience the qi of the tea. Living organisms have life energy flowing through them. When two or more organisms interact, there can be an exchange of qi. Under this cultural approach to tasting, the tea drinker is looking to understand how the qi of the tea interacts with their own bodies.

So, can the word "taste" encapsulate the multi-dimensional experiences that ingesting tea offers? A pretty tall order, given the way the word "taste" is thrown around. In our most everyday usage of "taste," "flavor," or "palate," it is likely that the fullness of range, duration, and variation of tea sensory experiences will go unrepresented by the general understandings of those words. There is need for a better word. "Savor" fits much of the bill. It is true that "savor" has associations with taste and flavor, but unlike flavor, its origins extend beyond the sense of smell. Savor shares an etymological kinship with sapient and the "sapiens" in homo sapiens. When referring to mankind, sapience often gets explained as "wise," or "intelligent." But even these words contain an earlier, more relevant meaning. Intelligence, sapience, and even our word "sage" (as in sage advice) refer to mental perception. Being able to savor something and being intelligent are both connected to the arts of understanding and perception. The concept of "taste" gets tossed around so loosely that it no longer communicates the depth of insight that "savor" suggests.

When it comes to tea, homo sapiens are the insightful, perceiving, savoring, humans. The extent to which we can savor a tea (or any food) is dependent on the extent to which we employ our minds and bodies to grasping and understanding that tea. It follows then, that all forms of savor are not necessarily equal. Savoring is an art, a skill that can be developed. Once the doors of perception are opened, it will take time to know how to recognize and greet each entering guest. Take apples for example. Go into the produce section of a grocery, and ask a person to pick up a red Fuji apple, a yellow Golden Delicious, and a green Granny Smith. Just holding and looking at these will likely evoke memories or impressions of how they differ. A good number of people can remark on the differences in crispness, juiciness, and sweetness of these three kinds of apple. The savor elements of these apples are more familiar guests.

Now compare awareness of those apple characteristics with the distinctiveness of Braeburn, Honeycrisp, and Gala apples. I would wager that fewer people can instantly recall and describe the differences as those distinctions become more nuanced. There may be a glorious diversity separating these similar-looking varietals, but without a more developed sense of savor, our consciousnesses may not capture these sensations.

If this rich variety of sensations can occur across apple varieties, it is realistic to expect even more with tea. The resulting savor experience of tea is due to both environmental and human factors. Teas like long jing, dian hong and Darjeeling, are expected to exhibit certain characteristics. These characteristics may vary across season and skillfulness of the processor. Just as one Fuji apple might taste a little more like a Golden Delicious than another Fuji, it is still expected to exhibit its Fuji-ness. The presence of defining characteristics is highly dependent on the when, where, and how of the apple tree's growth. A tea maker has the greater burden of building upon the work of Nature by enhancing or compensating for what has become inherent in the leaf. A long jing green tea may have grown to possess the right potential, but the tea processor can mar or exalt that sought-after savor through the work of his hands.

Savoring tea is a lifetime endeavor. It does not take a lifetime to discover new tea experiences and savor elements, but it does take a lifetime to collect and properly appreciate the precious experiences. A curator faces an ongoing challenge to determine which elements of the collection display the finest, the most beautiful, the most praiseworthy, the most valuable parts of the museum's treasure trove. Anyone who savors tea faces the same challenge in curating her finest tea sensations. This private collection may include broad canvasses of bold flavors alongside tapestries of intricate texture. There may be elegantly sculpted curves of aftertaste. There will be Early, Middle, and Modern periods, and maybe even a Renaissance somewhere in between. And you will regularly stroll through your collection to replace one experiential artifact with another, or tear down your walls to build a new savor-wing.

Certain conditions facilitate savor more than others. It is usually best to remove extremes and over abundance that may distract the senses. For me, this can even extend to eliminating fragrances from my clothes and skin. If I want to focus, I avoid savoring tea too soon after eating. Some foods linger in the mouth for hours. When a colleague or loved one eats garlic bread, you become keenly aware of this fact. Since water is the mother of tea, the water used can have a profound effect. The ancients were known to draw prized waters from famous springs. It isn't necessary to go to such extremes, but it is worthwhile to experiment with different sources of clean water. The mineral composition of water can serve to enhance or detract from the savor experience.

Then there is that most contested of points in savoring tea: preparation method. Professional tea tasters may pull out gram scales to measure precise amounts of leaf. Some use timers to control steep time. They use the same water temperature (often boiling water) for all teas. This procedure has its merits. Consistent treatment allows teas to be compared on an equal playing field. Fully boiling water can often reveal a fuller range of flaws and strengths contained in tealeaves. Tea should be treated this way every so often to more fully reveal the character of the tea. Some tea purveyors avoid sharing this kind of information, hoping the shortcomings of their teas can be masked with cooler water or shorter steep times.

A friend in the tea industry and I like to joke with each other by asking: "Which way is the right way to steep tea?" We don't say "brew" because coffee is "brewed." When he asks, I reply: "My way is the best way to steep tea." He smiles and agrees: "Yes, my way is the best way to steep tea." We both recognize that a person becomes attuned to drawing out slightly different sets of savor elements as he or she steeps tea. That may mean that a tea is too strong for one of us, but just right for the other. It may mean that I steeped the tea in a way that turned my delicate green tea into an overcooked soup. Never mind that steep; I just added a valuable (though possibly costly) experience to my collection of savor moments. The next time

I will adjust the parameters to draw out some other elements of the tea's personality.

Savoring a tea is like building a friendship. Steep the tea multiple times, squeezing out the variations within each iteration. Drink the tea while it is hot and while it is cool. Changing temperature reveals the personality of the tea. Drink tea in different seasons. You will find some teas more agreeable in the spring than the fall and absolutely crave certain teas some times of the year. Some friends come to you when you are alone and pick you up. Others carry the party and light up everyone's faces. Some friendships are lifetime bonds. Some are tenuously held together by a distant affinity or shared experience. In a similar way, savoring a tea is not always the same as liking a tea. Savoring asks us to recognize and accept a friendly tea for all that it is and can be.

Jason Walker learned to taste teas while living in China and traveling to Taiwan. He now publishes *Walker Tea Review*, writes, and consults with tea businesses.

Chapter 5

THE TASTE OF TEA

Suzette Hammond

"Can you tell me what I'm tasting?"

How many times have I been asked that in a tea class! To the teacher in me, it's both charming and also a bit heartbreaking. I smile because it poses a challenge: what a perfectly self-answering question to gently ground the budding student back in reality! (The tea taster's first koan, if you will.) But I am also disappointed. How I wish this student would have a more open mind (and palate), brave enough to seek the answer on their own. No, I cannot tell you what you are tasting. Yes, there is professional "tea vocabulary," but the truth of it is, if I describe this green tea as tasting like asparagus and you swear it's like fresh lima beans . . . we are both correct. My memory of asparagus might simply be more present and strong than my memory of fresh lima beans, while you may not have had asparagus recently enough to recall. Another taster might be reminded more of sweet grass or hay, perhaps picking up more on the slightly toasty, fired notes from the drying of the tea rather than the base vegetal flavor. What I'm trying to say is that it is all subjective. Does that mean there are no rules, then? How are standards maintained? How does the entire system not just collapse on itself?

"Pour yourself another cup, grasshopper, and do not worry about that which is out of your control."

It is far more important to pay close attention to the cup of tea in your hand, take in the aroma, examine the leaves from which it was steeped, sip slowly and focus your palate. That is how you will become a better taster—of everything. The novice tea student always seems to be in such a hurry, happily taking in everything they can learn once that fire is lit, sometimes becoming frustrated when obstacles are encountered. What I have found time and time again as an educator is that this rush leads to an unevenly paved knowledge road. There are places where the ground is perfectly smooth, meticulously maintained, and there are rough sections with lots of potholes. We all have a mix of expertise in topics that came easily, and large gaps where key experiences were skipped over.

This is not the fault of the student. After all, North America is not a traditional country of origin for tea. It's not in our blood as it is in other cultures, so we are rather lacking in strong, established learning institutions for tea. In fact, I often tell people with serious interest in a tea career that their best option is to find a reputable tea company that strongly values education and training and go work for them. Quite honestly, that is how many people in this market learn how to taste professionally. For those who find themselves in this situation—earnestly seeking knowledge, struggling to find words to describe the tea—I encourage them first and foremost to pause and realize what it is you're asking the brain and palate to do. Have some compassion for yourself as a human. Everything will come easier when you just let go!

Consider how you might answer the following: "How does that taste? What do you think of it?" You're asking the taster to put something that is inherently a sensory experience into words. You could be speaking of wine, cheese, beer, chocolate—it's all the same. This is exceedingly difficult, as this person cannot taste for you. They can only describe it to the best of their ability. That leads to the second part of this conundrum. You need your brain and your palate (taste and olfaction senses) to work together and summarize an incredible depth of textures, sensations, aromas, flavors and memories into a few words. Think of the sheer focus that takes! You realize quickly this isn't just a situation that applies to tea. How many other singular foods or food-enhancing items (spices, flowers) have you been asked to describe? It's like describing colors or sounds. You must find a frame of reference that the person with whom you are conversing can understand. This is where that compassion for your human-ness comes into play.

Amongst fellow trainers, my colleagues and I often say the "young" palate is like a muscle that hasn't been worked out in a long time. You must train and condition it to develop those skills; there's no such thing as a "gifted" palate, only a person with sharp presence of being.

Speaking of "being," it's worth noting here that the study of tea often brings up many connections between the mind and the waking world. Spiritually, whatever that means for you, tea is a vessel for deeper connectivity. One bowl can unite both friends and foes. How? Why? Speaking as someone who not only "works" but also "lives" in tea, I feel it's equal parts culture and science. The combination is rather miraculous. No other food or beverage on earth is as versatile biologically and as revered culturally as tea. All of this from one plant family! (Camellia sinensis, and a few related camellia varieties.) Consider this: In the category of green tea, researchers have identified one hundred fifty to two hundred unique chemical compounds that contribute to taste and aroma. In the category of black tea, by enrichment that happens through human ingenuity of controlled oxidation, over five hundred compounds have been identified. All from one plant! There's truly a tea for everyone on this planet, united by a common thread, a whisper of a familiar flavor that speaks to the taster in shades of white, yellow, green, oolong, black and fermented. Couple that diversity with wonderful chemicals like beloved L-theanine (revered for encouraging relaxing alpha brain waves, acute mental clarity and bodily calm), and you have a form of liquid meditation in every cup. Indeed, tea has much to teach us about life itself.

So, how do you learn to become a tea taster, then? A better appreciator of this gift to humankind? I suggest that you seek the common ground between you and everyone else—food. Remember our palate muscle analogy? Exercise that muscle by building stronger connections and memory to all foods. In order to describe a tea as "toasty with a slightly dry, walnut-like finish," you need to know what toasted walnuts really taste like.

So, pay attention to them in your next salad, both on their own and how they combine with the lettuce leaves, the cheese crumbles, the slices of pear (ooh! And what does that pear taste like, too? How is the crunchy skin different from the sweet fruit?) It just takes a moment. Breathe in. Exhale to relax. Chew and think to yourself, "This is a walnut." Remember that moment and try to recall it in vivid detail the next time you hear a tea being described as "nutty." Take a trip to a spice store, soak in the rich aromas one at a time. Visit your local farmers market and make sure to taste the difference between green curly kale and Tuscan kale. If you're up for a real challenge, walk through a large floral shop and try to smell each flower type individually and describe it. Don't forget that you have the ability to taste because you have the ability to smell. Thus, spending time tucking aromas into your memory bank is really important.

A quick story to illustrate this point: One day, when I was teaching a large class, I asked my students how they would describe a particular tea. I urged them not to be shy, and insisted that there were no wrong answers. One person raised her hand and said "concrete." The room started giggling in a friendly manner, along with some surprised "What!" reactions. I agreed with this person's taste observation and explained my reasoning. I grew up in the Southwest U.S., in the desert. I've since lived in many places across the country, in wildly varying climates; from ninety-five degrees and eighty percent humidity down to negative twenty-five with wind chill and white-out blizzards. Yet, my strongest sensory memories of climate are from the desert in the summer, during the monsoon. There's a distinctive sweet aroma when those nourishing rains flood the parched earth, washing over the pavement. I knew exactly what this person meant when she said "concrete." A more "consumer-friendly" description might have been mineral or damp river stones (this tea was definitely that, too. I was also reminded of a hike to the top of Multnomah Falls, Oregon). The lesson was, write down everything in your personal tasting notes. Whether it sounds nice or not, it doesn't matter. They're your notes and they strike a memory for you. In time, with some practice, a tea can go from being described as "bacon-like" to "salty", "savory," "seaweed," and "oceanic," or rich with umami (from amino acids present in high amounts for this particular tea). Here, I am referring to sencha, Japan's most famous green tea. Hmm, bacon. Who would have thought?

This leads to my final point. Rather than spend effort trying to memorize what others thought the tea tasted like, try to learn more about how it's made, what physically makes it different. In the case of sencha, some Japanese tea bush cultivars are actually bred to have higher levels of amino acids present in their cup profile. These amino acids create umami, the fifth taste (the others being sweet, salty, sour and bitter). Umami is savory, a unifying deep flavor in foods like mushrooms, cheese, meat, seafood, seaweed, soy sauce . . . and certain teas. Think of our walnut example from earlier. Some teas are roasted at different levels of their crafting. This roasting creates dry, nutty aromas and flavors in the cup. Understanding the intent of the tea maker can make forging a personal relationship to the taste of the tea—drawing out your own words and understanding of the flavor—much easier and more meaningful.

Cup after cup, hour after hour with tea, I am always reminded of how very fortunate we are to have tea in our world. Something so humble, so seemingly simple—just leaves soaked in water—bringing about such profound knowledge of what it means to be alive. Tea also taught me to eat and drink not just for sustenance, but more importantly, for connectedness. I could have lived my whole life consuming calories, measured units of "nutrition," bottled and bar coded for convenience. Instead, because of tea, I am learning the ways of slowly steeping, knowing when to release and when to hold back. To observe or participate. The depth of roasting, the savory of steaming. The curled up ball that gradually warms up and unfurls, or the flattened leaf that allows the water to wash over and purify. The wisdom of patience, one cup at a time. The taste of tea is the taste of patience itself.

Suzette Hammond is the Director of Education for Rishi Tea, a direct importer specializing in hands-on origin work. A passionate, engaged teacher, Suzette has been leading trainings in major markets across the country for over a decade.

Chapter 6

SOME PERSONAL REFLECTIONS ON TEA AND WINE

David Campbell

The wind was a torrent of darkness among the gusty trees,
The moon was a ghostly galleon tossed upon cloudy seas,
The road was a ribbon of moonlight over the purple moor,
     And the highwayman came riding—
Riding—riding—
The highwayman came riding, up to the old inn-door.

                                                          —ALFRED NOYES

Alfred Noyes's evocative metaphors help us to understand, unmistakably, the character of that dark night. That is the heavy lifting we expect of a metaphor. The same sort of heavy lifting is sometimes undertaken in aid of cross-cultural understanding of tea and wine: Tea is the wine of China, and wine is the tea of the west. As metaphors tend to do, however, the analogies break down when they are carried too far.

The realists among us might argue:

But the wind's not a torrent of darkness, and the moon's not tossed on the seas,

A road's not a ribbon of moonlight, and tea is not wine, if you please.

Yet surely there are some connections that can be made between these two greatest of all beverages, for tea and wine intuitively seem alike in so many respects. A strong simile might be the key: Wine is like tea and conversely, tea is like wine. Exploring this simile at length invites us to make comparisons and contrasts between tea and wine that can help us understand both better. In the West, where wine is part of the culture and is reasonably well understood, the tea/wine simile can serve as a guide to understanding tea. In the East, where tea culture reigns, the analogy can perform the same role for wine. Together they can serve as guides to understanding.

What can the parallels between tea and wine teach us? Although tea is made with prepared leaves and wine with the juice of vine fruit, tea bushes and wine-grape vines both have become important agricultural crops, each one the product of a separate single species of plant: *camellia sinensis* for tea and *vitis vinifera* for wine (although in North America a relatively small quantity of wine is made from vitis labrusca, generally this is not considered to be particularly noteworthy).

Two principal sub-species of *camellia sinensis* are used in the production of tea: camellia sinensis v. sinensis, which is cultivated widely in China, Japan and Taiwan; and *camellia sinensis v. assamica*, which is the sub-species grown in most (but not all) of the rest of the world. In the case of wine, there are no sub-species (usually just 12 bottles); however, following the spread of the *phylloxera* pest, *vinifera* vines in most growing areas must be grafted onto rootstock from resistant members of the vitis family.

In the beginning, both tea and wine were produced and consumed for their medicinal properties and healthful benefits. Only later did they become true beverages in their respective cultures. Although the health benefits that accrue from drinking wine and tea were never really "lost," many today are trying to "rediscover" them. Extensive research projects are underwritten by the respective industries to demonstrate and then bolster awareness of health related properties in each beverage. These include: extended life-expectancy, cholesterol and blood pressure control, and the reduction in the level of cancer causing free radicals, to name but a few. Nonetheless, although tea and wine are both healthful beverages, any given tea or wine must simply taste good for it to enjoy broad acceptance. How many of us, after all, take our regular daily dose of cod liver oil?

The origin of *camellia sinensis* is generally thought to be an area that stretches from the eastern edge of Assam, in India, through northern Myanmar and Laos, to Xishuangbanna in Yunnan Province China, a region known to cultural historians and anthropologists as Zomia. The wild growing variety here is *camellia sinensis v. assamica*, and some ancient trees in Xishuangbanna are estimated to be 1,700 or more years old. Curiously, however, some recent scientific studies have shown that the genetic diversity of *v. sinensis* is greater than that of *v. assamica*, suggesting that it, in fact, is the older of these two subspecies. If this is true, is *v. assamica* derivative? And if so, where *do* we find the true home of tea—in Sichuan?

Vitis vinifera grew wild in the area where the west meets Asia, in present day Georgia, Azerbaijan and Armenia. When the plant was domesticated, we do not know, but wine certainly was present at the very dawn of western civilization. Evidence of wine's early use, dating back some 7,000 years, has been found in archaeological digs in this region as well as in the Mesopotamian "fertile crescent."

By comparison, the evidence for tea suggests a more recent origin. The oldest archeological excavations that may show tea use are the Marquis do Dai burial site digs that began in 1972. Relics have been dated back to 186 BCE. We have testimony affirming the use of tea by 168 CE, for the gazettes of the day note tea production in Hunan and along the east coast as far north as Tai Hu, near present day Shanghai; but there is little or none demonstrating the use of tea BCE. Wine, it appears, is much the elder of these two enticing beverages. Archaeology aside, tea and wine both have mythological stories that attempt to explain their beginnings. The Book of Genesis tells the familiar tale of Noah and his arc. After the flood, when Noah and his menagerie landed on the peak of Turkey's Mount Ararat, he planted a vineyard, made wine and became inebriated. This ultimately led to much trouble for his son Ham and grandson Canaan, not to mention a bevy of latter day theologians. And no one seems quite sure where Noah's vines came from; but such is the way of mythology.

Tea's mythological origins may be found in the person of Sheng Nong, the fabled emperor who is credited with establishing Chinese agriculture (in Chinese "sheng" refers to the spirit or divinity, and "nong" is farmer). While wandering his empire in search of useful plants, Shen Nong, who tried them all, fell ill after ingesting a poisonous herb. Fortunately, a few leaves from a nearby tree drifted into his kettle of boiling water. The Emperor was revived and tea and its healthful properties discovered. Every region in China seems to have a story relating to how tea came to be there, the gratitude of the Iron Goddess of Mercy (Anxi Tieguanyin) and the eyelids of the Bodhidharma (Shaolin) being but two.

War and religion have been crucial to the spread of tea gardens and of vineyards, and to the wider acceptance of tea and of wine. These expansions follow similar, but by no means identical, paths. Tea plantings were first spread largely by monks traveling from northern India in their quest to bring Buddhism to China. Although tea itself had no truly spiritual significance, the monks found it to be extremely useful during meditation. Tea helped produce the wakeful yet calming state that is required for meditation. The caffeine content aided wakefulness and, although an unidentified contributor until quite recently, its theanine promoted the calm.

The spirituality, now such an anticipated part of tea culture, initially grew from tea's use by the monks living and meditating in solitude, high on their cloud-enshrouded mountain retreats. The notion of the spirituality of tea was boosted in the 8th century CE as it became more popular, largely through *The Classic of Tea*, Lu Yu's seminal discussion of the art of preparing and drinking tea. Proponents of tea and tea culture have appeared throughout the following centuries. The most famous of these might be the Huizhong Emperor: a cultured and dedicated apostle of the arts but a horrible ruler, the

Song dynasty crumbled under his watch. Huizhong wrote the *Treatise on Tea*, which, as well being as a learned piece on tea cultivation, was the most detailed description of the Song dynasty tea ceremony. The enduring early 20th century classic, *The Book of Tea*, by the Japanese master Okakura Kakuz, was written in English specifically to expose western audiences to the notion of *teaism*.

Tea and the rituals of tea were introduced to Japan during the Heian period of Japanese history (794–1185 CE) by monks traveling to and from Tang dynasty China. Later in Japan's Kamakura era, which overlapped with the Song dynasty in China, Japanese monks encouraged and supported the use of tea in daily life. But it was not until somewhat later, during China's Ming dynasty and the later stages of the Muromachi period in Japan (1336–1568 CE), that tea and tea culture became firmly established there. The practice of brewing tea by infusion rather than by whipping it into a suspension arrived from China after the fall of the Ming, during a period when Sino-culture and art were very highly regarded in Japan. Although most Japanese continue to drink infused tea rather than whipped tea, the rise of Japanese nationalism in the late Meiji put the latter into a societally favored position. Most today recognize the chadao tea ceremony; far fewer are aware of senchadao. A similar tale of wandering Buddhist monks led to tea and tea culture coming to the people of Korea and Indochina. *The Korean Tea Classics* stand as some of the finest and most revealing of all writings about tea and the spirit of tea.

War and its needs were also instrumental in the spread of tea. China's constant demand for military horses led directly to the development of the "Tea Horse Road" at least as early as the Tang dynasty. Along this road, tea was carried from Yunnan and Sichuan to Lhasa in Tibet, where it was exchanged for horses that had been raised on the high Tibetan plateau.

Centuries later, a signal event ultimately led to the development of tea gardens in India. In one of the most pernicious acts of 18th century commerce, traders from the British East India Company began paying for their Chinese tea purchases with opium that they produced in India. According to plan, hundreds of thousands of Chinese became addicted to the drug. Attempts by the Daoguan Emperor to eradicate the addiction and eliminate the trade led to the British invasion of China known as the Opium War. The war resulted in the complete humiliation of China, the establishment of foreign treaty ports in Shanghai and elsewhere, the loss of the island of Hong Kong, a mortal wound to the Great Qing, and British resolve to find other sources for their tea. That source was India, where plantations, initially operated by the same British East India Company, came into being.

Similarly, wine has been spread in the west both by religion and by war. Unlike tea, however, wine has a direct religious relevance, and its use spread as Christianity came to be the dominant religion in Europe. Wine is required for the Christian sacrament of communion during which, by the doctrine of transubstantiation, it becomes not just a symbol of the blood of Jesus Christ but the actual blood itself. As with Buddhist monks in the east, Christian monks established abbeys and monasteries in new territories as they sought to spread their religion. Once entrenched, they planted vineyards in order to provide the sacramental wine they needed. Many of the great vineyards in Burgundy, Champagne, Avignon, Bordeaux, along the Rhine and throughout Spain continue to reflect this monastic heritage.

No recent conflicts appear to be caused by wine (although the level of port trade between Portugal and England is the best single correlate of all European wars fought since the Renaissance), but this has not always been the case. As Rome's legions marched through and over what is now known as Europe, subjugating Gaul, Hispania and Brittania, Legionnaire commanders planted grapes to provide wine, the only sure source of potable liquid at the time for their armies. Many of these vineyard sites, particularly in southern France and in Spain, remain planted to this day.

Tea and wine exhibit the two widest flavor spectra of all beverages consumed by humankind, and both tea and wine come bearing psychoactive drugs: caffeine (and importantly theanine) in the case of tea, and alcohol in the case of wine. These drugs act upon the central nervous system as a stimulant and a depressant respectively.

Caffeine, the preferred drug of most humans, promotes wakefulness and alertness and suffers from very few prohibitions against its use. It is scarcely surprising therefore that, as commonly observed, tea is the world's second most highly consumed beverage (after water.) Less frequently noted is that wine is the fourth most widely consumed natural beverage (only caffeine laced coffee, with its comparatively narrow flavor spectrum, comes between tea and wine.) Unlike caffeine, however, alcohol is prohibited by large swaths of society and closely regulated in those where it is not. That wine holds such a high place, despite these inconveniences and the well-known effects of overuse, attests to the powerful attraction of alcohol.

As tea and wine are both agricultural products (the wild growing tea trees in parts of Yunnan and in Taiwan aside), understanding the nature of these crops is important to many, not least the tea farmer and the *vigneron*. For most, tea and wine are simply beverages to enjoy, but for the romantic devotees of either, pilgrimages to the tea garden or the vineyard are often treated as obligatory rites of initiation. Every encounter with a tea master or a *vigneron* will be notched on the holster of the psyche. At one level this is an unsurpassable learning experience; however at the extreme it descends into a technical snootiness that turns off many people and distracts attention from what is truly important: tasting, savoring and simply enjoying the hedonistic, healthful and spiritual benefits of tea and wine.

Crops are cultivated plants deliberately grown and nurtured by humans to fulfill some particular need, be it for food, clothing, medicine, or simply pleasure. Specific plants are selected and grown for their particular desired qualities and yields and display a wide range of genotypes and phenotypes. This has given rise to the notion of the "cultivated variety" or "cultivar." Whereas the number of cultivars is declining for most crops—as plant breeders winnow down the available selection in order to foster increased yields, or heartiness, or to increase the ability to stand up to mechanized agriculture—the number of cultivars available to tea farmers and *vignerons* is increasing. Growers seek more and more diversity in what they grow, and plant breeders at tea and wine research stations are eager to oblige.

There are more cultivars for tea plants and grapevines than for any other crops. The most basic ampelography will list hundreds of different wine cultivars such as pinot noir, chardonnay, sauvignon blanc and carmenière. The number of tea cultivars is even more mind-boggling. The *Great Chinese Tea Dictionary* alone lists thousands, though it is unclear to what extent these are all distinct. Examples include *qing xin* and *jin xuang*, which are widely grown in Taiwan, *tieguanyin* and *Anji bai* from China, *yabukita* and *benihikari* from Japan, and the unromantically named but very important B157 and AV2 from India. And all this is before the subject of "clones" has even reared its intimidating head. This diversity of plant material, coupled with the vast differences in planting sites, has led both tea-masters and winemakers to the importance of what is known in the wine community as "terroir" might be more apt. Wine literature is replete with tiresome, sterile debates about the meaning of "terroir." Is it just soil? Do people matter? Where does one draw the line with respect to mesoclimate? The beat drones on. Part of the problem is that although one French word for soil is *la terre*, the translation of "terroir" into English is devilishly difficult. Mostly it's translated as, well, "terroir;" or at a stretch, something like rural agricultural region, or perhaps locality. The British, the Americans and even the French, whose term it is and whose intellectual history is replete with notoriously hard to define but intuitively understood concepts, are engaged in the fray.

I am unaware of any single Chinese or Japanese term that captures, for tea gardens, the sense carried by the word terroir; the Chinese *"wotu"* (fertile ground) seems to come closest ("terroir" itself has been borrowed for tea writings in English and French). The importance of the concept is well understood, however, and the effects much discussed in Chinese, Taiwanese and Japanese tea circles. For my part, I'll leave all of the arguments surrounding the roles of drainage, and aspect, and elevation, to others and use "terroir" simply to mean "a sense of place."

Lest I sound churlish, let me elaborate. Neither tea nor wine should be, or can be, reduced to some fixed set of technical specifications. The growing of fine wine and tea, the transformation of must and of leaf, are practiced arts that are far greater than mastery of any set of techniques. By way of example, Thelonius Monk was a middling piano player at best; he could not hold a candle to the technical flair of, say, Fats Waller. But Monk was an artist—and not just any artist, but one of the most brilliant in the history of a music genre that has produced many greats. His command of the music and his influence on the jazz medium are without parallel. So, too, with wine and tea. Winemakers and tea-masters must achieve at least some minimal measure of technical skill, but no amount of this can compensate for the lack of the artist's touch. The greatest technical winemaker or tea-master extant may produce an impeccable but essentially soulless beverage. Conference of soul rests in the hand of the artist.

Happily, access to the soul both of tea and of wine is available to all of us who approach either one with nothing more than an openness of mind and a willingness of spirit. This soul can be found in the simplest as well as the loftiest of wines and teas. A true connoisseur of wine or tea does not need to know, much less feel compelled to seek out, the pH or TA of what they are drinking in order to be moved by it. Knowing beforehand whether the crop was mechanically harvested or hand picked does not enhance our appreciation (and it may well detract from it). None of these, or any others, is an *a priori* reason to approach or to recoil from any given tea or wine, for we ought to approach them all. Our truth is found only in the cup or glass. To be sure, just as learning the theories of perspective may enhance our appreciation of a masterful painting, the overall pleasure we get from a cup of tea or a glass of wine may be increased by coming to understand some of the technical reasons it tastes the way it does. But that is, at most, merely an option. And it is also why for "terroir" I favor the admittedly imprecise but evocative "sense of place" over the technical concern with aspect, elevation or drainage.

So, does a "sense of place" reveal itself in the taste of tea and wine? The straightforward answer is yes, absolutely. On a broad level there are recognizable taste differences among Taiwanese, Chinese and Japanese teas. On a narrower level there is a noticeable difference between Alishan and Lishan, Shizuoka and Uji, and Darjeeling, and just about everything. Similarly, wines from New Zealand and Italy each display their own very recognizable taste profiles, and the differences between Pauillac and Margaux do show up in the glass.

When tasted, tea and wine show this "sense of place" more than any other agricultural products; more than grains, or cash crops or tree fruits. This doesn't mean that we will always identify a precise location when we taste, and that isn't the point, but almost all of us can recognize that there are differences among what we taste. As to identifying the place, this, more often than not, is a parlor game used principally in the pursuit of one-upmanship; the finer distinctions stymie us all. This does not mean that some producers don't tilt at the windmill of an international style that tries to erase "sense of place" altogether; they do. And all of this brings us to the nub of the whole exercise, which is simply the *taste* of tea and wine.

It does not take more than one cerebral synapse to recognize that tea and wine taste nothing alike, smell nothing alike, look nothing alike and use very different utensils (although there is a total git in London England who is attempting, with the cooperation of the Riedel crystal company no less, to develop stemware for tea tastings – heaven help us all). The simile is in the approach to tasting, in the very fact that we *are* tasting. We drink tea and wine for the pleasures they bring; we taste them to learn, and when we learn our pleasure increases.

There is nothing profound in noting that the human physiology, whether tasting tea or tasting wine, is a constant. At our current level of knowledge, humans are thought to be able to recognize only five distinct tastes: sweet, sour, bitter, salt, and *umami*. Everything else that we commonly think of as taste is really smell. The human sense of smell is far more developed than the sense of taste; there are far more neurons carrying sensations of smell than there are carrying sensations of taste. Although all five senses are carried to the brain by one of twelve cranial nerves, only the olfactory nerve and the optical nerve attach directly to the cerebrum, the most highly evolved part of the brain. All others, including the nerves carrying sensations of taste, attach to the brain stem, the least evolved part of the brain.

We approach "tasting" either tea or wine first by looking at it, then smelling it and finally tasting it. Once in our mouths, some of the volatile components in the beverages are carried to receptors at the base of the nasal passages and from there, by way of the olfactory nerve, to the brain. This process, known as retro-olfaction, is why we often think that one thing tastes just like something else smells; *gaoshan* tea like cinnamon, sauvignon blanc like fresh mown hay (to be polite).

Although each beverage sector has some vocabulary unique unto itself (e.g. case-hardened in tea manufacture or shot-berry in viticulture), the terms used to describe what we actually taste are remarkably similar: long in the mouth, astringent, balanced, complex and so forth. These terms, along with a multitude of descriptors, mean the same thing whether expressed in the language of tea or that of wine.

In one crucial area, however, our simile falls apart, and tea and wine diverge markedly. When we have a bottle of wine, we are holding the finished product, the final expression of the winemaker. Certainly, a wine meant for ageing (and relatively few are) will continue to develop over the course of its journey through time. Two bottles of the same wine stored in different locations may, and often do, age somewhat differently, but it is always our expectation that the wines, if sound, will taste very much alike, if not identical.

Not so with tea.

Yes, some teas may be stored and aged with benefit (relatively few) but all teas must be brewed before they can be savored, and brewing can amount to a skill unto itself. How we brew influences taste very substantially. Whether we are casually plopping a bag of

PG Tips into the Brown Betty so we can enjoy a "cuppa", listening with rapt attention while Laoshi explains, yet again, the subtle differences in the taste of this tea versus that one, or have donned a *kimono* to participate in the formal *chadao*, the teas we are tasting come to us with the final step incomplete. The final step is up to us: we actively participate in creating what we hope to enjoy.

Let us give the last good word to Lewis Carroll:

> "Have some wine," the March Hare said in an encouraging tone.
> Alice looked all round the table but there was nothing on it but tea. "I don't see any wine," she remarked.
> "There isn't any," said the March Hare.
> Heaven forfend there should be no tea either!

David Campbell is the proprietor of Tillerman Tea in Napa, California. He travels regularly to China, Taiwan and Japan, where he purchases tea directly from family growers. In addition to his work in the tea business, Campbell has been active in the wine industry for over thirty years.

Chapter 7

THE ALCHEMY OF TEA

Sat Hon

Alchemy is a metaphor for resurrection,
while tea is the living manifestation of rejuvenation itself . . .

To explore the deep connections between tea and alchemy, we must divine its Neolithic roots and oral history. The dawn of alchemy arose from our common ancestor of the last great Ice Age: the mythic shaman Pan Gu, the Primordial Old Man. In this epic legend of genesis, Pan Gu cleaved the chaotic darkness in two halves, light and shadow, and thus sparked the birth of our universe into a dynamic interplay of Yin and Yang. The reciprocal action of these two polarities, complimentary opposites, is the essence of alchemical cultivation, which, in turn, is deeply connected to the development of shamanic rituals that involved tea.

To understand the profound connections, we must first divine the Neolithic roots of alchemy and its relationship to shamanism and tea. The origins of alchemy are infinitely mysterious, but we may suggest a timeline that begins around 30,000 years ago, at the conclusion of the final stages of the last Ice Age. Splinter groups of early humans descended from the Himalayan plateau and populated the

Asiatic plains and melting glaciers, while a small die-hard contingent of these tribes clung onto the high plateau. Those faithful adherents of the high plains would eventually evolve and become Tibetans, Nepalese and other aboriginals of the peaks, while the others who made the descent would eventually develop into the proto-Chinese. Further along, a few of these pioneers of the Asiatic plains ventured across the Siberian strait into the Americas, and over the course of several thousand years became Native Americans, the First People of the New World. Hence, Tibetans and Chinese share a common ancestral tongue. The linguists call it Tibetan-Sino language. Since these two ancient races share a common heritage, Chinese shaman and indigenous Tibetan Bonpo share a strong resemblance and a kind of cultural "genetic" lineage.

During the next 20,000 years, this archaic form of shamanism remained essentially unchanged. Around 10,000 years ago, the practice of shamanic healing reached a critical mass. The metal, pottery and herbal medicines discovered from this era all derived from the experimentation of the earliest alchemists, as can be seen on the wall paintings of our Paleolithic ancestors. In the caves of Northern Spain and Southern France can be seen Neanderthals dancing in shamanic ecstasy encircled by flickering glowing embers of light, swaying in the shadow-play and transfiguring into part animal and part man. This image is epitomized in the famous Shaman of Lascaux, which captures the shape-shifting capacity of these proto-magicians. Other drawings depict the shaman's slow lumbering gait, which portends the sudden transmogrification into a lean scruffy hungry bear, emerging from a cave after a long winter sleep.

With a leap of fantastic imagination, the shaman-turned-alchemists inferred that by ingesting these most toxic concoctions, mortals could, by esoteric analogy, transform into immortals. Many modern people, imbued with their modern scientific sensibility, would laugh at such farfetched correlations between ingesting liquid gold and achieving immortality. But don't forget in our 21st century, earth is still inhabited by a large population who refute the existence of evolution as a scientific confabulation and believe that God is a masculine theistic being. Farfetched indeed!

The invention of the compass was based on the landscape alchemy of geomancy, *Feng Shui*, wind and water. The mineral alchemists used lead, silver, copper and mercury to transform base metals into gold: the mineral realm of immutable immortality. For the practitioners of mineral alchemy, it is most unfortunate that mercury is highly toxic, although its usage, in trace amounts, has persisted even to date in immunizations in order to combat infection, as well as in dentistry and Indian Ayurvedic medicine.

After generations of alchemists ingested such toxic elixirs with tragically fatal results, a few individuals started to shift their attention inwards, resulting in the alchemical inner cultivation of the Song dynasty, circa 1400 AD. The study and practice of inner alchemy became wildly popular, simply because its adherents were able to achieve great longevity. For instance, it is reputed that one contemporary alchemist, Li Ching Yuen, lived to the impossible age of 250 years. My own late master told me that he personally met the venerable old alchemist during a banquet held in his honor.

I believe that essentially we practice alchemy to reconnect to our human core. During the turbulent years preceding the Cultural Revolution, at the time of the Communist era of *"letting a thousand flowers bloom,"* the Chinese Doctor, Lui Gui Zheng, transplanted feudalistic archaic forms of inner alchemy and gave it a modern name, *Qigong*, the cultivation of energy. However, the essence of Dr. Lui's Qigong is fundamentally alchemical meditation and mind training. During the 1950s, with the patronage and support of the ruling members of the Communist Party, Dr. Lui would establish the first historic Qigong clinic to treat many common illnesses in China.

But how do these esoteric details about the origins of shamanism and alchemy relate to the mystery of tea?

Healing. The mysterious connection is the power of healing, which is realized by the use of tea in shamanic rituals.

THE SERENDIPITY OF ALCHEMY

In my case, I stumbled upon the practice of alchemy quite acciden-
tally, or depending on how one views the events of one's life, by fate.
I had expected to find the very stuff of myth—sorcerers and wizards,
shuddering magic spells, shamans with sun-bleached skulls wearing
iridescent cloaks and beating mightily on sealskin drums. The truth
was far more profound. It was something akin to falling in love, the
haunting sensation of a native son coming home.

For instance, in the single gesture of waving my arms above
my head, my movements are suddenly transfigured into a heron's
pale ghostly flight. When I practice this move I feel myself plunge
abruptly into a luminous and mobile liquid that is none other than
the pristine element of time. I share it just as excited bathers share
gleaming saltwater with the denizens of the sea. These creatures are
not oneself, but are joined to one by time's common flow.

This is an ancient trail. By following it I began to recognize that
alchemy starts not in the physical, but in the metaphysical plain of
the sacred. Over the course of many years I learned to practice this
archaic inner alchemy in order to transform, like the lowly leaf grub-
bing caterpillar, into a full fledged monarch with ocelot wings, free
from its humdrum existence in low lying shrubs. I learned to drink
the honeydew of life and shed the skin of mortality.

In the passages above, I hope to have instilled a taste of the mystical and ecstatic tongue of alchemy. The Taoist approach is never
direct, always taking an oblique trajectory toward understanding.
Defining the meaning of alchemy too concretely or rigidly (if this
is even possible) would be both fruitless and misleading, giving the
reader a misguided sense of certainty that perhaps alchemy is easily
knowable through one's mind alone and fits into a neat box. In doing so, I would have transgressed a principle tenet of the Tao and
a philosophical underpinning of all alchemical practices. The Old
master Lao Tzu warned that what is captured in words will inevitably
be false. But words are all I have to help make clear the mysterious
healing power that occurs when alchemy meets tea.

STONE ALCHEMICAL TEA

Legend tells us that the earliest case of tea's medicinal use was as a healing antidote, a cure for the effects of poisons. Shen Lung, the numinous herbalist, became gravely ill by testing and ingesting hundreds of herbs to assess their herbal and medicinal properties. He had become so ill that the toxic poisons turned his whole face blue. With three cups of tea, his entire ailment vanished. Henceforth, tea was commonly used as an antidote against the effects of mineral toxicity caused by material elixirs that the external alchemists believed could be formulated.

Teakettle

In my teacher's tale, a young Chinese lieutenant led his starving battalion on a heart-breaking ascent of Mount Konga in the early days of World War II. There they met a mysterious old master of alchemy, who devised a way to supplement the soldiers' diet by resurrecting an extremely rare and ancient tea ceremony.

His use of the natural concavity in a boulder as a teakettle was an ingenious use of nature. Moreover, the lichens, mosses and other small vegetation growing within its surface were rich both in essential minerals and vitamins. This type of tea has a modern derivative called the Yen Wu tea, tea of the cliff boulder.

Accompanying the brewing of this tea was the Old Master's elegant gesture of using his forefinger to trace in the air the sacred script, *Fu*, a spiritual mandala, which was intended to transform the mundane act of drinking tea into a divine ritual of the spirit. The particular *Fu* script, as shown in the illustration on page 72, depicts the mountain spirit. By drawing the energetic pattern of the mountain, the alchemist symbolically harnesses the forces of the earth into the tea, imprinting the tea's watery molecules into a crystalline form that is beneficial for health and well-being.

Water

The use of a silken net to collect the morning dew for the tea is a time honored method of survival in the high plateau, where water sources are extremely scarce. By using the earth as a passive filtering system, such liquid is both pure and endowed with the essence of the flowers. In his book, *The Art of Alchemical Qigong Remedies in Therapeutic Application*, the author, Dr. Zhou Chien Quan, notes that a rare source of water for brewing alchemical tea comes from the liquid trapped inside hollow geodes. In extremely extraordinary and precious instances tiny aquatic creatures are found living inside these naturally self-contained and self-sustaining biospheric geodes.

Hence, for the alchemist, this liquid is clearly endowed with life-sustaining vitality and rich in curative minerals. Further on in his book, Dr. Zhou wrote that another natural filtration method uses bamboo to filter water by drilling a hole in the upper segment, letting it filter down into the lower segments, and finally tapping the purified liquid at the lowest section of the bamboo. This is very much akin to a method Vermont farmers use to tap the sap from their maples in the process of brewing maple syrup; it is believed that the unadulterated maple sap is rich in vital benevolent bio-cultures.

As an aside, the popular Kombucha, an effervescent fermentation of sweetened tea, is very much akin to the alchemist's process of bio-filtering and fermentation of the water in their bamboo filtration process. Furthermore, since bamboo grows in segments with a permeable membrane in between each section, the alchemist would calibrate the section with the length of time for filtration. Hence, by using the direct one-to-one correlation between segment and month, water filters down at a length of nine segments requiring nine months of maturation (in parallel with the gestation and maturation of a human fetus).

Fire

The hand gesture (or mudra) used in holding the teacup where the middle finger is folded in toward the thumb symbolizes the fire pat-

The Fire Mudra drawing.

tern. Thus, in one hand, the tea master illustrates the nature of the fire mudra below that supports and cooks the tea water in the cup above. This most profound archetypical relationship of fire and water is ultimately reflected in the balance of mind and body, the polarity of the masculine supporting the feminine, light and darkness, heart and kidney, and finally the Shakti, the spirit imputing from below the Parvati, matter. It's often said that, especially in the Japanese *Chaidao*, drinking the green powdery sea foamed liquid whipped by the tea whisk is akin to swallowing the whole ocean symbolically.

Rite of Transmission

When an alchemical teacher accepts a disciple into the fellowship of his guild, his act of offering tea, either informally or formally, symbolizes the offering of a powerful transmission. This rite of passage is akin to the vow of taking refuge in Buddhism, the baptism in Christianity and the coming of age ceremony of the Bar Mitzvah in Jewish culture. And in my own lineage of the Dragon Gate, the master will dip a single finger in the offered tea and touch the disciple's third eye in a symbolic gesture of transmission. This ancient knowledge is directed into the novice's mind and is given as an empowerment to help him open his wisdom eye, *insight*.

At still a deeper layer, by drinking the tea with the fire mudra, the master is demonstrating the ultimate context of Taoist alchemical cultivation, the balance of water and fire, yin and yang, the life and death in a single cup of tea. It is through harmonizing these polarities that one can derive nourishment. Hence, for the uninitiated, the grind of life's hardships depletes their life force and vitality, but with esoteric insight and skillful means, the sorcerer's apprentice learns to harness obstacles, disasters and conflicts as a source of enrichment and ultimately liberation.

Truly, then, alchemy is a metaphor for resurrection, while tea is the living manifestation of rejuvenation itself, its leaves springing to life in scalding hot water, then blossoming and yielding its sea-green fragrance. Bringing these worlds together in a single cup of tea is, for the alchemist, an act with esoteric meaning. Simply drinking a cup of tea makes real the ultimate harmony between yin and yang, heaven and earth, mortality and immortality, life and death.

Alchemy and Tea

One of the central tenets of alchemy is the process of regeneration or rebirth, a form of resurrection from near death. As the tealeaf is rejuvenated from its shriveled state back to its full vigor with scalding water, so is the alchemist returned from a death-like state by a jolt of awakened consciousness. The semi-biographical book, *Opening the Dragon Gate*, translated by Thomas Cleary, is the story of an apprentice, Wang Liping, who embarks on a journey of alchemy under the tutelage of three Taoist grandmasters.

In one story, Wang enters into a state of almost cryogenic coma through the ingestion of special herbs. His respiration is slowed down to the point that a mirror placed under his chin does not capture any sign of moisture. For six days his masters perform the rite of passage for the dead, even erecting a wooden headstone for him, and chanting the Taoist Book of Dead. After the sixth day, Wang wakes up and relates how he entered a palatial hall where he met with ancient Taoists and was given advance esoteric alchemical teachings.

The resurrection of the tealeaf is a parallel process. The leaf gives out an essence that enlivens our mind and spirit to a wakeful state of clarity. No wonder the myth of tea is attributed to the Indian monk, Bodhidharma, who during a deep meditation in which he kept falling asleep, sliced off his eyelids and threw them on the ground; from those miraculous eyelids sprung forth the sapling of the first tea tree.

There is, of course, a price to pay even for the more seasoned alchemist. A seeker is required to decipher a macabre atlas of shamanic rituals and tunnel into the nether regions of startling darkness with its unfamiliar flora and fauna. The revelations about the human spirit that await us make the dangerous descent worthwhile. Now and then a sumptuous vista will suddenly emerge, a slice of nirvana with gleaming limpid deep sea-creatures lurking at the depths of our collective consciousness. No wonder the great tea master, Lu Yu, in his book, the *Tao of Tea*, proclaims that in holding a cup of tea, one beholds the transmigration from death to life.

Sat Hon, MFA, a native of China, is a multi-faceted teacher, a Taoist adept who interprets and transmits this quintessential and age-old wisdom of healing movements: *Qigong, Taiji*, and *Alchemy*.

Taiwanese Tea Ceremony, Photography © Phil Cousineau, 2007.

Part II
THE SPIRIT OF TEA

Chapter 8

THE PARABLE OF STONE ALCHEMICAL TEA

Sat Hon

I have been the guardian of the following origin story about one of the most magical aspects of tea's relationship to alchemy for over four decades. I was entrusted with knowledge of Taoist alchemy that is still entirely reliant on oral transmission passed down from master to disciple in a living lineage. Likewise, Buddhism in its first five hundred years was also completely passed down through oral tradition without written works. Only at the first Buddhist conversion did they realize that without written sutras, sacred texts, the teachings of Buddha would have vanished.

As the Swiss psychologist Carl Jung would have noted, there is great synchronicity at work as I complete this essay in a Manhattan that has been darkened by Hurricane Sandy. There is no power in our building, and so I must write by candlelight, which seems appropriate for the story I am about to tell. It is during trying times such as these that the ancient disciplines of alchemy and tea will prove to be of solace.

What follows is my gingerly attempt to paint a portrait of alchemy and its connection to tea by relating encounters of my own Taoist master's initiation into the fellowship of the alchemist's guild.

The Sacred Script of the Mountain Spirit, drawn by Sat Hon.

The alchemists' use of tea in saving lives under the most dire of circumstances illustrates the power of tea to restore health and extend one's life beyond imagination.

Here is my story:

During the darkest hours of the epic Sino-Japan War (1937-1945), massive columns of soldiers swarmed ant-like across the abandoned rice paddies at the foothills of the Daxue Shan Sentinel mountain range. A young lieutenant named Gu Luxin, who had been drafted during the late stages of the war, paused at the narrow mountain pass and gazed into the distance as if staring into the gaping jaws of *Yama* at the threshold of the underworld. The lieutenant's eyes shone with a dark steely glint mixed with a forlorn, dreamy quality. His cheekbones were high and round, and curved lines etched his cheeks. His upper lip was thin, and as he had a slight overbite, his lips stretched to shield his teeth when he clamped his mouth shut. Far beyond, the surging peaks could be seen penetrating through the morning mist and vanishing into an ominous gathering cloudburst. The golden yoke of sun wavered behind a thickening lace of mist, which shrouded the mountains and turned them ghostly pale.

As Gu stood at the entryway 7,000 kilometers above sea level, time seemed suspended. The worst atrocities of the war faded away in his mind—the grisly Nanking massacres, the muffled cries of babies suffocating in their mother's arms as they attempted to shield them from an agonizing death, the relentless aerial sorties rifling down soldiers and civilians alike, and the bombing of cities. Amidst the eerie silence of the Japanese army's final retreat, China's forces were withdrawing to the mountainous region of Szechuan to take their final stand for one last battle.

The young officer was not yet thirty, but he had done and witnessed things well beyond his years. He felt old before his time, tired, and burdened with all the demands upon him. Above all, he was utterly overwhelmed by the responsibility of so many lives placed in his hands. Time stood still as Gu silently prayed, "O, hear me, spirit of the valley, gods of the ethereal peaks, please grant me and my men safe passage."

The young lieutenant had been given command of a unit of one hundred and fifty soldiers, which was called the "Green Dragon Company." The lives of these young men, all teenage peasants with only a few short weeks of training, were placed in his hands. Their mothers had pleaded with him: *"Please bring our sons home!"*

This is what he was thinking about as he squeezed through the narrow mountain gap created by two gigantic boulders, he read an ancient inscription etched on one of the stones: "Anxious Pass Cliffs, even wild geese are frightened."

"Ah, how appropriate," Gu thought.

He caught his breath, and as he passed through a narrow stone archway, memory surged in. He recalled his graduation day at Beidai College. He was moving slowly in the long line of graduates who were about to receive their diplomas. In college, he had been fresh and almost agonizingly self-conscious, burgeoning with growth and thrilled with the anticipation of what lay ahead. Ahead of him were long strings of firecrackers popping cheery bursts of light and sound, permeating the air with sulfurous smoke. Children zigzagged through the solemn procession with their colorful silk streamers. He was only twenty-one years old and the world was in front of him.

After the ceremony, his Taoist professor approached him to offer congratulations. He placed a hand on Gu's shoulder, and said rather oracularly, "Finally, you have made it to the finish line."

The finish line was the professor's perplexing expression for his belief that life is an existential relay race, a struggle to the end, a competition between the self and circumstance, opponent and a nemesis that will surely obstruct you, make you falter or even fail. The professor believed that life was one long struggle, an obstacle course

"Aren't Taoists unconcerned about attaining goals?" Gu asked him in a gentle challenge. The professor raised an eyebrow, and proclaimed that he had never encountered any true Taoist presence at the school—inferring that even he shouldn't be considered with such eminence.

"Do you know why they light firecrackers at celebrations?" the professor asked him.

"To chase evil away," Gu replied. Then he added, "Ah, a deeper question would be 'Why is evil always present at these momentous events?' Perhaps danger is inherent in great events, hence the presence of evil spirits."

The professor turned to Gu and spoke so softly that Gu had to lean close to him: "Remember this word, *Weiji*. It refers to a dangerous opportunity, but in dangerous times there are also hidden opportunities for awakening." With a wave of his hand, the professor slipped back into the crowd of well-wishers.

"But awakening to what?" Gu asked.

The professor spun around and laughed, "Look for the extraordinary in the mundane."

Smiling, Gu shook hands with him and dissolved into the mass of onlookers, and as he walked away he became filled with a sudden sense of foreboding.

While his professor's words hovered in his mind, Gu was startled back to reality by a loud burst of what sounded like the firecrackers of his graduation ceremony. But these sounded ominously close.

"Duck!"

The shout came from his personal attaché and was so violent it brought Gu back into his body, back into real time, back into the war.

Crack-crack!

Those weren't firecrackers, it was the sharp staccato sound of gunfire echoing eerily across the valley. His attaché recognized the imminent danger to his commanding officer and instinctively leapt on his back to protect him. Gu lay underneath him until the gunfire died down, then rolled over on his back.

In one of those desperate moves that wartime brings out in soldiers, Gu grabbed a handful of pebbles and threw them in the direction of the gunfire. When the snipers fired back, his soldiers were able to locate them by tracing the trajectory of their shots and firing back. An old oak tree shuddered, and Gu watched in horror as two Japanese snipers tumbled out and fell in one fluid motion, like Olympic divers leaping off a springboard, returning fire until they hit the ground with a dull thud.

When the gunfire had ceased, Gu approached the fallen bodies and barked to his men, "Bury them."

"Those *gaoshi* (*dog shits*) don't deserve to be buried," muttered the gruff old cook, Ah Song. He was the lieutenant's personal servant and had cared for him since childhood. Ah Song spit on the ground and growled, "Let the wild dogs have their feast."

Shaking his head sadly, Gu walked over to the dead bodies and searched their pockets. According to custom, each soldier had a small packet of folded origami in the shape of a lotus blossom. Hidden in the center of each packet was a small family portrait of wife and children. Gu respectfully took the packets and slipped them into a hidden pocket in his own military jacket.

As a kind of impromptu eulogy, he said quietly to the fallen enemy, "If I survive this war, I vow to deliver these packets to your families."

The old cook was perplexed by the gesture, even angered.

The young master must not be right in his head, he thought. *To be kind to your enemy is cruel to yourself.*

A TEA PILGRIMAGE

The Daxue Shan Mountains were formed by the tectonic plates of two massive landmasses pushing against each other. Like gigantic hands pressing against a piece of clay with relentless pressure, the fault line between them rises and becomes a swelling ridge of heaving peaks. In the last millennium, the crags and pinnacles have surged well beyond 7,000 kilometers above sea level.

The Tibetans called this range Minya Konka, the Crystal Mountain, and they considered it to be their most sacred site. During peacetime, Buddhist and Taoist pilgrims would trek to the Konka Monastery for its legendary tea, the Snow Lotus of the Himalaya. During wartime, pilgrims of another sort desperately sought refuge in the peaks of Minya Konka, hoping to escape the unrelenting aerial assaults of the Japanese. The enemy planes couldn't breach the insurmountable elevation or the ever-present misty veil of clouds. With an almost inborn homing instinct, the Chinese people retreated to their sacred mountain for protection and safety.

After days of leading his soldiers up the mountainside, Gu looked at the torturous trail ahead of him and saw a long and undulating line of slowly marching human bodies. They reminded him of a writhing dragon whose head was disappearing into the clouds. The sight was dreadful. He realized that his regiment formed the tail end of this human chain 300,000 links long. The coiling legions of infantry scaled the jagged, steep precipice. Heaviness dogged their every step. Their faces became gaunter and more haggard, and streaks of dark brown sweat ran down their cheeks as hope drained from their hearts.

Gu watched his men with a leaden sensation in the pit of his stomach. He thought, *Some of my men may not make it to the top.* Already after the first day, the cold wind had worsened, scraping their faces like razor blades. Strewn along the trail within the crevices and small caves loomed the grotesque corpses of men who had fallen into the deepest of slumbers, never to wake up. He was stricken with grief and thought to himself that it was a romantic lie that the dead looked peaceful and had simply fallen into some kind of eternal slumber. He wanted to scream at the absurdity of any nobility in the sight of the bodies lying in front of him, contorted in rage and agony. These soldiers had left behind trails of frozen tears and caked blood, cracked, blackened lips with teeth marks depicting searing pain. And etched in each face was the horror of the final moment, as they grasped the enormity of their lonely mortality at a small overhang in a dirt hollow, hungry, cold, without loved ones; then, the last gasp before darkness enshrouded them.

Being at the tail end of the 5th brigade, Gu's regiment had been given the assignment to take care of the dead. With the Japanese army in hot pursuit, Gu calculated that he didn't have enough time to bury so many bodies, but took some consolation in the possibility that perhaps in death they could return to their beloved farms down below. He feverishly prayed to himself, *Let earth return to earth.*

He felt emboldened and ordered his soldiers to collect their personal belongings and family photos. Then he instructed his soldiers, "Roll the bodies down the cliff."

As noble as the effort appeared to be, he knew it was a gruesome task. The bodies had frozen and bonded to the earth. Having no other choice, Gu's soldiers hacked at the limbs and bodies with pickaxes, bits of flesh and bones splattering their faces. His men worked in silent fury.

A STRANGE APPARITION

While lost in painful reverie, Gu saw an extraordinary sight. From out of the corner of his eye he saw a wizened old man ambling up an impossibly steep path that joined with theirs. The climb must have taken extraordinary effort, but the old man wore an aura of undeniable jubilation. He left behind him a sparkling iridescent afterimage, as if a torch was waving from side to side in the dark. This sight evoked a long lost memory in Gu of a sea monster swimming on a moonless night, leaving behind its wake of fluorescence, tiny sulfuric algae furiously emitting pulses of luminescence. As the Old Man of the Mountains came around the final bend of the path, Gu could hear fragments from a song he was singing:

"Ha, ha, ha, hey, hey, hey,
first cup kisses and moistens my lips,
second cup disperses lonesomeness and such dull tedium,
third cup eviscerates all worries and fears . . .
Where lies Penglai Isle,
I'll ride the cool zephyr and return . . . "

The Old Man of the Mountain had beaming eyes and wild whitish eyebrows that curled up like the antennas of a moth. He wore a tattered saffron robe with long flapping sleeves that billowed like a small parachute and had a yellow silk sash tied at the waist. He shouldered a long bamboo staff with a small bundle tied on its end swinging pendulum-like from side to side.

"Ha-ha-ha," he laughed. "Make way for the living, make way for the living . . . "

He kept chanting as he threaded his way through the collapsed piles of soldiers. He gave off a subtle scent of divinity. It was as if an immortal had briefly touched the dusty surface of the earth with one sandaled foot, observed all the silly self-inflicted trouble, and decided that there was no hope of redemption for any mortals. So, he resumed his place in the ethereal palace with transcendental joviality, having reminded the children of earth of their butchering of each other—brothers killing brothers, fathers murdering fathers with such lethal monomaniacal focus. They could not be trusted to manage their own affairs, and further atrocities would surely bring the wrath of heaven on them.

Look for the extraordinary in the ordinary, Gu thought, as his old professor's words rang in his ears.

Gu crossed the road to greet the bearish old man. His saffron robe flapped like the wings of a great albatross. His eyes twinkled as he performed his karmic duty, a compassionate vow to save all sentient beings.

"*Sifu*, Your Reverence, please, can I offer you my officer's mount and serve as your transport up the cliff. It's a seven day hike up the steep trail."

Impulsively, Gu dropped down into a full prostration, touching his forehead at the master's feet. It was an awkward moment. He had surprised himself. The whole regiment of Gu's fighters was also stunned as they saw their beloved commander prostrating in the dust, *kowtowing* to an old wizened man who wore little more than rags.

Even the old man was embarrassed, behaving as if somehow his true identity had been revealed. He bent down and lifted the young man up from the ground, noticing that Gu's eyes shone with tears and his hunched shoulders quivered with weariness.

Ah, poor lad, the old master thought, *he is burdened with a load way beyond his youth and capacity. It is indeed a great burden to hold so many lives in one's heart. Underneath this officer's authoritative veneer lie all the makings of a romantic, a spiritual seeker. But how can I save him?*

"Don't be deceived by outward manifestation and phenomenon," he said. "This old bag of bones may indeed still make it up the mountain one last time."

To most people, the old man would have appeared to be no more than a foolish peasant who was staggering up the dangerous cliff, but something told Gu to look closer. As he looked closer, he could detect the old man's aura pulsating like a small sun. And in the depth of his eyes, Gu could see far back into the long corridor of human existence, as if the old man had defied time itself.

The vision into the old man's soul triggered something in the young lieutenant. He reminded himself that he was an officer in a terrible war, the commander of a small ragtag band of men who had entrusted their lives to him, and that he could surely fail.

He thought, *didn't the Japanese snipers almost kill most of my men? It was pure luck that the snipers chose to capture me instead of my soldiers. They know that an officer is a much better trophy.*

Slowly, Gu realized that the old man was no mere wandering peasant. He was a venerable old Taoist who saw the extraordinary in the mundane, the rare opportunity in dangerous times, just as Gu's college professor had predicted. Now he had a glimmer of hope for himself and his band of warriors. The old Taoist could be his only hope of scaling the precipice and keeping all his men intact.

The old Taoist observed Gu arriving at precisely this assessment, and softly chuckled, "Who taught you your keen skill of seeing?"

"My Professor Chandao at the Beidai College," Gu replied. "He taught us the ancient art of the oracle and the *I Ching,* the *Book of Change.* Long ago he predicted that I would encounter remarkable men in ordinary circumstances and dangerous times."

The Old Taoist's eyes opened wide with surprise. "Oh, *him* . . . that son born of a turtle fled from the monastery years ago. He certainly has a *long tongue,*[1]" the old master lamented.

Gu was familiar with authentic teachers' reluctance to reveal their true natures in worldly circumstances. They knew most people would misunderstand their behavior and take them to be utterly foolish, or worse, charlatans.

"Then you are my *tai sifu*[2]." Gu started to flatten and prostrate himself again in front of the old man.

"Don't! You're scaring your men."

The Old Taoist pointed to the semi-circle of half-frozen soldiers surrounding them, a strange reminder for Gu just how stunned and shocked his soldiers had become by the incessant fighting and marching. Gu nodded wearily. But it was the old cook, Ah Song, who seemed to know what was truly happening and how his young master was fighting for all of their lives.

Ah Song had a dark past. In his younger days he had led a group of famished peasants to rebel against the local magistrate. Unfortunately, their rebellion failed and he was captured and sentenced to be executed within three days. On the last night, he saw one of his death row cellmates sleeping unconcerned and without a trace of fear. Just as Ah Song was thinking that his fellow prisoner possessed incredible forbearance, he turned to Ah Song and said, "Go to sleep, my poor man. By tomorrow, the Manchu will be overthrown and we will be free."

The next morning, they were freed by the revolutionaries, who had succeeded in overthrowing the Manchu Dynasty.

The prisoner turned out to be the Old Taoist who had been locked up for months without any resource of news from the outside world. That was when Ah Song realized that the Old Man had the power to see the future.

"Please, Your Reverence, will you help my young master?" Ah Song asked. "He hasn't slept for days now. At night, he wanders

---

1. (*Eng.* a busy body.)
2. (*Eng.* Grand master)

around the camp kicking at the soldiers who have fallen asleep too deeply, fearful that they might not wake up. He has depleted his own rations in order to feed the hungry orphans trailing behind us, and he gave away his coat to an old woman freezing on the side of the road. I don't think he will last another day."

Ah Song's voice quivered like a bowstring. The company was not aware of all the covert deeds of their young commander. Now, as one body, they converged on the Taoist master, the master of clouds and thunder, the shape-shifting sorcerer.

The Old Man of the Mountains seemed genuinely moved. After a long silence, he sighed, "Okay, I'll have a cup of tea with you good men."

A shadow passed over the soldiers' puzzled faces.

"Tea?"

The Green Dragon Company was mystified by the mysterious old man's request of sharing a cup of tea amongst friends, as if they were living in peacetime. Only Gu and the old cook grasped the full significance of this invitation to enjoy a cup of tea. Gu instructed his personal attaché to bring the utensils and a small coal stove to make the tea, but the old Taoist waved him away, "Today, we'll brew stone tea."

STONE TEA

The ancient wizard selected a granite boulder veined in deep dark marble streaks, with white sparkling quartz threads crisscrossing through its whole mass like a giant spider web. The stone was mottled by patches of green lichen, and rusty brown moss clung to its slightly concave form. Using his long sleeves as a brush, he gently swept away dust, debris and small insects from the boulder.

The old man's hands danced with the liquid grace of a tea master. Every gesture was performed with minute precision. He flicked his fingers as if strumming the invisible filament of an ethereal harp. Long after, Gu realized that the old man's movements were derived from the classical Taiji Quan. Specifically, he came to discover, the flicking of his fingers was inspired by the Taiji gesture, and the hand strums from the Pei Pai gesture.

"Hmm, let's start a hot little fire," the tea master said.

He spoke softly to himself, a habit developed from years of living in solitude. At the bottom of the rock there were piles of debris: loose conifers, small twigs and leaves. He scooped up a handful of these elements and rubbed them gently in his hands while huffing and puffing a steady stream of air into them. The air throbbed as he sang an eerie incantation: *Hung ba xu fu si . . . so bum, bum, bum, ba, ba, ba . . .*

The mantra looped in a slow circle then increased in tempo and volume that reverberated across the valley. A thin veil of mist slowly drifted in. Tiny particles of vapor penetrated everyone's clothes until they sensed the faint tingling sensation of a sentient presence. The master of clouds and mists was calling upon the spirit of the valley to come and share a cup of tea with him. For her, humans were mere temporal creatures, miniscule ants crawling over her abode, Mount Konga. She knew humans were destined to last but for a few moments, like the fleeting existence of morning gnats.

Suddenly, the ingredients in the old master's hands burst into flame, shining through the mist in a vermilion radiant orb. He dropped the hot embers into the pile of refuse, where they quickly ignited and a small fire started to burn. Reaching into his pocket, the old Taoist took out a handful of jade green stone eggs and dropped them into the blaze. Then he upended his bamboo staff and unplugged a stopper in the last section. As if by magic, water started to trickle out into the hollow of granite.

Ha, the old fox, the old cook thought, *he still has tricks up his sleeve— and in this case, up his staff.*

After filling three quarters of the basin, the tea master grabbed a bunch of green shoots from nearby pine trees and dropped them into the water. From his bundle he added a handful of Goji berries and half dozen red dates to the brew. The stone eggs became translucent from the searing flame. Using two long twigs as prone, the tea master picked up the heated stone eggs and carefully dropped them into the tea. Within minutes, small bubbles the size of shrimp whiskers percolated up to the surface. "The tea is ready," the tea master intoned. "Now, everyone make yourself a tea cup with bamboo leaves."

The master used his index and middle fingers and traced an alchemical transformational hieroglyph that hovered above the surface of the steamy tea. Silently, the tea master invoked the esoteric mantra: "*May this be transformed into the life essence of numen and qi and may this tea be given as an offering to the mountain spirits to assure everyone present safe passage. Om a hum, sohum.*"

He folded a large bamboo leaf into a cone, and using it like a ladle, he sprinkled the first taste of steamy tea skyward and then to the valley gorge below. The mist abruptly evaporated, the clouds parted, and the sun emerged like a diamond in the crystalline cobalt sky.

THE CHANGES

One hundred fifty men were fed and nourished by the Taoist Master's strange brew of Stone Tea. They had taken part in a sacred ritual that reached far back to the dawn of time, before the discovery of bronze, before the use of pottery. For the first time in the agonizingly drawn-out war, Gu and his bone-weary men were filled with a sense of optimism. Their hopes for survival seemed brighter, and, for the first time in weeks, they dared to talk about surviving the war. Uncannily, one thought occurred to each of them: "*Yes, we are the masters of our destiny.*"

After serving the brew, the Tea master dropped into a deep meditative *Samadhi*. His breath became so silent that if a feather were placed under his nose, it would remain utterly still.

As he rested, Gu drank deeply from the tea bowl, like a thirsty stallion plunging its whole nose into the stream. He swallowed the cinnabar red tea with the mild pine fresh scent deep into his soul, into the pit of his sex. He felt a stirring of the coiled fire serpent unwinding at the base of his sacrum, *the sacred sanctum*. The dragon was undeniably rising in him, his spirit irrevocably awakening as they drank what they would eventually call *Yen Yu tea*, Stone Alchemical

Tea, which is supremely rich in minerals, vitamins and its most essential ingredient, the hieroglyphic sacred script that can disperse the chill and fog in the hearts of men. This sacred brew they would make three times a day, morning, afternoon and night.

Miraculously rejuvenated, Gu and his company paid their last homage to the old alchemist. Each of them prostrated themselves before the still wizened old man seated on the boulder. Some would later claim that the old wizard seemed to float a few inches above the rock. Is it possible that their consciousness was slightly altered by the mild hallucinogenic effects of the blue green lichens?

FAREWELL

After bidding farewell in silence, the renewed Green Dragon Company resumed their relentless march toward the mountains. The bluish mountain peaks spread out toward the heavens like colossal columns with glistening snowcaps that shimmered in the sunlight. A solitary peregrine soared and swirled overhead, its shrieks piercing the air, awakening the dog-tired soldiers.

Struggling to keep up with the quickly receding shadow of his young master, the old cook whispered softly to the Tea master, "I'll keep an eye on him. I won't let him overdo it. He just wants to save the whole goddamn world."

As evening approached, the air grew cold with moisture. Gu stared ahead, hypnotized by the summit vanishing in the blood-red clouds. It was so beautiful he couldn't peal his eyes away. He folded together his long fingers, which seemed more suited to holding a brush than a rifle. He was worried about the old man, recalling another of his professor's strange quips, "Even an immortal could be killed."

His professor had explained to him that Taoist immortals are not *the undead* like the vampires of modern fiction. Alchemists are flesh and blood, but have attained a higher plain of existence: the ability to step in and out of time. In essence, they can slow the process of time by entering into a catatonic somnambulistic trance, hence freezing the body in a state of cryogenic hibernation. Subsequently, while common folks toil ceaselessly day and night, the immortals will only spend a fraction of their life span in doing what is absolutely critical. When humans live in fear, hunger corrodes their stomachs and hearts in the fight to secure food; when men hunger for love, they destroy all that which is lovable inside of them; when seeking to build a safe haven, they pollute the very land they live in. In a world ruled by myopic boars, trampled by ravenous goats, and scavenged by laughing hyenas, the immortals step gingerly amongst these wild beasts caressing their neurotic egos, moving with liquid grace, side-stepping all the traps and pitfalls of fame, fortune and sexual obsession. The alchemists flow along with the mortal stream but never get caught in it. While the rest of humankind march furiously toward death, Taoists float on their backs, cease all striving, and return to a state of deep absorption, rejuvenating their being within sublime cosmic potencies.

With sudden clarity, Gu realized the old man must have been living all along right there in the Konga Mountains. *And we have brought this calamity of war to him,* Gu thought to himself, sadly shaking his head. *We have compelled the dragon out of his cave.*[3]

Night approached slowly. The soldiers were enveloped in pitch-black darkness that the stars couldn't penetrate. The encroaching fog and the wet vapors sent a piercing chill into their bones, and the cold Himalayan air made breathing painful. Small clusters of fire failed to spread warmth beyond the little circle of huddled bodies. All over the mountainside, tiny dots of flickering fires blinked on and off like tiny fireflies, signaling to each other, *yes, we are still alive.* The thick fog shrouded everything in bone crushing heaviness, which threatened to squeeze out the last bit of hope.

In the middle of the night, the fog lifted and Gu fell asleep. In that time beyond time between sleep and waking he heard the

---

3. (Subsequently, later in the march, the high commander, Yang Xin, discovers another alchemist, a two hundred and fifty year-old herbalist, Lee Ching Yuan, and bestows on the ancient wizard a celebration banquet. Gu is amongst the few hundred honored guests.)

prowling of wild beasts searching for food scraps in their camp. Startled awake, Gu assumed it must have been a pack of wild dogs trailing behind the company, so he fell back asleep. He dreamt of a vast cerulean sky with a lone kite soaring above the velvet clouds. A bamboo wind flute that was attached to its tail trilled a high-pitched shrill, and a long, brightly colored streamer extended from the kite making small loopy curls in the sky, a diamond instance of eternal sunshine and innocence.

The next morning he woke to the sight of lacey scarves of mist draped across the pine forest, their needles saturated with droplets of twinkling dew. Squealing squirrels chattering and scattering pinecones below woke the soldiers. The fat squirrels were enraged over the invasion of their territory and the kidnapping of their kind. During the night, the ever-resourceful old cook had trapped a few, and the aroma of meat stew wafted through the camp. He was their lifeline against starvation. One by one, the famished soldiers were drawn to the warm meal.

That was one lucky squirrel, Ah Song thought, *someone saved it from the jaws of death. If only we could be as fortunate.*

THE ASCENT

Ceaselessly, the soldiers marched forward like one gigantic centipede. They scaled the precipices and overhangs, the treacherous, icy wet trails across the razor edged mountains, which looked like the back of a fire-breathing dragon angrily raising up its dorsal crest and thrusting it at the heavens.

In the early afternoon, Gu led his men through one of the most dangerous passes. They had to form a human chain, linked arm to arm, bodies hugging tight against the cliff face, their feet barely able to secure a foothold on the crumbling ancient corridor chiseled by a long forgotten band of warriors from another era, also fleeing their enemy. Gu was so focused on leading the company he hadn't noticed that the old Taoist Master had disappeared. The thought was terrifying that he may have fallen, but Gu felt obliged to keep moving.

When the path became so narrow even a mountain goat would have had trouble finding footing, he had to dismount his beloved mount, the brunt stallion with a pale white diamond star on its forehead. The noble horse reared on its back legs and neighed its frustration as Gu was forced to abandon it.

"Go! Find another way up," Gu shouted and smacked its side.

Without looking back, he urged his men to keep scaling up the mountain toward the seemingly insurmountable snowy peak.

The men crawled over the overhangs, sometimes dangling precariously with fingertip holds. Over time, the men adapted to the mountain. They even resembled it. Their sweat-soaked clothes turned the dusty ochre color of the earth. From a distance, they appeared to have merged with the mountain. After seven days of relentless climbing, Gu and his unit finally reach the plateau at the summit of Mount Konga.

"Ha, welcome, welcome, my friends."

Waving from a cluster of pines, the old tea master smiled and called out, "I've been waiting for you for three whole days."

Gu was flabbergasted. It wasn't possible. *How could he have surpassed us?* Gu wondered. *Did he knows a shortcut and didn't share it with us?*

The old man noticed the slightly annoyed expression on the young soldier's face and explained, "No, my young friend, there is no shortcut up the mountain. Four nights ago, I passed your camp and stumbled into one of your cook's squirrel traps." The old man shows a torn frail silk sash.

Gu looked even more perplexed and asked how anyone his age could have scaled the cliffs in the dark?

The old man laughed. "There was plenty of light under the full moon. While other people sleep during the night, I stroll in a meditative state, which rejuvenates my body even better than a long night of slumber. As you've witnessed, a deep sleep could be deadly in this climate."

His cool honesty convinced Gu that the old man was telling the truth. The old wizard may possess the means of keeping his regiment alive, and his soldiers must acquire such skill. In turn, the tea master saw how Gu arrived at his decision and was concerned, asking him, "You're so busy trying to save others, but will you be able to save yourself?

His heart was moved.

"Come find me this evening. We have much to speak of. "

"I am so grateful and honored," said Gu. "Nothing between heaven and earth will prevent me from seeing you this evening."

A low hum of conversation emerged from the regiment. They looked at their commanding officer with newfound respect, even awe.

Emboldened, Gu turned and headed back to look after his soldiers. "Our journey has just begun," Gu said quietly, "there is still a long path ahead of us."

A gust of wind sprinkled flakes of snow over the ground around him. Then a strange thing happened. Gu seemed to hear a tingling music emanating from the dancing particles of snow. He didn't say a thing, just reveled in the moment while the men drank their wine and stirred the fire. In the middle of the night the men lurched to their feet and stumbled into their make shift tents, rolling into their dusty blankets. They bunched close together to stay warm under the soft milky moonlight.

The young lieutenant bent down and untied his laces, slipping off his boots. Then he peeled off his socks and unfurled his damp feet on the moist buoyant needles and thick dark purple moss. He wriggled his toes until the stiffness drained out of his body and soul. The furrows on his forehead gradually smoothed out and his eyes brimmed with a burning urge. He shed his sidearm and placed it beside his boots; instinctively he knew such a place had no need for a weapon.

Finally, Gu moved up the footpath, rolling each foot silently from heel to toe, with the moon shadowing right behind him. For a few moments he tread onward, the deep needle beds hushing his footsteps and the cloud-layered valley below soaking up all sounds except the murmuring needles of the treetops.

When the mash of vines and brambles blocked his way, he would crouch low to crawl through the small opening between low hanging branches, and sometimes he had to hack through thick curtains of tightly woven bamboo. The effort was like an initiation, a rite of passage into the realm of the unknown and unknowable. Although his face was badly scratched and his clothes torn, Gu finally penetrated through the bramble enclosure and stood up. His eyes widened with awe at the circle of trees surrounding a clear flat stone at the center. His gaze rested on the massive, warped glowing cobalt flagstone. A deep silence reigned; the presence of ancient magic—the old kind of primal forces—emanated from this place. The moss covering the slab was thick as a bear hide, and the sweet ferns sprouting from its crevices imbued the place with the faint sweet scent of a musty monastery. Gu clambered on top of the slab and folded his legs in the lotus meditation asana with his palms resting on top of each other. His gaze fell on a spot about three feet in front of him, and as his thoughts diminished, all his senses expanded outward so that in the stillness he perceived the tiny rustling *pat-pat* of meadow mice tunneling through dry crinkled leaves, the hoarse chirping of crickets, and the encroaching thumps of footfalls toward him.

An endearingly familiar figure emerged from the thicket, lumbering along with a bear-like drunken gait. Gu heard the familiar lilting nasal rendition of a Peking operatic aria with its high-pitched glass shattering supersonic wail.

"*Ai,e-e-e-e*, look at what the cat dragged in," the approaching figure greeted Gu with wild merriment.

"Yes, master, I have come according to your wishes." Gu prostrated himself in front of the tea master. He lifted his palms upward and pressed his forehead to the ground, a profound Buddhist gesture of reverence.

"Bah!" the tea master gently scolded, "None of this formality now."

But he was quietly moved by the demonstration of respect from the classically trained young officer who possessed the old time elegance of a gentlemen scholar. He thought that the young man just might have the potential to acquire the alchemical skills that he wanted so badly to pass on to the next generation.

"Master," said Gu with all due respect. "I have come to ask you to teach me the art of inner alchemy. I have come to see that your skill will help my men survive this war, and I have made a vow, a blood oath that I will, with every fiber of my being, bring them all home alive."

"Ah, well, a great undertaking indeed," murmured the sorcerer of the white light. "But the art of inner alchemy is not for the faint-of-heart, nor frivolous fools. What do you have to offer for such great wisdom?"

As if in a trance, Gu took his military knife and calmly sliced open his palm. Crimson blood gushed out. "I offer my blood, my body and every cell of my being." Kneeling at the flagstone, Gu's disheveled hair was slick with sweat as his lifeblood drained away. He was as wild as an ensnared wolf caught in a steel trap. The old man pressed his thumb at a point just above Gu's wrist. Instantly, the bleeding stopped.

"There, there, my son, you shall offer me a cup of tea."

Gu's last thought before falling into darkness was: *I have finally been accepted.* When he woke up a few hours later, his hand had been bandaged and a pot of water was boiling on the campfire. The tea master lit a small oil lamp, a shallow dish with a single wick flickering a soft golden light, and sang a hypnotic incantation.

In the wavering shadows, Gu saw strange forms dancing in the darkness. The old man held the steamy cup of tea in his right hand with the middle digit curled back. With his free hand, he traced a sacred script, *Fu*, the energy pattern of the mountain. He offered the tea to the valley spirit, the bright full moon, and called on all his ancestral teachers to gather and witness this transmission. He was passing the torch of wisdom to the next generation, the 20th lineage holder of the Dragon Gate.

Gu knelt and offered another cup of tea to the old man, saying, "Teaching father, *Sifu*, I offer this cup of tea as my eternal devotion to the Tao, to benefit all sentient beings and achieve liberation."

Emerging through the cloud layers, the moon looked on this ancient rite of transmission. Gu gazed up into the dark sky and the oddest thought occurred to him that one day human beings would plant a flag there.

The old wizard stared intensely at him. His bemused smile told Gu that he was reading his thoughts, or more, had created a small window for him to peer into the future.

So, alchemy is mastery of time and space.

The idea hit Gu so strongly that he reeled backwards and fell to the ground.

"Ah, this is a fine cup of tea."

The old master drank deeply of the pale green liquid.

"Now, let's begin," he said slowly. "The foundation of alchemy is in meditation, in coming face to face with one's true nature."

Without a word, the old man folded his legs, rested his palms on his lap and dropped into a deep state of *Samadhi*. Gu became utterly still.

Steadily, he felt something roiling at the edge of his consciousness. Some skittery awareness, a pale amorphous skein of shimmering nimbus studded with pulsating lights, like a blind, monstrous deep-sea creature lurking in the dark black ocean, a fusion of psychedelic vision and the radiant Indra's net spanning the space of galaxies and a multitude of realities. A small voice rose up in him from his very depths.

So, this is it. This is my true nature. Still. But it's too easy, way too simple. How can this be it? You have struggled all your life to gain enlightenment, and on this god-forsaken rock you attain the supreme awakening, the state of nirvana.

Soon, even the voice was extinguished. Gu's mind exploded, his ego shattered and his consciousness was stretched far enough to cover the whole universe.

Then, total silence.

Time stopped.

The only movement was the beating of their hearts. Bright moonlight illuminated the seated figures sitting quietly on the stone.

A lone red fox crept out of the hidden crevice and moved through the brambles to the perimeter around the flagstone. Soundlessly, it edged forward on its belly toward the men and stopped a stone's throw distance away, resting on its haunches with its tail tucked beneath like a cushion. There, the fox remained motionless with only the tips of its white furry ears flicking and twitching toward every little noise. The fox crept closer toward the men, and its whiskers jerked. With a soft bark, *bup*, that sounded eerily human, it broke the mesmerized circle, and the little creature silently retreated back to its cave and burrow. An early morning drizzle started to fall but was deflected by an invisible force surrounding the seated figures. Their clothes remained completely dry.

Slowly opening his eyes, the old alchemist observed how his young disciple was still deep in meditation. The old man bowed his gratitude toward the retreating shapes of the little critters, for they had borne witness to the crowning of the next lineage holder of the Dragon Gate.

The old man thought, *that is a true tradition that dates back to the beginning of the last Ice Age.*

Gu was awakened by the sound of swishing fabric. Opening his eyes, he found a curious sight. The old man stood on the edge of the flagstone and used his bamboo pole like a fishing rod to hurl a silken net over a field of clover. With a flick of his wrist, he jerked and wrapped the net around the pole. Completely soaked from the dews of the clover, he squeezed the moist net, and a dribble of liquid fell into the teapot.

"Ah, I see you are awake," he said, cool as the morning breeze. "Good. Now help me collect clover water for the tea this morning." The old master handed the pole and net to Gu, who proceeded to collect a quart of clover-scented water.

So this is the secret of collecting water in dry mountainous Taoist sanctuaries, thought Gu.

"Master, I'm eternally grateful for the power and wisdom you have bestowed on me." Gu prostrated himself at the feet of the old man and said, "Now will you show me the Cloud Walk, so that I can teach it to my men? I think it would help them survive the rest of this war and to keep the faith that our war with Japan will end and that China will be victorious."

The Old Tea Master beamed with pride and joy. He felt the burden of carrying on the lineage begin to lift. Slowly, he unveiled the most esoteric knowledge of life: the art of transformation and transfiguration.

"The secret of the Cloud Walk," he said, "is in the pendulum swing of its waltz-like step. Most men would be exhausted by a day-long march, and they would need extensive rest and sleep. But the Cloud Walk, which was discovered by our Ice Age ancestors during their long desperate struggle against the forces of nature, enabled our tribes to trek across deserts, continents and the Siberian strait. The essence of the walk is in its gait: a long step forward and two short, then rock backward and step out with the alternate leg forward. The loop is circular and coordinated with the breath."

He went on to demonstrate the Cloud Walk while telling the young lieutenant that most wandering Taoists were able to travel both day and night if needed without prolonged rest. "For we can slip into a state of light wakeful sleep," he said, "restoring our strength and vitality during our walk."

Each word was etched indelibly in Gu's mind.

As the old master spoke, Gu noticed snowflakes falling around them. They stuck to his face, then melted and ran down the back of his neck and cheeks. Somehow, the old man remained completely dry. The snowflakes were deflected from him as if an invisible dome was shielding him. Without a word, Gu moved closer to the old man. The old master shrewdly noticed Gu's actions and laughed the laugh of one who knows. His laughter rang out in the white surrounding silence like a bell ringing in the silent sky. Then, the old wizard fell into prayer, "This young disciple of mine will one day travel to a foreign land and be reminded of this moment when he shakes a glass dome filled with water—a miniature man with a white beard encased in a watery world where flakes of white drift and fall just like now. May the Bodhisattva of all Compassion, Kuan Yin, shine her light on Gu, my dharma son."

Over the course of the long night in the mountains, the gentle snowfall turned into a heavy snowstorm. This was fortuitous, since it forced the battalion to remain stationary for three days and nights. During that brief time, Gu learned a lifetime of inner alchemy and Taoist magic from the old Man of the Mountains. In turn, Gu was able to teach the Cloud Walk to his regiment, which became one of the few in the battalion to survive the long march without fatalities.

Gu never saw the old master again, though he felt his presence in his dreams.

AFTER THE WAR

Years after the war had mercifully ended and peace reigned, Gu retraced his path to the mountain and tried to find the old master. But the ancient wizard had returned to his hermitage like a deep sea turtle diving into the timeless mystery of the oceanic realm of consciousness. When Gu reached the flagstone at the peak, the place where he was initiated, he discovered a small slip of yellow silk wedged between the crevices. Written on it was a poem left behind by the old alchemist:

> Like silken clouds we met by the winds of karma,
> life is but a brief stay on this floating opera,
> why grasp with such dreadful might power and fame;
> when time passes,
> all that remains are but a few strands of hair and bones
>   fallen to the earth.
> Be careful of doing good, my young friend,
> Without wisdom, it will cause great harm and catastrophe.
> In time, a tsunami of crimson will awash our continent,
> Walk, my son, and never stop walking in the clouds.
> —*Your old teacher, Cloud Wanderer.*

That was the last message that Gu received from his teacher, but it was enough to help inspire his own vision of saving the new China. Only then did he realize the true nature of time. Past, present and future existed in one simultaneous moment. To be an alchemist, he realized, meant being capable of traveling between the slices of time.

Ah, but the old man did not teach me such traveling, the young lieutenant thought as he folded the slip and placed it in his inside pocket, like a precious talisman. As he began his journey of descent, a lithe red fox watched in silence Gu's departing figure until he vanished, and then bounced nimbly back to a cave hidden in a recess.

Decades passed.

The young lieutenant grew wiser and wiser, and at the same time more and more disillusioned. After several failed business ventures, he then traveled across the wide ocean to the Land of Gold, America, and discovered that instead of gold, it was paved with the sweat and labors of slaves, indentured serfs and generations of destitute immigrants. His previous education and training in China was utterly useless in America, except for the teachings of the old alchemist. Being a stranger in a strange land, Gu, at the age of seventy-six, finally met a disciple who also went down on his knees out of sheer respect. Now a master in his own right, Gu reached for a steamy cup of Stone Alchemy Tea. His hands shook slightly, and he could see in the eyes of his young apprentice a reflection of himself as a young man kneeling on a flagstone in a land far, far away and a time long ago. With gladness in his heart, Gu passed the cup to his student.

After a lifetime of searching, Gu had come to know that tea is a liquid thread that links all the different generations in a long strand of shamanism. Whenever Gu drank hot tea, he felt its warmth coursing down to the base of his spine, and he became thoughtful and philosophical, knowing that the foundation of alchemy is in meditative practices. When the survivors of the Green Dragon Company returned home, they were often asked to tell the tale. One by one, they explained that three things enabled them to survive the extreme hardship of their dangerous march into the mountains, three small miracles that had saved their lives: the Squirrel Broth, the Stone Alchemy Tea, and the Cloud Walk Qigong. The valiant soldiers felt grateful for the three elixirs that had helped them hold onto the tough cord of life and saved them from the jaws of death. A few of the survivors expressed their gratitude by teaching the Cloud Walk called *qigong* when they returned home. Others passed on the practice of Stone Alchemical Tea.

Chapter 9

THE FOOL AND THE TEAPOT

J. L. Walker

A friend from Yueh presented me
With tender leaves of Yen-His tea,
For which I chose a kettle
Of ivory-mounted gold,
A mixing bowl of snow white earth,
With its clear bright froth and fragrance,
It was like the nectar of Immortals.
The first bowl washed the cobwebs
From my mind—
The whole world seemed to sparkle.
The second cleansed my spirit
Like purifying showers of rain.
A third and I was one with the Immortals!—
What need now for austerities
To purge our human sorrows?
Worldly people, by going in for wine,
Sadly deceive themselves.
For now I know the Way of Tea is real
Who Immortal Tan Ch'iu
Could find it?

—Chiao-Jen (*Tang dynasty* 618-906)[1]

1. John Blofeld, *The Chinese Art of Tea* (Boston: Shambhala, 1985).

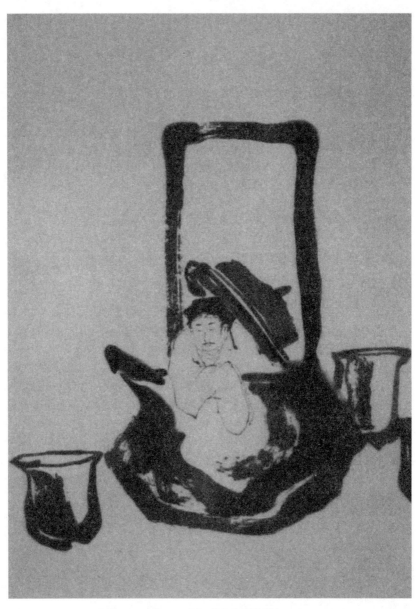

"Contemplating Tea," J. L. Walker, 1981

Chiao-Jen's three cups of tea open a window onto a whole universe that points out a refreshing view of human nature, one that inspires us to shift our attention away from the complexities of day-to-day life through the Way of Tea into an immediate, simpler, more "foolish" perspective. To evoke a recognition of the essential wholeness of Heaven, Earth, and Humanity is the function of the fool in the teapot.

This fool has wandered in many guises through the literature and philosophy of traditional China from its very beginning. To the eye of common sense, the sage is a fool:

Everyone says that my way of life is the way of a
    simpleton.
Being largely the way of a simpleton is what makes
    it worthwhile.
If it were not the way of a simpleton
It would long ago have been worthless.[2]

The difference between Lao-tzu's simpleton and ourselves is one of cognizance or awareness, of fully tasting all the possibilities of experience. Having realized the Tao, perfect presence is what the fool actually *is*, an Immortal, and thus the fool is a gift essentially inherent in the world. He or she will offend the self-righteous, outrage the worldly-wise, and shock those who take themselves too seriously. Without the simpleton we complacently sleep on.

Lao-Tzu again states forcefully:

When superior persons learn of the Tao, they practice it
with ardor. When mediocre persons learn of the Tao, it
leaves them indifferent. When inferior persons learn of the
Tao, they laugh loudly. If they did not laugh, it would not
be worthy of being the Tao.[3]

There is no institutional dogma, no doctrine, no set of directions to becoming an Immortal. There isn't really even a single, universally

---

2. *Tao Te Ching*, Chapter 67.
3. *Tao Te Ching*, Chapter 41.

agreed-upon definition. We seldom see them, yet we can recognize them: they are the ones who play the fool. Like a certain famous Zen master, they will fill your teacup to overflowing and keep on pouring. When you ask them why, they will tell you that you have to empty out your cup before the ultimate teaching can be poured in. The Tea Immortal may invite you someday, "Have a cup of tea."

The Chinese character we translate as Immortal, *xian*, is composed of two particles, one meaning "person," the other signifying "mountain." Thus, the Immortals (and there were far more than the famous eight) are those who belong to the mountain. The mountain is a symbol of "Tao," the immutable, changeless origin of change. The second dictionary definition of xian is "divine." There are to this day divine eccentrics who wander in quest of the Tao, of original nature or purity, of freedom from the churning world of *yin* (the receptive) and *yang* (the dynamic). The action of the Tao is returning, yin ceaselessly changing to yang and yang back to yin, and so the Immortals also reach back into the world—the Tao must go to town. Taoists say that the greatest masters are found not in the mountains, but in the cities and villages.

Having achieved the Tao, Immortals are called *Zhenren*, "realizing" (*zhen*) "people" (*ren*). Fully realized, they move freely between Heaven and Earth, sometimes serving as intermediaries between the gods and human beings. Their very strangeness of dress and manner symbolizes their rejection of quotidian norms and points to their radically transcendent state of being, masters of both creation and

The Chinese character for Immortal, Xian

THE SOUL & SPIRIT OF TEA

rest. They exist not to set an example, but to create an opening for us to unlearn our accustomed patterns of perception. They demonstrate the complete attunement of all levels or aspects of our being necessary to unfold our potential. Dame Ch'en, an old woman of Tao, wrote:

On the high slopes and low plain,
You see none but woodcutters.
Everyone carries in his bosom
The idea of knife and axe;
How can he see the mountain flowers
Tinting the waters with patches of glorious red.[4]

Anyone who truly sees the mountain flowers, the tinted water, is already reaching beyond most of us. We are the woodcutters, heads bent to the "knife and axe" of daily life. Fool's mind is our liberation. It is the radical revelation of the primordial nature that concerns the fool or Immortal in the teapot. The utterances of any divine fool or innocent are difficult for us, because they belong to a mode of understanding that transcends our everyday, objective mode of knowledge. They presuppose a kind of unitive knowing that lies beyond and within the play of opposites, in which things and minds are not separate and isolated from one another.

So how do we discover this different kind of relationship between ourselves and the universe? The Immortals have left us some suggestions. The early fifth-century work, *A New Account of Tales of the World* (*Shih-shuo Hsin-yu*) tells of the eccentrics devoted to the Taoist point of view of *tzu-jan,* or naturalness, who became known as the Seven Sages of the Bamboo Grove. Their leader was Hsi K'ang (223-262 C.E.), a poet and musician who installed a forge in his garden where he enjoyed iron-working, an odd preoccupation for an aristocrat, though perhaps a suitable hobby for a Taoist alchemist. Hsi K'ang argued that there were two ways to achieve immortal status: some can attain the Tao by "nourishing nature," i.e., by a gradual path of cultivation including meditation, diet, lifestyle, and alchemi-

---

4. John C. H. Wu, *The Golden Age of Zen* (Taipei: United Publishing Center, 1975).

One of the Seven Sages of the Bamboo Grove, Hsi Kang, the musical alchemist with his instrument on his back. . . . the perfect tea guest if
you ask me!

Detail

cal elixirs, whereas only the few "are given a special breath. They are endowed with it by nature."[5]

Hsi K'ang's constant flouting of the strict rules of social propriety and his bitter enmity to the tyrants of the age brought him eventually to prison. As he awaited his execution, Hsi K'ang wrote these words describing the essence of the path of the sage:

> Committed affectionately to Lao-tzu
>   And Chuang-tzu,
> I have devalued things and valued my
>   Own person.
> My ambition has consisted in guarding
>   The Uncarved Block,
> In nourishing the Undyed Silk, and
>   Preserving Reality whole.[6]

Only the Tao is absolutely free, and yet our original nature, uncarved by conceptual thought, undyed by emotional attachments, is also the Tao. Therefore, fullness of being, life, and expression with-

---

5. Robert G. Hendricks, *Philosophy and Argumentation in Third-Century China: The Essays of Hsi K'ang* (Princeton University Press, 1983).

6. *Shih-shuo Hsin-yu: A New Account of Tales of the World*, translated by Richard Mather (Minneapolis: University of Minneapolis Press, 1976.)

out limit lies within us all. It lies beyond assent to truth, beyond dissociation from the world, beyond the relative altogether and yet paradoxically within it. As a human being, one ideally strives for harmony within the Great Ultimate (*Tai Chi*) "reality whole." For each individual the way will be different, easy or effortful, fast or slow, by immersion in the words of the sages or by sudden illumination, or even completely by accident. We can only create the conditions in which the divine innocence of Tao may reveal itself. The philosopher Kuan-tzu (ca. 400 B.C.E.) wrote:

> If you reverently clean its abode
> It will come of itself.
> You will recover your own true nature,
> It will be fixed in you once and for all.[7]

Chuang-tzu observed that the Tao cannot be conveyed by either words or silence, but it is found in that state that is neither speech nor silence. There are first two things that have to be cultivated. First is the harmonic resonance of *ch'I* (*qi, ki*), or bio-energy, in oneself, and second is mindfulness. Because this is usually very difficult, such disciplines as ink painting, calligraphy, meditation, and Tai Chi Ch'uan can be essential points of entry into the lifelong process of cultivation that leads to freedom. The Chinese art of tea, less formal than the highly stylized Japanese tea ceremony, is another such path: heart and hand in accord, a sense of relaxed fitness, of grace and spontaneity without affectation, leading to dignity, harmony, and refinement of character reflecting the Tao of nature.

Throughout the ages in China, certain people were posthumously raised to divine rank. Such men and women were held to have become Immortals, living forever in the shining courts of heaven. To be so elevated, by imperial decree or popular acclaim, a person had to prove him—or herself—a model of excellence and benefactor to humanity. The Tea Immortal was Lu Yu (Tang dynasty), author of the first literary work on the subject of tea, the *Cha-jing* or Classic of

---

7. Stephen Karcher, *Ta Chuan: The Great Treatise* (London: Carroll & Brown Limited, 2000).

THE SOUL & SPIRIT OF TEA

Tea. Like all Immortals, Lu Yu began life as an ordinary person. He was abandoned by a river as an infant, only to be found and rescued by the abbot of a nearby Zen monastery. The abbot raised the boy kindly, but Lu Yu showed no interest in the mystical doctrines of Zen. Preferring instead the philosophy of Confucius, he eventually ran away with a band of traveling players. He had an excellent sense of humor and skill at cutting and editing plays, and he became an accomplished musician, poet, and an expert in everything to do with tea. He eventually settled down, and his gifts won him an official post that carried with it a theoretical responsibility for the literary output of the heir to the Dragon Throne. His almost miraculous sensitivity to the subtlest differences in the quality of water used to brew tea and his amazingly discriminating palate, both important components of the tea master's art, were legendary.

Voyaging once on the Yangtze River as the guest of a high-ranking official, Master Lu Yu was invited to taste a jar of water that his host had asked to be drawn from the pure midstream of the river, where the water was reputed to be of the finest quality. However, after one sip Lu Yu put the ladle down in disgust, declaring that the water came from close to the riverbank, where it could be expected to be polluted or turbid. The officer who had been sent to draw the water insisted that he had followed his master's instructions exactly. Lu Yu took another experimental sip and allowed that it could have been midstream water, but it had been diluted with water from near the bank. The awed officer then admitted that he had spilled a little of the water from the jar, and so had topped it off with water from near the place where the boat was moored. "Ah, Master Lu," cried the rueful officer, "you are clearly an Immortal!"

A Tang dynasty poet and contemporary of Lu Yu, Fei Shi-yi, visited a spring located in a monastery where Lu Yu had lived for a time to enjoy brewing tea with its fresh, clear water. Finding the monastery in decay just a few years after the master's sojourn there, he wrote:

Reaching the West Tower Temple,
I found no trace of people

Where nobles once had thronged,
And Master Lu had dwelt!
The weed-encrusted building
Was inhabited by frogs,
The lonely well by fish—
Yet something of his greatness lingered.[8]

Another story tells that Lu Yu's adopted father, the abbot of Dragon Cloud Monastery, was so fond of tea prepared by the incomparable hand of his son that after Master Lu left home for the second time, the abbot gave up tea drinking altogether.

Contemporary tea votary John Blofeld wrote in his own tea manual: "The spirit of tea is like the spirit of Tao: it flows here and there impatient of restraint."[9] To approach the unfettered freedom of fool's mind, tea mind may be of use even now. A Zen saying asserts that since there is no meditation without tea, and thus no enlightenment without tea, tea also cannot be described in words, but only tasted directly right here and now.

A session of drinking tea, thoughtfully prepared in the traditional way—listening to the softly seething kettle, dissolving idle concerns in the patterns of the rising steam, and simply rejoicing in a few carefully chosen, beautiful tea things—may lead to a more permanent awareness. Perhaps the alchemy of tea is, after all, the true elixir of immortality.

J. L. Walker lived in Taiwan for four years where she studied Ch'an Buddhism, Chinese painting, and learned to play the guqin. Her tea master was her guqin teacher, Professor Sun Yu-ch'in, who appears here as the Sage in the Teapot. Under his guidance she learned to appreciate the interwoven delights of tea, teapots, poetry and ancient Chinese music which enrich her life to this very moment.

---

8. Blofeld.
9. Ibid.

108   THE SOUL & SPIRIT OF TEA

Chapter 10

MOHAWK TEA

Douglas George Kanentiio

During the late 19th and early part of the 20th century many Mohawk men from Akwesasne found work as lumberjacks in the Adirondack Mountains and in the forests of Ontario. Mohawks had a long tradition of being expert canoeists whose skills took them across the continent as employees of the various fur trading companies. They were, without exception, the best at shooting rapids or portaging across miles of narrow trails with 200-pound packs on their backs. Their narrow canoes required exceptional balance and sensitivity to the movement of waters and the shifting winds. They also had to travel light, move with speed and use the resources around them for food, shelter, heat and, when necessary, medicine.

The managers and owners of the timber operations used jobbers to recruit Mohawks who were given, or chose, the most dangerous part of tree harvesting. The Natives were the high riggers (those men who climbed to the top of trees), choker setters (the ones who placed cables on downed trees), sky hookers (men who oversaw the stacking of cut trees on wagons and trains) or river hogs (those who rode the great rafts of timber from the cutting sites to the mills). They used all kinds of axes and saws but for the river hogs, the pike and gin poles along with the peavey was most important. River hogs were held in high respect, for they had to dance across slippery logs—their movements as light and quick as Broadway dancers—above freezing waters while the rafts rushed through rapids, knowing that if they slipped and fell, death was a certainty.

Despite their hard work the Mohawks were not paid the same as their non-Native compatriots. In addition, the Mohawks would bring their entire families into the Adirondacks. While the men were in camps, their wives and children lived nearby, with some of the women laboring as cooks while the youngsters were hired as bullcooks (sweepers, helpers, wood splitters for the many stoves in the kitchens and bunkhouses). Still, money was scarce and food carefully doled out according to need. The non-Natives did not have their spouses nearby and on their days off rushed to the nearby boomtowns to patronize the bars and whorehouses scattered along the edges of the mountains and alongside the railroad lines. The Mohawks refrained from boozing, preferring to give their wages to the family's matriarch. Other than coffee, tobacco and salt they preferred to live off the land as much as possible. One of the things they did to save a few pennies was to make their own teas. In the forests and fields they found ginseng, snakeroot, sassafras, hellebore and witch hazel, all of which were natural medicines in the form of teas. For food the children gathered blueberries, sumac, wild leeks, milkweed and nuts of all kinds. These would be preserved or added to the traditional cornbreads boiled by Mohawk women, or added to pan breads for flavor.

After weeks in camp the workers would become sick, primarily with colds and other infections. Wounds resulting from the use of sharp tools and falling tree limbs were common, but while the non-Natives took long to recover, the Mohawks seemed to heal more quickly and were rarely ill. The reason for their robust health was mysterious to the other workers, who marveled at the strength and endurance of the Natives.

My uncle, Angus Sohahiio George, was a lumberjack in the late 1920s and early '30s. He and his family, including my grandmother, would retreat into the mountains every fall, and return to the reservation after the snows melted. He became an expert with the various axes used to cut, trim and shape logs while also mastering the heavy motorized chain saws that were becoming common after World War I. He made his way from his family's log cabin, which he and his brothers built, to the work camp ready to labor ten hours and more. He was never sick and thought his better-paid co-workers stubborn and foolish for not using what he called "Indian medicine" to stay healthy. He said that his family was poor but used the things around them for comfort and nourishment. If he ran out of tobacco he used willow shavings blended with sumac; if he had a sore throat he chewed sweet flag; if he wanted to hold off hunger he drank sassafras or slippery elm.

One plant in particular kept the Mohawks from influenza or the common cold: the blue spruce. He would take the needles from the tree and dry them over a stove, then place them in a pot of water and let it steep. He drank cups of the tea, sometimes softened with maple syrup or sugar, throughout the day and said he never lost time due to sickness. In addition, his "poor man's diet" meant he healed faster whenever he was cut or bruised. My uncle told me that the "white men" may have made more money for doing the same job as the Mohawks, but they were sickly types who knew little or nothing of the woods around them. Worse, they refused to learn from the Mohawks and as a consequence died from injuries or fluid-filled lungs. The fact that the Mohawks did not have the money to spend on black teas or ground coffee, tobacco or bleached flour, actually saved them from similar fates.

MOHAWK METHODS FOR SELECTING PLANTS

The Mohawk-Iroquois people have specific practices for selecting plants to be used for food or as medicine. All plants have their own reality, their own duties and powers. Each is not only unique but is given the gift of life, and it must be respected if its full potential is to be realized.

There are individuals within every community who have, by nature, been given the ability to find medicine and food plants that are often hidden to others. Most people trudge through forests and stomp across fields insensitive to the plants around them. They neither see nor feel how plants react to their presence. When asked to do so humans generally lack the patience or innate awareness of the plant nations, while others are overwhelmed by the energy surrounding them at any given step into the natural world.

The plant harvester works with the seers, those who are able to prescribe specific plants which effect healing. They are either told or instinctively know where the plant may be found. Before they begin selecting which plant to take they do the following:

- Refrain from taking the first plant, as it is the one that watches over the others and has such an important duty that it is not to be removed from its place. If the first one dies by picking the others will react in fear and may remove themselves.

- Refrain from taking more than what is required. Over-harvesting will weaken the plants and disrupt the balance with other species. It is an absolute rule that the sisters of the taken plants are left behind and enough so they may flourish. Each plant is given to address the specific need and no more. Some plants may be selected and preserved, but the harvester must leave enough behind for reproduction and to insure the other plants remain in good health.

- Before selection, the plant is spoken to and told why it was chosen and how it will be used. Permission is asked before selection and gratitude expressed to the plant for using its power and life force. Plants, like animals and humans, respond to the voice and to individual songs of thanksgiving. It is important to approach the plant with a clear mind and without anger or negative emotion as this affects the healing powers of the plant and causes it to become defensive.

- Almost all plants are harvested in the morning, during the growing sun since this is when they have the most power. Morning is also the time when they draw water from the earth and are most flexible.

- Women experiencing menstruation harvest plants for themselves and no one else since they are becoming physically and spiritually renewed. Women during this time have the gift of creation and birth so their powers may eclipse that of the plant life.

- Plants are to be placed in wooden baskets, glass or enamel. Their power is diminished by contact with metal. They should also be used with natural flowing water, since the life and energy within the liquid adds to the healing and nutrition of the plant. If this is not available then distilled water may be used, with the understanding that this kind is better than water that has chemical additives. The water must also be addressed and thanked for its use.

- Harvested plants work best when stored in natural fibers or a leather bag out of the sunlight. They should not be in a place that has heavy human traffic, as this interferes with their power. Never put the plants adjacent to salt.

THE MOHAWKS AND TEA

The Mohawks are a part of the Haudenosaunee, the Six Nations Iroquois Confederacy whose homeland is that area south from the St. Lawrence River, north of the West Branch of the Delaware, east of the West Canada Creek and west of the Hudson River; over 11,500,000 acres of mountains, forests, valleys and meadows in one of the most ecologically rich regions of the planet.

Here the Mohawks arrived after an exodus from the distant southwest, a journey beginning in the continent's arid lands, across the Great Plains and into the green northeast. Their place of entry was at the mouth of the Oswego River and eastwards past the Finger

Lakes until they ended their trek on the banks of the river that bears their name. Here they built towns, tilled the fertile soils and hunted the great forests to the north for elk, bear, caribou, moose and deer. They called themselves the "Kaien:ke:ha:ka"—the "People of the Flint"—after the stones used to make arrow heads and spear points. .The Mohawks, a name taken from their Algonquin neighbors in deference to their fame as fighters, was how our ancestors came to be known throughout the world. They stood before all other native peoples in defense of their home territory and their ancient freedoms.

The land was good and generous, giving, in return for their skills and labors, fields of corn, beans and squash: the three sisters, or the "sustainers of life". In Mohawk, the food plants are called "Kaien:thoh:se:ra," and from the beginning of time have provided not only humans but other species with the ability to survive. Each time a planet is taken and consumed, it is to be acknowledged and given verbal gratitude which, in Mohawk, is expressed as *"nia:wen,"* or thank you, at the end of each meal.

A SAMPLE OF MOHAWK HEALING PLANTS

Ken:niio:hon:tes:ha, Strawberry

This is the leader of all plants that grow near the ground. All parts of the plant are used, and it is particularly good for the heart. Its roots help the intestines and flow of blood while the leaves reduce fever. Its berries assist the kidneys and bladder and may relieve toothache and skin problems. It is the food that sustains the spirit along the journey to the skyworld.

O: rhoh:te:ko:wa, Burdock

Its shape is similar to the veins and arteries in the human body. Its cap is like unruly hair. Its roots are deep into the earth, strong and fibrous. The roots are used to purify the blood, the stems to reduce hunger, the leaves for ulcers and kidney problems.

Wah:ta, Maple
The leader of all trees, its sap is a source of renewal for the Iroquois as the spring approaches. The sap not only provides energy but the bark and leaves may be used for liver and spleen ailments.

Eh:sa, Black Ash
The black ash is used to make splints for the basketweavers of Akwesasne. The pulp is pliable, strong and durable. The bark may be used to reduce fever while the leaves are a laxative and also heal kidney and urinary infections.

Oh:sah:ken:tha, Cattail
This swamp-based plant is a source of prime nutrition. It is edible from stem to root. Boiled, it makes an excellent tea, particularly the roots, which aid the kidneys and bladder.

Oh: nen:ta, Eastern white pine
This is a sacred tree among the Mohawk. The tallest of all trees in the northeast, it was planted by Skennenrahowi, the Peacemaker, at the formation of the Haudenosaunee (Six Nations Iroquois) Confederacy over 850 years ago. Its five needles on each stem represent the five nations of the Confederacy. The needles are used in teas to prevent scurvy, while the springtime buds purify the entire body.

Te:io:ne:ra:to:ken, Wild Clover
The leaves of this plant prevent infections and scurvy while reducing nervousness. It is an excellent way to cure indigestion. The flower has many uses: it heals wounds, relieves skin irritations, helps in curing liver ailments, reduces coughs and purifies the blood.

The medicine plants, which include all teas, are called "O:nonh:kwa:shon:a". These plants were given specific powers to affect healing and clarity of mind. They are highly sensitive to the presence of human beings while responding to speech and song. They come in many shapes, with the Mohawks believing that the form of a plant reveals where it is best used in the body. These plants may be used in a number of ways, from teas to poultices for bruises and wounds.

Mohawks believe that human beings may trace their origins to another world, a place where light itself has consciousness. From there a celestial being descended to the earth carried on a beam of light. This being was female, with the name of "Aien:sek," the Skywoman. She brought with her strawberries and tobacco. Ken:nio:hon:tes:ha is the Mohawk name for strawberry while tobacco is called Oh:ion:kwa:io:we.

Skywoman eventually died but from the heart place within her body grew strawberries, from her mind came tobacco, from her chest corn, and from her feet potatoes. The planting methods of the Iroquois followed the shape of her chest, as mounds were used for most crops until the introduction of the iron plow after the American Revolution and the beginning of reservation life. This was also the time when gender roles changed; because of movement restrictions to small reservations, men's hunting practices were largely curtailed, which meant they began to intrude on the ancestral farming duties of women. Also compromised were the soil cultivation techniques used by women with a switch from mound plantings to the linear methods used by Europeans.

But the harvesting, preparation and consumption of teas made from plants remained an important part of the Iroquois diet. Teas were far more than refreshment drinks or sources of caffeine. They were a way of maintaining a connection with the natural world, of sustaining culture and knowledge. Teas were a way of fostering personal relationships through conversation. A pot of tea was always part of the normal social rituals. Teas were also used at ceremonies where a large kettle with healing herbs was, and is, left on top of a wood burning stove, its aroma lending to the day's events. Each person was free to take a cup of tea, stand before the people and give verbal thanks for its healing properties.

THE SOUL & SPIRIT OF TEA

Douglas George-Kanentiio, Akwesasne Mohawk, is the former editor of the journal *Akwesasne Notes* and was a member of the Board of Trustees for the National Museum of the American. Kanentiio resides on Oneida Territory with his wife, the singer/composer Joanne Shenandoah. Kanentiio is the author of *Iroquois on Fire* among other books, and is a contributor to Phil Cousineau's *Beyond Forgiveness: Reflections on Atonement.*

Chapter 11

THE MAGICAL SPIRIT OF TEA

Melanie Carpenter

When we sip a cup of uplifting peppermint tea or are soothed by a chamomile tisane, a story is there in the steam, in the flavor, in the essence that dances on our tongue and slips into our body. It is a story of a long journey. It is a story from the green nations that begins with a seed's genesis of life, and travels through its growth cycle to harvest. It's a story that mirrors our own human journey, and as we drink in the healing properties of tea, with each sip, we can hear the lessons that the plants have to teach us and feel their truths reverberate in our own. A simple cup of tea holds infinite possibilities and insights.

The spirit of tea begins with a seed. Seeds are remarkable things. As an herb farmer and lover of plants, I spend lots of time with seeds and am touched deeply by the lessons they hold. To some it may seem like simple biology. To me it is nothing short of miraculous. The strong spirit found in tea comes directly from the adversity and wonder that shapes the birth of plants. Some seeds take heat to germinate. Fire must burn them. Their tough exterior is so rugged that nothing can penetrate them and nothing can escape until flames crack them wide open. Fire releases the possibility of new life and rejuvenation. To these wild herb seeds, what looks barren and blackened is fertility lying in wait. Other seeds, by comparison, need to stratify in cold isolation. No life will begin without a frigid, almost monastic retreat into hibernation. In that deep icy sleep the sweet dormant shoots dream, waiting to explode with the coming of spring. And there are still other seeds that need scarifying. Their strong protective walls must be broken down by the elements. They must become vulnerable and open, with this opening, growth and all things are possible.

Tea, brewed with intention and drank with an open heart, carries this message from the seeds to our spirits. Be vulnerable. Be open. Be the phoenix rising. Be comfortable in silence. Search it out. Grow. Tea can remind us of how to trust and can teach us how to be human.

How does tea do this? Some people believe that tea is "simply" a combination of water and plant matter. Brewed at the right temperature, the heat extracts the chemical constituents from the plants into the water and voila—there you have it, an herbal beverage. And they are right. On the surface, that's what tea is—simple solubility and extraction in action. Need to sleep? Decoct some valerian root. Having indigestion? Try some peppermint. Baby has a fever? Catnip's your friend. Teas of medicinal herbs will certainly take care of the body.

In fact, it is one of our greatest healing preparations. However, dive beneath the surface and the tea drinker will find so much more: a way to not only fortify the body but to enliven and soothe our souls. Tea is alchemy, the transmutation of common substances into something dear, something precious. Water, the life-blood of our planet, mixes with the plants and coaxes from them their sweetest essence, their pungent flavors, their ancient lineages and memories. The tea holds the plant spirit medicine and its deep holiness. When I drink tea at the end of a day, I can see the plants swaying in the fields. I remember the harvesting of their leaves and the plucking of their blossoms. I can hear the conversations our family had as we laid the roots and leaves to cure in the drying tunnel. The smell of the earth is there. The rain and sunshine.

On any given day, an herbal tea blend may consist of multiple herbs, steeping together, their spirits joining in harmony—the natural world distilled down into an itty-bitty cup. Even when I'm on the run and grab a tired old tea bag from the convenience store, I think about those green angels tucked inside and wonder where they grew, whose hands harvested them, and feel comforted as the herbal brew seeps out and their ancient spirits swirl into the water. I am comforted by tea because tea has a spirit. It is the spirit and essence from each plant carried in the water and on the steam. Many people in modern society believe that only humans have higher consciousness, only humans are sentient intelligent beings, but that has not been my experience. I have felt the spirit of the plants touch my heart deeply and speak directly to me, evoking emotions, teaching lessons, and caring for me.

Some people may think I'm overstating the mystical, poetic nature of plants and tea, but I'm not. Tea can perform miracles. It can capture a moment, heal a heart, bring beauty back into a world that is too rushed and harried to notice the divine waiting there. Not only is the actual tea, the liquid that one drinks, transformative, it is the art of blending, brewing and sharing tea that brings the magic back into the world. This lesson first came to me through the teachings of my step-mother, whom I prefer to think of as my glorious, green fairy godmother, Rosemary Gladstar. Rosemary is an herbalist, author, and visionary who has taught thousands of people about the beauty and healing power of plants. When our families joined I was thirteen, and I didn't really understand the significance of her herbal wisdom or the great work she was doing in the world. I was a teenager.

Enough said.

What did blow me away were all the amazing things you could do with plants. I was turned-on by this vivacious woman who took me into her heart as a daughter, introduced me to the magic of the green world, and taught me to listen to the spirit of the plants. We were living, breathing, eating and drinking plants. Herbal teas, baths, poultices, extracts, facial steams, cream, and salves, we made it all. Our house, more precisely our kitchen, was in a constant state of herbal preparation. It was glorious, messy, and fun. Healing wasn't something that happened in a doctor's office. It was what you ate for breakfast. How you cared for your neighbors. What you slathered on your skin after a long bath. It was the teas and extracts you brewed. It was a way of living and being *alive!* That's what the plants brought to us each day with such bounty and grace. Rosemary raised me as her grandmother raised her, in the folkloric herbal tradition, where the plants are your greatest teachers and one of the most important skills to master is making a cup of good tea.

In the folkloric tradition, it is not enough to simply have a nice tasting beverage. A cup of tea needs to awaken all the senses, maintaining the spirit and vitality of the plants that compose it. Like the seed that is catalyzed to grow by the elemental forces of nature, the human spirit needs beauty, aroma, explosions of taste (pungent, sweet, bitter), and all manner of stimulation to grow. A tea needs to *do* something to your body, needs to break you wide open. And then in steps the magic, and the spirit of the plants commune directly with the sacred inside us.

The first *transformative* tea I ever experienced was blended in the basement of our Vermont home. Rosemary had out her herb jars and we were talking about a teenage dilemma that was troubling me. I sat on the counter, legs swinging, watching her work. As we talked, she grabbed a pinch of this and handful of that, tossing it all in our blue-speckled crock bowl. She mixed. Smelled. Paused to comment on something I said, all the while, her hands were dancing around her apothecary. Into the brew went one herb and then two more. More blending and she was satisfied.

I remember her commenting on how pretty the tea looked as she led me back upstairs to put on the kettle. Getting out two matching cups and her good teapot, she sat me down and brewed the tea. As the minutes passed and the tea steeped, we continued to dissect the inner workings of my fledgling love life. After a while, she strained the blend and served the tea in her fancy cups with saucers. We took our first sips. It was delicious! Growing up on Lipton, I was blown away. Who knew tea could taste like this? There were so many flavors, mint with a hint of citrus, and something warm underneath. The tea was slippery on my tongue, not acrid or drying. Even the color was beautiful! When I looked at the tea it had a bluish purple hue (very impressive to a teenage girl!) We didn't add any honey or cream (a first for me at that time), and it tasted outrageously wonderful. The smell was comforting and I remember feeling, well, special.

At the time I couldn't articulate what was so magical or great about the moment. But years later, as I helped Rosemary with her classes and programs, I began to learn what made that experience so memorable and why tea is essential, why it speaks to the soul. First, tea takes time. Sweet Rosemary took time that day. She paused and changed her focus from work and the busyness of life to make a cup of tea for me. This is a profoundly important lesson—to take time for tea, for ourselves, for our families and friends. That alone, if nothing else, is the magic of tea. If you want to make a good cup of tea, you can't hurry it along and make it brew faster. It just doesn't work that way. Leaves brew differently than blossoms, and roots have their own needs altogether. To make an out-of-this-world tea, or even one that's passable, it takes time. In this frantic world, carving out time, even if it's twenty minutes for tea, can almost feel like an act of revolution and self-reclamation. It's a way of saying I am worth it. You are worth it. And at the end, I get to drink something delicious, good for me and full of spirit—nirvana.

Second, the act of blending and serving an herbal tea is both satisfyingly artistic and also a beautiful healing art. At the time, I was oblivious to the fact that while Rosemary was blending the tea, she was distilling my words, feelings, needs and secret desires into that bowl. These plants were her dear friends, and she knew them well. As kindred spirits they worked together to mend a young girl's heart. I saw her mix scarlet hibiscus, milky oats, spearmint, and blue malva. I could smell the spicy star anise and heady sweetness of rose petals. What I missed at the time was that she was doing more than just making a tasty drink. She had added herbs to lift my spirits, warm me up, please my eye and bring me joy. She chose the cups, fine China, to communicate subtly but clearly that this time together was significant. It was important to her that the tea look lovely both in the bowl and in the cup. She was brewing beauty and healing. Tea can do this—bring beauty into your world and create a communion between the plants and the human spirit. It not only connects us to the green world but also to one another—plant-to-human, human-to-human communion. Blending, brewing, and serving tea is not the same as turning water into wine, but it's darn close.

Since that day in Rosemary's basement, I have watched countless people blend teas, and I also make teas myself. On our farm, when I see a client or host a visitor, the first thing I do is offer them tea. What I am repeatedly struck by is the heightened awareness that comes from doing this. The ritual of making tea is ancient and familiar. It feels good to make tea. It feels human. When I think about why this is, I come back to the herbs. We have co-evolved over thousands of years with the plants. We breathe each other's breath. Plants provide our food, our clothing, our medicine. Almost everything we have comes directly or indirectly from the plants, so it's obvious that we should, as humans, feel reverence and connection to them. But so often we do not. So often we are disconnected. Looking around my community, I see people who are stressed, sad, lonely, and overwhelmed. Many individuals that I work with speak of feeling unmoored, lacking spirit, and I certainly have experienced this myself. From the herbal tradition, there are many things we can offer to ease these feelings and restore wellness. Tea to me is a high priestess of healing. I think it primarily has to do with two things. People get to touch and work with the plants, and they have to participate in the creation of their own medicine. Unlike a pill that can simply be swallowed on the run or a tincture that is ready-to-go medicine, tea needs us. We have to be involved or the tea just won't get made. The water won't get boiled, herbs won't get steeped, and no tea will be strained. This involvement in our own healing process is part of the magic; working with the plants directly helps us connect to our own divinity and the spirit of the plants.

THE SOUL & SPIRIT OF TEA

Every day on our farm, I see how working with the plants is what heals people as deeply, if not more so, than any chemical constituent or herbal preparation. When people touch the plants, feeling their leafy bodies between their fingers, something begins to stir in their own bodies again. Something primal. Something good. When people smell the aromatics of the herbs or the humus of the soil, the limbic part of the brain is stimulated, and memories come back. Connections to past, present, and future begin to be reestablished. And when the vibrant, out-of-this-world orange of calendula blossoms stun people's eyes, the colors of the world return, and everything seems brighter. After a hard day of farming, everyone is tired for sure, but underneath the grime and fatigue is a rejuvenation of spirit. We have tended something well. We have worked hard. We have taken care of the plants and spent time with these dear green friends. Our human bodies are in concert with plants' bodies, our senses are awakened and we feel alive. While not everyone lives on a farm in rural Vermont or cares to get dirty and back-to-the earth (although highly recommended), they can have the same ineffable experience while blending, brewing and drinking tea. That is the magic of tea; it's the mother earth, the spirit of the green, in your cup. You don't have to have two hundred species of herbs in your pantry. It can happen with just a few favorites. The key is to roll up your sleeves, tune in with your heart and put your hands to work. Blend. Sniff. Taste. Live.

All this leaves me thinking about Mary Oliver's beloved poem, "The Summer Day." In this poem, Oliver writes:

" . . . I don't know exactly what a prayer is.
I do know how to pay attention, how to fall down
into the grass, how to kneel down in the grass,
how to be idle and blessed, how to stroll through the
    field. . . . "

Oliver ends the poem with the provocative question, "what will you do with your one wild and precious life?" To reclaim that one wild and precious life, we must, if not pray, then at the very least pay attention. We must make time to fall down into the grass or into a cup of tea. To stroll or to steep, it really doesn't matter. What matters is to plant our seeds, like the green teachers tell us. To trust that the fire, ice, isolation, and deconstruction of life is part of the growth cycle and that the spring will come again. When we start to feel alone or ungrounded, we must grab up our kettle, turn off our phones and sit with a friend. Talk or be silent. Take in the steam, take a sip; the spirits of the plants will awaken ours, and the magic will begin.

Melanie Carpenter is an educator, herb farmer and community healer in Hyde Park, Vermont. She lives with her husband and daughter on Zack Woods Herb Farm, where together they care-take the land and grow medicinal herbs.

Chapter 12

TEATIME WITH CHILDREN

Babette Donaldson

"Talk and tea is his specialty," said Giles. "Come along inside . . .
We'll see if tea and buns can make the world a better place."
—KENNETH GRAEME, *The Wind in the Willows*

My fascination with tea began as a child, reading the stories from authors Lewis Carroll, Beatrix Potter, A.A. Milne, C.S. Lewis and Kenneth Graeme, who scripted scenes of sharing tea with family intimacy, friendly companionship and comfortable humor. They made my world a better place by giving me an escape from the day-to-day and by teaching me to use the teacup to serve myself a sip of serenity. Their literary teatimes preserve images of security and elegance, peacefulness, playfulness, celebration and a commonsense wisdom, all brought to be by sharing a teacup and sipping the warm brew. These stories have become classics, and the characters remain never-aging companions we introduce to our children and grandchildren. Their fictional tea times perpetuate a symbol of solace and everything being right with the world. Along with nursery rhymes, songs and movies, the stories infuse a deeper meaning and importance to teatime. It is a way for Christopher Robin to teach Pooh Bear to be "proper" and for Mr. Tumnus to welcome Lucy through the magical wardrobe into Narnia; for Mother Rabbit to nurse and comfort Peter and for Alice to try to make sense of a completely upside-down world. As children, we were reassured by the promises of the teapot.

Over the years, my association between tea drinking, reading and writing generated the desire to write something as meaningful and as beloved as these timeless stories. Without realizing at first, my characters were tea drinkers and my settings were teashops until I eventually created a collection of tea themed stories for children and families, *The Emma Lea Books*. My visits to schools, bookstores, libraries and tearooms have expanded my own feelings about what tea means to me, and what teatime means to children. I'm often asked to speak on "manners and etiquette," as if teatime is an opportunity to teach good posture and grooming. But I have to be honest and say that I much prefer to open a dialogue with children about the sensory experiences, the cultural rituals and the fun that teatime and a tea lifestyle can be. With children, I consistently affirm that their real relationship with tea and the way they share it with family and friends lives here too.

> *"A Proper Tea is much nicer than a Very Nearly Tea,*
> *which is one you forget about afterward."*
>
> —A. A. MILNE

TEACHING TEA TO CHILDREN

Teacher Karen, a local kindergarten teacher, organized a Mother's Day tea party for her class. She phoned and asked me to speak to the children and their mothers about "What tea is all about." Since tea history and culture is thousands of years old, it was difficult to know where to begin. Realizing that very little of this is relevant to children I decided to let them do the talking and pointed the question back to them. What were their stories? When we were finally settled into a circle on the carpeted floor, Teacher Karen first chose a little girl who was sitting still with her hand politely raised to tell how she prepared tea parties for her dolls. But a boy named Jeremy was bouncing around in the background, waving his hand in the air with a mischievous Peter Rabbit smile, impatient to tell his story. When Karen finally called on him, he rambled on about his dog and nine new puppies. Eventually, she had to interrupt and remind him that we were supposed to tell stories about tea. Turning from him, she chose a few other children who reminisced about going to tea-rooms, having fancy, dress-up birthday party teas, wearing tiaras and princess dresses, having tea with grandmothers when they visited and being allowed to pour the teapot. "In England, they say that the person who pours is being mother," one girl shared.

Throughout the other children's stories, Jeremy squirmed, becoming increasingly desperate to finish his story. The teacher couldn't ignore him any longer and called him, reminding him that if he told a story it had to be about tea. After three false starts, and rising tension, Jeremy finally reached the point of his story. Slowly, the boy described how his mother had given an outdoor bridal tea party at their house and the women had left the tables filled with half-filled teacups and plates of goodies as they were saying goodbye. He confiscated the beautiful porcelain and extra sweets and created a tea party for the entire litter of puppies. Jeremy finished his story with, "Puppies like tea. Now I do too!" I imagined Jeremy as an adult and a father telling his own children the story, encouraging traditions that are fun and memorable, because that's what teatime was about for him.

Jeremy's struggle to be heard reminded me that teatime isn't just about talking—it's also about listening. Tea is often said to loosen lips and encourage conversation, and teatime is when we are reminded to focus on what our children have to say and practice the patience we sometimes need to allow them to get to the core of what they need to say.

For children, there is a clear distinction between tea as beverage and the way sharing it becomes part of our lives. For them, the event and the trappings always trump what's in the pot. They know the teapot holds a potential for simple joys that have already resonated through several generations and are likely to continue for dozens more.

"Harry found the [tea] . . . seemed to burn away a little of the fear fluttering in his chest.

—J.K. ROWLING, HARRY POTTER

A TEA PARABLE

One of my most memorable book signings was at Amy Lawrence's Afternoon To Remember Tearoom. Every table was crowded with children and their adults at teatime, as I read one of the stories and visited at each table. Later, an eight-year-old girl, Lisa, bought one of my picture books and a teapot for her best friend. While I was signing the book, she explained that this was a gift for a friend whose father was home under hospice care. It was a frightening experience, knowing that the time with her father would be short. There was so much they wanted to say before the end, but speaking was difficult because of the tubes, the pain and the medication. Most of the time her friend did all the talking while her father could only listen. The two girls would sometimes talk to each other to fill the room with happier sounds. But sometimes Lisa's friend couldn't make the words come out and it was difficult to keep from crying. Lisa had a thought during our tea party that this was something her friend and the dying father could share without words and would make a few minutes of the day seem happy. The girl could prepare a different tea each day and sit and read to her father during their teatime. Maybe that was even more important than trying to think about the end of his life—just the most precious moments each day.

One of my favorite tea quotes is by a Vietnamese Buddhist Monk, Thich Nhat Hanh. "Drink your tea slowly and reverently, as if it is the axis on which the world earth revolves—slowly, evenly, without rushing toward the future." I have loved his words for many years and repeated it during many of my tea talks, but I'd never felt it as deeply as I did, and had never considered the importance of sharing tea, until I saw the possibility through Lisa's eyes. When I think about those two girls, Lisa and her friend, knowing they are now teenagers, perhaps preparing to go away to college and leave home, I'm reminded that teatime is also a support system and a lifestyle. I wonder how many bedside tea parties she shared with her father. Did it help? Did that simple tradition give her and her father some peace and sweet memories? In the face of great loss and sadness, was the warm cup of tea a moment of comfort?

IMPORTANCE OF FAMILY TEATIME

My first public presentation about the importance and potential for family teatime was at the Northwest Tea Festival in Seattle, Washington in October 2010. The audience was a mix of ages from six to eighty. It wasn't a big crowd and I was nervous that my audience wouldn't last through my intro. I launched into my talk and ended with, "Family teatime is when we create a setting for conversation and relaxation. We behave with respect and courtesy. We listen. We pay attention to the small details. In so doing, everyone who joins us at the table feels important. It is one way that we honor our children and teach them how to honor and respect others." The remainder of our hour was spent remembering as my small audience opened up with memories of when they had been made to feel special at a family teatime; one recollection of a grandmother's cracked teapot inspiring another of a favorite aunt's shelf of teacups collected from around the world. They remembered teatime as storytelling time, favorite book reading time, talking about anything time, art project time, cookie baking time and cakes so warm from the oven that the frosting melted into the surface. Children recalled when they were first allowed to use the china cups instead of plastic and how much they enjoyed stopping at the local teashop to choose a new blend.

What struck me was that the way children feel about sharing teatime and the way most adults feel about it are exactly the same. Even though our world has changed radically in the last decade, sometimes causing a schism between the pre-tech generations and the ones who don't remember a dial telephone, the ambience and calming effect of teatime has not changed. It is one of the few things that remain comfortably multi-generational and fun. The phrase, "Would you like a cup of tea?" is still an invitation to conversation sweetened by a snack.

FAMILY TEATIME HUMOR

One of my favorite comic strips, *Rose Is Rose*, by Don Wimmer and Pat Brady, recently picked up on the family teatime theme. The father Corky takes a break at the office to have a video conference "tea party" with his wife and young daughter, Mimi. Teatime for children is when adults stop what they're doing and pay attention to them.

There's a frequently told joke about another father and daughter that may be based on an actual event. As the story goes, a father was home babysitting one evening while his wife was out. When she called to check on them, he bragged that everything was going well. He was reading and their three-year-old daughter was keeping him supplied with cups of tea from her toy set. The mother replied that the only water their daughter could reach was the toilet bowl.

Sharing a cup of tea isn't the same thing when we fail to give our attention and respect to our children. If we fail to give full attention and involvement to our children when we have the opportunity, allowing distractions to be more important than they, aren't we teaching them by example to do the same?

TEATIME WITH CHILDREN

Inspired by what children say is most important to them, I offer the following teatime suggestions.

- Make it special. Use your best tea ware. Buy or blend their favorite teas.

- Honor them with your undivided attention. Turn off the electronics. Don't answer the phone.

- Involve them in planning and preparation so they feel valuable and capable. Let them pour the tea even if they spill.

- Make it a personal ceremony they can take with them, so they can feel connected to their family roots wherever they go.

- Let them know that, in having tea as a part of their life, they are connected to something great and substantial that is shared around the world.

THE NEW LITERATURE OF TEA FOR CHILDREN

The classic stories that defined tea for me as a child continue to be popular with children, but other writers like myself have also been inspired to include teatimes in their fiction. From the "American Girl Books" to "Fancy Nancy", the meaning of teatime for children is scripted as something more than a simple beverage. Like Giles in *Wind In The Willows*, we drink tea "to make the world a better place." Once I was the speaker at an American Girl Tea Party at Barnes and Noble in Sacramento, California. In a small space in the back of the store, twenty girls plus their dolls, parents and a few grandparents crowded around tables as we read, talked, sipped and nibbled. Even in the middle of the crowded store, there was a peacefulness that seemed to buffer the noise and insulate what we were doing. Girls became friends quickly and families felt the closeness that teatime inspires. It also inspired communication—actual talking—not fragmented texting. Around the tables we maintained eye contact and heard real laughter, rather than reading virtual LOLs on mini LED screens. The tea party magic engaged even the shyest child and the most reluctant dad. We all need this, especially our children—especially now. It's becoming ever more difficult to feel confidence in the future and joy in the present small moments when things change so rapidly and when the news is full of daily violence and speculation about the end of the world. How do we help our children feel safe and not get overwhelmed?

Teatime's stereotype serves us well. It's a tool we can use from the time our children are very young until we are very old and they return to visit us, at which time they can delight that we still have tea ware in a cupboard or displayed on a mantle that stores moments of family history. It's a tool that can be taken away to college or to a new job in another city when our children leave home and need a reminder to relax and find their inner peace. Teapots and teatimes are time machines—transporting us through our carefully crafted and most cherished remembrances. We can begin with our children at any age. I wasn't one of the little girls who had a toy tea set and pretended to serve tea to my dolls. The tea things in our home were kept in a cupboard, never used. They were considered the good things we weren't allowed to touch. My first family tea was when I was in my twenties and my grandmother gathered the women of the family together, her daughters, granddaughters and great-granddaughters. I still remember the glass plates with a holder for the matching teacup. There were pumpkin bread sandwiches with cream cheese squares, pimento cheese on white bread triangles, and rounds of rye cut with a biscuit cutter on which a proper slice of cucumber perched. The tea was one of the only flavored blends at the time, Constant Comment, and Granny sat as proud as a queen at the head of the table. It was the last time we were all together. I always wondered how much closer we would have been if Granny's tea had become an annual event.

WHAT IS TEA WITH CHILDREN ALL ABOUT?

When Teacher Karen first asked me to speak to her class, I was just beginning to understand what tea can mean in our daily lives. Now that I've studied tea culture and history for more than ten years, traveled to Chinese tea gardens, sipped fine whole leaf tea with tea masters and have chosen it for my work, I confess that it is the children I've met who taught me what teatime is about.

• It's the way a cookie melts.

- It's how much jam can be piled on a hot scone.

- It's the way you make a sandwich for lunch seem like a party.

- It's the way Grandma's kettle whistles and sounds like a bird.

- It's how to sparkle-up a plain-ol' regular day.

- It's when we bake muffins and eat them when they're still hot.

- It's a party for two or a party for everyone we know.

- Inviting someone to tea tells them you like them.

- It's when you feel like a dress-up princess or special even in regular clothes.

- It's when pretending becomes real.

- Teatime is when children are grownup and grownups are children.

- It's how much more beautiful mother is when her face relaxes into a smile and she closes her eyes with the teacup under her nose.

- It's when Grandma tells us about how the old days were. Then you help her understand how the new days are now.

- It's when you find that there are some things that have stayed the same.

There are thousands of simple things that teatime has been over the years and what it can mean to us. Children remind us to look to the simple things and value them all. Something as quaint as a little teacup or an old chipped china teapot can become the beginning of a family tradition. It can be one of the most meaningful traditions a family can share and endure through generations. It can comfort us through loss and disappointment, through illness and grief. Teatime can celebrate birthdays, graduations, weddings and the birth of the next generation. It can become part of every day when we stop our work and relax together in the middle of the afternoon, or it can be an annual over-the-top extravaganza. Tea can be what we need it to be.

A FINAL SIP

We think of children living in an un-knowing world, where we can keep the stress and violence from touching their innocence. My experience with children is that they are like sponges that absorb our tension and fear. In the same way, they draw on our calm and confidence and feel safe when they sense this in us. How do we find our own inner peace and share this with our children? Teatime can be a few moments of peace within ourselves, an escape from the fear of things happening in the world beyond our control; it allows us to focus on the comfort of our family. Peace in the world—one cup of tea at a time.

There is a song by Jill Jackson Miller and Sy Miller, "Let There Be Peace on Earth". The lyrics continue, "And let it begin with me." The language of peace begins with individuals then; like dropping a pebble into water, it radiates out from each of us. What teatime offers is an opportunity to share this with young children, joyfully, without lessons or lectures, as we locate that place of peace.

Babette Donaldson is the author of *The Emma Lea Books*, a series of family teatime storybooks, and a contributing writer to *World Tea News* and *Tea Magazine*. She is also one of the organizers of the San Francisco International Tea Festival.

Chapter 13

THE KI OF TEA

Michael Goldberg

INTRODUCTION

In Japanese, *ki* (*chi* in Chinese) is the primal energy or vital force that is present in all living beings. Some cultures feel it even in inanimate things like trees, rivers, and mountains. It took Einstein to postulate the amount of energy there is in an atom. From whence it comes, where it goes, is a subject of science, religion and philosophy. In the Orient, it is thought that this energy flows within and between us. This has had profound implications in medicine, acupuncture and pressure massage, the martial arts—it is the "ki" in Aikido and "chi" in Tai Chi—and tea, to mention a few.

I have lived in Japan for thirty plus years and was honored to be chosen as guest editor for this chapter. I do not feel qualified to interpret the deep meaning that tea, more specifically the Tea Ceremony (called *Sado*, *Chado*, or *Chanoyu*) has in this culture, and felt I should learn from those with better understanding than I. What I have gleaned, I share with you here.

Until it was popularized at the end of the 19th century, the history of green tea in Japan had two interwoven strands: one, that of Zen Buddhist monks who turned the simple act of drinking the frothy liquid made with tea powder (*Macha*) into a ceremony that may be seen as "religious"; and second, the ruling elite and Samurai class. I find it interesting that it was an Occidental, Gilles Maucout, who described a strong attachment to the aspect of Tea Culture related to the Martial Arts. The Zen tradition is represented in this chapter by Emiko Koseki, who is a mentor to me.

For the contemporary aspects of green tea, I turned to Yoshi Watada, a specialist of *Gokuryo* (high end) tea and a *kissa* master in the trendy Omote Sando district of Tokyo. I also asked to meet with a representative of the Japan Tea Exporters' Association and was received by Kotaro Tanimoto, whose English is excellent.

After the discovery that green tea plants were contaminated by fallout from the Daiichi nuclear plant in Fukushima, I—ever the skeptic—drove through tea plantations in Shizuoka for two hours with a Geiger Counter and GPS, mapping the data for Safecast, a voluntary organization that shares the results with specialists and the general public alike. Their raison d'être is to make known where there are hot spots and where it is safe. Lack of openness by the authorities led many to worry about radiation everywhere, though it is not warranted. I can assure you that the highest reading I got near and in the tea fields in November 2011 ($0.133\mu Sv/h$) was less than a typical reading at my home in Tokyo ($0.16\mu Sv/hr$).

Finally, no chapter about tea in Japan would be complete without a heart-to-heart chat with Mihoko Okamura, the secretary of Buddhist philosopher D.T. Suzuki, who is widely known as "the man who introduced Zen to the West." Though not a *Sado* practitioner, he drank it almost daily. I would go so far as to say he did not have to practice tea—all his life was a demonstration of what students of the arts (and perhaps the martial arts) in Japan aspire to, putting "realization into practice."

EMIKO KOSEKI

Emiko Koseki is Executive Secretary of Japan Inter-Culture Foundation. She devoted many years to Zen practice at Enkakuji Temple in Kita-Kamakura, and has long practiced tea under the Iemoto of Chinshinryu.

The Practice of Tea

Zen Buddhist monk Sen no Rikyu (1522–1591) is considered to be the father of Chanoyu, the tea ceremony. He refined it to the form that it is practiced in to this day. In his later years he performed it—if that is the appropriate term—in a tiny, rustic hut of his own design. Built exclusively for the tea ceremony, it can seat only five people. Among Rikyu's innovations was having one entrance for the host and a smaller one for guests, forcing them to bow low in humility when entering. He placed emphasis on the moment, purity of spirit, equality of standing and honesty, as well as Wabi Sabi, a concept that is difficult to explain, combining refined simplicity with natural roughness.

Japanese cultural disciplines are called "do," which means a "way" or "path." Chado, or Sado, means the way of tea. Kado (also called Ikebana) is the study of formal flower arrangement. Shodo is the art of calligraphy. Each is a way of putting one's spirit in order. In Kado, there is a rapport between you and the flower; with Sado, it is in relation to the tea. It is a form of ascetic practice.

"As bowls truly suitable for Sado, more of them are of an asymmetrical shape. There are bowls . . . with the left and right sides of different shape, ones without symmetry, ones with an uneven surface consisting of bumps and indentations with a high foot or base of crooked shape, and ones in which the glaze does not completely cover the whole tea-bowl. Rather than a bowl of regular and symmetrical shape, this type has something of interest and arouses a feeling of appreciation . . . I think of it as something that destroys perfection."

—Hisamitsu, Shin'ichi
(translated by Patrick MacGill James / Abe, Masao in the
Eastern Buddhist, Oct. 1970)

It's said that Sado is an art form, as is Ikebana (flower arrangement), and of course Shodo (calligraphy). Japanese etiquette is also consid-

Emiko Koseki.

ered an art form, for example the forms of bowing. Even the movement of one's feet while walking is connected to good cultivation. These are all part of the concept of art in Japan, at least they were in times past. It all used to be inter-connected, but this is less true now.

Zen and Tea

Tea practitioners today don't do Zazen (Zen meditation). Originally, almost everyone practiced both. Action on its own tends to disquiet the soul. The basis of Zen meditation is sitting still. One puts the spirit in order, concentrating on the act of breathing. In Sado, there is "a path," so there is movement. Doing nothing serves to quiet the spirit. There is a need to discover how to use this in action while maintaining the calmness one has found. In the tea ceremony, your thoughts and movements flow naturally. This way of internalizing and disciplining the self is learned from Zazen. In the early days, it was thought that both were necessary to bring the meditative process to fulfillment.

Zazen does not mean "doing nothing." The body is motionless, but the soul is active. It is an act of putting one's ki (spirit) in order. An expression we use for training the spirit in Zazen is to "knead the ki" the way a potter works a lump of clay. One measure of how well your spirit is tempered is through Sado, the Way of Tea.

The Tea School Tradition

Chinshinryu, the Tea Ceremony branch to which I belong, is part of the Buke-cha (Samurai) tradition. It has a three hundred year history. The tea service used to be practiced by Zen monks, the feudal lords, and the samurai class. Woman weren't allowed to participate. During the Edo period, after the country was unified and became peaceful, women were allowed to take part in the tea ceremony. Nowadays most practitioners are women.

The head (Iemoto or sokeh) of every tea school in Japan has always been a male, though male practitioners now comprise around twenty percent, perhaps less. The traditions with Iemoto at the top are old systems, which some say are no longer relevant. Now that Japan is an affluent society, tea schools have large numbers of students. Historically, when Japan was poor and seemed at times to be on the verge of collapse, the Iemoto were resolute in preserving their traditions. In my opinion, there are some things in these systems that can be criticized, but it is truly thanks to them that there has been cultural continuity.

When us ordinary folk can no longer afford tea lessons, we can stop at any time. Lots of people do in fact drop out. Urasenkei Tea School now has several hundred thousand students. But during the Edo and Meiji periods, the Iemoto were reduced to poverty and had to pawn their own treasures to keep the school going and protect the traditional teachings from being lost. It is certain the tea ceremony would not have been handed down intact through the generations were it not for Iemoto at the top.

In the tea ceremony you pay attention to the bowls, all of them different and marvelous pieces of ceramic. Of course in Japan, and also to a large extent in China, you cannot be a thinker, an intellectual, without being an artist at the same time.

— *Huston Smith*

One of the things that impressed me when I first started was the way the drinking bowl is handled. Until then, I'd wash a cup under the faucet and stick it carelessly in a wicker basket, all with the same hand. I was struck by the gestures of the person conducting the tea ceremony, washing and reverently turning over the bowl before putting it down—holding with one hand, putting the other underneath, tilting to spill out the cleansing water, then placing the bowl down carefully. Since then, I've treated the things I handle with more thoughtfulness. I became conscious of that thanks to Sado. The Japanese term for "taking notice" is *ki ga tsuku*—your *ki* becomes connected with something. Decades later, I'm still in the process of learning.

"Watch Rikyu preparing tea, and you will discover that his entire body is filled with ki. His precise, deliberate gestures are like those of a great warrior! There is no gap into which you can penetrate . . . his concentration is flawless."

—*Toyotomi Hideyoshi*

GILLES MAUCOUT

Retired in Paris after being based for decades in Asia, particularly Japan, Gilles Maucout is a certified tea ceremony master in the Sohenryu tradition, as well as a practitioner of Kodo (incense recognition), and Kyudo (archery).

Chanoyu

At first I was struck by the mysterious ritualization of the Chanoyu, Japanese tea ceremony, and by its beauty. These are two things you notice when it is performed in the right environment. When it is conducted in a small four mat room specifically designed for Sado, there is a framework. It is almost bare. There are no frills, few objects—a flower, a hanging scroll. Yet there is elegance, and the beauty or power of the person conducting the tea ceremony.

Sado is the purest and most complete expression of Japanese civilization. In the tea house, you have architecture. In behavior, you have Japanese manners, the relationship between people and with nature. There is precision, quality and beauty in everything before you, the way everything is handled. There is parsimony—you are given a tiny piece of cake, and the tea bowl is not filled to the brim, yet they suffice.

Chanoyu is not easy. You sit on tatami (straw) mats seiza style (on bended knees). After ten minutes, Westerners experience pain in their knees and get cramps. Next, you have to learn to do each gesture in the ceremony precisely. Thirdly, you have to do the same thing again and again for months, even years, before gaining a deep understanding. Slowly but surely you enter a space that is absolutely amazing—a sense of communion—a symbiosis with nature, the surroundings, the people there, and the quality of what you are doing.

The ceremony is an expression of Japanese culture, and at the same time it is universal. Yet the tea ceremony was once in crisis. At the end of the Edo period, tea masters found themselves out of work. The tea schools had to come up with ways to survive. They came to realize there was growing interest in tea culture. The gentry discovered that by studying tea, they acquired skills of politeness, respect, harmony with nature, and more.

In the 20th century, all the tea schools went through a transformation from their elitist origins into institutions for popularizing the tea ceremony, especially among women. The men were busy working. Unfortunately, widening the scope of tea practice led to a lowering of standards. Practitioners didn't go through the same self-training as in the past.

In the art of swordsmanship, it's really a struggle of life and death. Therefore, you have to be really earnest about it, if the great problem of death is involved. . . . The study of tea, the tea ceremony, is also selfless mastery of the art. No self is to be let there. All traces of the ego-centric concept are to be wiped out.

—D.T. Suzuki

The Samurai Tea Tradition

The disciplines of the Japanese "ways," or practices, are centered on clearing the mind and finding the natural energy within. In my experience, when you practice tea energetically, you do so with the very same spirit as in the martial arts. In Japanese archery, the target is twenty-seven meters away. It may seem strange, but you must assimilate the target into your consciousness in a way that the arrow will find the mark on its own. In Western archery, one takes the arrow, fits it into the arrow rest, pulls back the bowstring, then takes aim. The Japanese method is very different. Of course there is a target, but in a way, you must forget about it. If your mind is emptied, your awareness heightened, and you have self-control, the arrow finds the target! Of course, it requires a lot of technique as well.

If you were to ask a tea master today about a connection between the tea ceremony and the martial arts, he likely wouldn't see any connection. When you participate in a tea ceremony, you have a bowl, and that's it. The more you practice, the closer it is in your consciousness. It's amazing that the Samurai practiced Sado, even though they were warriors. The more you practice, the closer you come to your target, so to speak.

The Tea Pavilion

The relationship between Japanese culture and tea service evolved over hundreds of years, until Sen no Rikyu codified it. When the tea room was created, it was purposely built outside the house. The samurai served tea to invited guests in that special place, specifically designed with intimacy in mind, either for oneself, for one's connection with the universe, or for one's relationship to the other guest(s). The surroundings of the tea pavilion—the ceremony, the silence, nonverbal communication with the other people present and with the cosmos—imbue the tea ceremony with spirituality. The mystical aspect is never far away, even though it is ethereal and never mentioned. The tea pavilion can act as a catalyst to connect with the beyond. It is closed, with almost no openings to the exterior,

Iho-an Tea Hut in Kodaiji Temple, Kyoto © Dennis Wright.

yet in it you are connected with the universe. The tea pavilion is a space where one can withdraw or extricate oneself from the crowd and the daily grind, the pressure. This is something that is needed all the more in the 21st century.

The "tea pavilion" can be any space at all, even in one's home. Ideally it is somewhere that you have tidied up to which you can withdraw and remove yourself from the tedium of daily life, from which there seems to be no escape. I recently went on a three day trek in the Moroccan Sahara with a student of mine, accompanied by two Tuareg guides and several camels. There, we held a tea ceremony in the open. It was absolutely wonderful. We could feel cosmic energy (I know this sounds like a cliché). After walking several days in the barren desert, you experience a relationship with the cosmos. This experience parallels that of the tea pavilion. It too is empty.

There was an eclipse of the sun over Paris, I think it was 1998, and for five minutes it was pitch black in the middle of the day. The birds went silent, and in the middle of summer it suddenly went cold. We realized at that moment that without cosmic rays, the earth dies. This energy is the wellspring of life; indeed, it is the source of ki within us. For me, ki is transmitted through the practice of tea.

YOSHI WATADA

Yoshi Watada is the owner and tea master of Cha Cha no Ma, a modern tea house/restaurant in Omote-Sando, Tokyo.

Tea and Silk

When Japan opened to trade with the outside world in the late 19th century, there were basically two exports—silk and green tea, the latter mainly to America. Japanese teas developed a reputation for high quality and commanded high prices. In 1941, an allied embargo was put in place, exports halted, and consumption of quality tea was promoted domestically. Until then, most Japanese drank lower quality roasted teas. Green leaf tea was an export commodity, too expensive for any but the elite.

During the Second World War, many Japanese men were killed, including those who cultivated tea. The industry found itself back where it was in the 1870s. Slowly but surely, quality green tea returned to the slopes. Kissa (which literally means "enjoying tea") became popular as a place to meet and enjoy excellent teas. In time, the ubiquitous coffee shop took over, and Kissa-ten became synonymous with "Coffee Shop." Tea houses are now a rarity.

Yoshi Watada.

Quench the Thirst, or Savor

There's no description in written records of what tea ordinary people drank daily in the early days. Most tea sold today is bancha, made from leaves and twigs left after the picking of choice leaves. Served fairly weak, people drink it to quench their thirst, like water. This bancha used to be steeped in a teapot at home; now it is mass-produced and sold in plastic bottles. That's not to say it is bad for you.

Macha (powdered green tea), which Sen no Rikyu used in the tea ceremony, is a luxury item. So is Ryokucha. Both were reserved for the elite. The way to enjoy good quality tea is to serve it strong. It is meant to be slowly savored on the tongue. Tea can be judged by a number of characteristics: color, sweetness, flavor, uniqueness, fragrance, and pungence.

Soft water (low in mineral content) is preferable. If you can't get a hold of that, ultra-purified "baby water" can be purchased in some upscale supermarkets or where infant formula is sold. Mineral water is not best, though it's not bad; some brands are suited to Japanese tea.

The Nature of Tea

The most important thing is to drink good tea. There is a plethora of inexpensive, green colored liquids that are called tea. While they may be good for your health, you feel no association with nature when drinking those. One of the fundamentals of good quality tea is that its aroma reflects the environment in which it was grown. Even if it is not where you were brought up, or you live in a big city, it's nostalgic. The origins of good tea—the earth, the mountain, the climate—are evident when you drink it.

In order to meet demand for bottled green tea in supermarkets around the world, tea plantations expanded rapidly. Huge machines were developed to handle the volume, with "homogenized" characteristics of the tea controlled by computer. There is no ki, no spirit, no aura to be found there. Although it may be considered a health product, it's not meant to touch your soul. Teas grown and prepared with care are something else; for me, they are like diamonds. The ki

The most important thing is to drink good tea.

or spirit of tea is the result of communication between nature and human beings. Simply by adding water, tea can be prepared anywhere. It's a wonderful beverage. If there is one fundamental thing to tea, I would say that it should be enjoyed.

KOTARO TANIMOTO

Kotaro Tanimoto is Vice President of the Japan Tea Exporters' Association and President of Hellyer & Co., Inc, a tea import & export company. He is also the bass guitarist in superhero-type costumed Shizuoka rock band.

The Meiji Reformation

Tea came to be exported from Japan toward the end of the 18th century. After China lost the Anglo-Chinese War (or "Opium Wars"), the British monopolized their tea market and planted Assam tea shoots from China in India. The Dutch controlled tea plantations in Indonesia. America had become independent after the colony's rejection of the British tax on tea. The U.S. needed a stable supply, and decided that Japan—despite three hundred years of isolation from the outside world—would be the source. Admiral Perry's "gunboat diplomacy" did the trick. Most of the tea exported from Japan to the

U.S. then was Chinese style gunpowder tea (rolled into small, round pellets) and Oolong pan-fired tea.

During the Meiji Reformation that followed, education and the tea ceremony were opened to women. There were many widows after the Russo-Japanese War (1904–1905), and one of the few ways they could earn a living was to become Ikebana (flower arrangement) or Sado (Tea Ceremony) instructors. The teachers' licensing system grew out of this—basically a pyramid marketing scheme—and the philosophy of tea was lost.

Tea Affected by Radiation from Fukushima

After an initial period of uncertainty and fright over the discovery of tea contaminated by the Fukushima nuclear disaster, control by Japanese authorities was strict. Tepco (the power company that owns the crippled Dai-Ichi nuclear plant) was obliged to compensate the tea farmers for loss of revenue, one reason that monitoring was able to become systematic and effective.

The green tea plant (*Camellia Sinensis*) has the unusual property of absorbing nutrients other than Carbon Dioxide through its foliage and transferring them to new growth leaves, a phenomenon known as Foliar Transmigration. In a study at Oregon State University, tea plants that were contaminated solely on their leaves became much more radioactive than plants growing in contaminated soil. The study applied the same quantity of radioactivity (Cesium-134) to potted tea plants either on the leaf surface or in the soil column. While there was more uptake from the roots compared to "control" plants, when Cesium levels in the new growth green tea leaves were counted, it was found that radiation in the tea that was exposed via the leaves was thirty-four times greater than the root-spike group. If one spike in the foliar group is excluded, the average was twenty-four times higher.

Tea Plantation.

Cesium from rains after the reactor explosions fell mostly on the tea leaves, with comparatively little on the ground. In fact, you can barely see the soil in tea fields, only the leaves. In 2011, the National Tea Institute conducted studies in many tea fields in Shizuoka Prefecture. They concluded that almost all the Cesium contamination came from the leaves, not from the ground. Each growing season after that, tea farmers pruned the plants more than usual and discarded the harvest. In 2012, one eighth of the Cesium content remained, and a year later, only one sixty-fourth should remain.

Japan's reaction was far better than what happened in Europe after Chernobyl. Turkish tea was also highly contaminated by radioactive Cesium, up to 80,000 Becquerels per kilogram (three hundred times higher than Japanese tea after Fukushima). The average was 25,000 Bq/kg. Instead of taking it off the market, the leaves were mixed with earlier crops. The tea squeaked under the EU's legal limit, which was much laxer than the Japanese safety standards. In April 2012, the allowable levels in Japan were further tightened, and now limits are much more stringent than in the U.S. and the EU. In a word, Japanese tea is safe.

THE SOUL & SPIRIT OF TEA

The Making of Japanese Tea

The top leaves of the tea plant are picked by hand and steamed immediately afterward, to preserve their color. This Aracha ("raw tea" before the curing process is completed) contains leaves, stems, dust, etc., separated by aerating in a wicker basket or using a wind sifter. The leaves are kneaded, separated, then heated, and are then gently rolled into Japanese tea's characteristic long, needle-like shape. Later, the leaves are separated by size. The process is done entirely by hand for boutique teas and by machine when it is an industrial process.

Handling of Macha is different. The bushes, as well as those of Gyokuro, are shaded from direct sunlight, so the leaves are darker and higher in Amino Acid. After special drying, blending, and storage in a cycle of up to eight years, the leaves are slowly stone-ground to a very fine emerald green powder.

All tea in Japan is heated yearly for re-drying. Until the Taisho Era seventy or eighty years ago (before refrigeration), Tencha (the source of Macha) was kept in large pottery urns in high mountain areas. Nowadays storage is tightly controlled, so moisture from summer humidity isn't a problem. Still, heating the leaves once a year during maturation changes their flavor.

Aracha is not completely dried. Its moisture content is kept around three to five percent of volume. When it is ready to be sold, the moisture level of blended green tea is around one percent. Drying time and temperature differ for the various ingredients. The col-

The top leaves of the tea plant.

or and flavor of tea come from parts that must be kept partly fresh, with more moisture. The larger leaves, which give the tea blend its aroma or bouquet, need to be dried well.

Virtually all Japanese tea is blended. It's impossible for a consumer to find tea from a single source because it's never "perfect." It's like a symphony. One violinist or pianist may excel, but they can't compete with a good orchestra. Blending masters called *cha-sho* spend up to ten years apprenticing. Each tea brand and wholesaler has its own expert with a sensitive nose and tongue who must know how to roast and blend to achieve the particular qualities desired by their clients.

Choice of good ingredients is very important. The characteristics of growing tea plants change every year, depending on the environment and the weather. The farmer can only produce the raw materials. Merchants must choose leaves from plantations, which are producing the right ingredients for the balance they want of color, flavor, and aroma. Like a chef, the Master Tea Taster designs the tea, controlling its "body" and taste by mixing from various sources, the way a conductor brings out the best in an orchestra.

MIHOKO OKAMURA

Mihoko OKAMURA was born in the United States and now lives in Kyoto. She was personal secretary to D.T. (Daisetz) Suzuki, the renowned Buddhist scholar who is credited with introducing Zen philosophy to the West.

Mihoko Okamura.

THE SOUL & SPIRIT OF TEA

Suzuki-sensei said: "Come in. Please sit here." He took a very old bowl and a kind of container with tea, which he scooped out and put in the bowl. He brought boiling water, poured it in, and whisked it up. This must have taken at least ten minutes, maybe more. Then he said, "Please, have this tea." He hadn't said anything the whole time. It really impressed me a lot at the moment—the quiet dignity. Later I learned a lot about how he taught Zen. I think that initial contact was probably the best introduction to Zen that I could have had.

—*Dr. Albert Stunkard*

Being Religious About Tea

The Tea Ceremony is not simply a matter of drinking tea, or how to brew and serve it. *Sado* is a philosophy. There's nothing like it elsewhere in the world. You have to treat the utensils with great care, in the same way you are supposed to treat yourself. It's an exercise, the next best thing to being in a monastery. You try to learn from the higher things of life. In Western religions, people have to enter a monastery to be in contact with the highest being. In Japan, this is within yourself. When I was a teenager, I posed the following question to Suzuki: "Japanese don't go to church for religious instructions. How do they relate to religion?"

"In Japan," he answered, "religion and culture are in the same drawer."

Whatever you do, it is not separate from the highest quality of life. Tea, shamisen, dance, kendo, judo, archery—any of these are exercises in developing your being. The "do" in Sado means the way to satori, to enlightenment. You must have "uniformity of mind." That was Suzuki's phrase for it. Your mind must be uniform all the time, not going up and down.

Mushin—"No Mind"

I studied Japanese dancing from when I was three years old (in the internment camp), and the teachers never felt "religious" to me. It's in teaching of the arts that they transmit traditional values. They call it *mushin*, "no mindedness". Mu is Buddhist "emptiness." There is no English equivalent, nothing in Western language that's comparable to mu. No matter what branch of art you practice, Japanese teachers talk about mushin. "Mushin ni naru koto desu," they tell you. You attain a state of "no-mind." The word mushin is really a synonym for the Buddha. Most Japanese don't know that. They don't have to know it. By saying mushin, they intuit the quality of Buddhahood they are expected to aim for. But as soon as you take aim, the arrow goes the wrong way, because the very instant you aim at something, you are going off the goal. Mushin will do it for you.

Dr. Suzuki told me that the best-qualified teachers always talk about this, and the ultimate point of all studies is to become mushin. Subject and object become one. They are one! In the Tea Ceremony, when you are whisking tea in a bowl, it is not something outside of you. The tea bowl and yourself are not separate.

The Cosmos

To see a World in a Grain of Sand
And a Heaven in a Wild Flower,
Hold Infinity in the palm of your hand
And Eternity in an hour

—*William Blake*

The potter Bernard Leach used to recite William Blake's "The Songs of Innocence" to Yanagi Soetsu, founder of Mingei—the folk pottery movement in Japan inspired by unknown Korean potters. The first four lines are pure Mingei, and pure tea. They are also Buddhist enlightenment. It's fantastic that Rikyu would try to bring all of that into Sado.

Tea is performed in a four and a half straw mat hut, the smallest room in Japanese architecture. You remove your shoes before you enter, and find yourself immediately inside the tea room. There's no corridor, no foyer—like huts found in Korean farmhouses in Rikyu's time.

The size of the traditional tea room is inspired by a Buddhist text called the Vimalakīrti Sūtra. In Japanese it's called Yuimakyo. Yuima is Japanese for the Sanskrit name Vimalakīrti, the only lay student of Shakyamuni (the Buddha). All the other disciples were monks. Shakyamuni felt that Vimalakīrti's understanding of Buddhism was far deeper than that of his other students, and he would recommend that the others visit Vimalakīrti whenever they could. But Vimalakīrti always reproved the monks for their lack of understanding, and they didn't like that.

One day, Vimalakīrti was said to be sick. As it turned out, he feigned illness because all of humanity was not well, at least that's how it is described in the sutra. Buddha instructed his innumerable followers to visit and pay their respects. They went together, and all fit miraculously in his tiny room. The Sutra says that thousands attended, without feeling crowded. All felt totally free. The entire universe fit within the walls of the tiny room; the bounds of the room were limitless. So goes the parable. In the tea ceremony, as in Pure Land Buddhism, you have to repeat. Practicing something ten million times allows you to become mushin. You forget what you are practicing and you forget your self, which allows you to become free. This is the true meaning of jiyu (the Japanese word for "free").

Sans Cérémonie

When Jack Kerouac and Alan Ginsberg visited, Dr. Suzuki made tea for them. I happened to have had a cold and couldn't join them. I was in the next room and I could hear what they said. It's probably the first time they'd ever had macha. Ginsberg said: "it's like pea soup . . . but it's very good."

Suzuki worked on his manuscripts morning 'til night, so he'd take a tea break every day around three or four pm. His favorite was fresh powdered green tea, which he had sent from Japan. He would whisk it, or I would when I was around, sans cérémonie. What is ceremony? If you have a guest, you go through the whole process of purification, observing the vessels in which you drank the tea, cleaning the whisk, the myriad things you do in front of your guests. But at home, with the whole set in the kitchen, there was no ceremony. A whisk of tea: how much simpler can it get? He did that every day. Between lunch and dinner is a long time, don't you think? It's not unusual in America to have tea in the afternoon. He needed a break; we all need a break!

When I make it, sometimes it's bad tea. It's not as good as it should be. Dr. Suzuki was a great tea brewer. He'd serve tea in a teapot no bigger than the palm of your hand. He had a way of knowing when the hot water, which he brewed in an iron kettle, had come to the right temperature. He would pour it into the tiny teapot and cradle it in his two hands until he could feel it had brewed just long enough. Then a wonderful liquid would come dripping out—two or three drops at a time. There were no more than two or three sips all told. The tea would spread out in your mouth, hugging the surface of your tongue in a way that you could savor it for a long while. One could tell the kind of patience he had from the way he made tea. He was able to identify himself with the tea being brewed, the teapot, the tea bowl. All were present in the one person called Suzuki, Daisetsu.

Michael Goldberg has lived (fully!) 30 years in Japan. With a background in video art, he freelances as cameraman/director for overseas television networks and magazines, and is producer of the documentary *A Zen Life: D.T. Suzuki*.

Chapter 14

A TIME AND PLACE FOR TEA

Jonathan Wimpenny

"Architecture is basically a container of something.
I hope they will enjoy not so much the teacup, but the tea."
—YOSHIO TANIGUCHI

Architecture sets the frame for all human activity, the space and stage where we all play our part, making entrances and exits on its Euclidian stage. For architecture and human ritual are inevitably linked, whether it be the grand approach to an imposing palace or the simple, intimate space of a Japanese teahouse.

My earliest memory of ceremonial space is of a very modest building in Yorkshire, a place where my grandmother would organize that quintessential of all English ceremonies—"high tea." In summer, come rain or shine, she would hold court in her garden gazebo. "Simmer down then childer," she'd insist. "Time must stand still for high tea." The proceedings always began with two aunts helping my mother to carry three silver trays from the main house. Of course, we kids knew what was on each: the first had 'Sunday Cold' sandwiches—tongue or cucumber—thin, quartered neatly and trimmed of any crust. The second had china cups and saucers, rattling alongside the stout silver pot of Darjeeling. Finally the third tray (the one we'd regard with rapt attention) was piled high with portions of treacle parkin, ginger-snap biscuits and Mountbatten cake.

The gazebo, painted pale green with white trim and glazed on three sides, was entered by two wide steps attached to the bottom frame. The whole structure, measuring at least twelve foot square and ten foot high, was placed very proudly (in full view of the passengers on the double-decker omnibus trudging up Cowlersley Lane) in the center of her front lawn and mounted on a circular metal track that allowed it to be rotated towards the warm sun and away from the prevailing breeze. Inside was her cream-colored wicker chair, and flanking her daybed (aligned along the back wall) were two cabinets painted white and piled high with Baedekers and her other travel books. My aunts retrieved the three luggage racks stored below the daybed, unfolded them for the silver trays as Grandma offered us plates and napkins, 'played mum' and poured the tea. After we ate our sandwiches and scoffed the final rinds of marzipan, she would read aloud as we drifted off to sleep, dreaming of distant lands.

"'Appy as pigs in muck we were," as they say in Yorkshire. Recognizing both safety and comfort, the peripheral ganglia of my reptilian brain had been triggered to memorize every minute detail of this ceremony—a tidal wave of sensations and flickering images fixed securely on the back of my retina. If you think about it, spatial recognition is an extraordinarily complicated thing, for along with the physical sensations of smell and taste and the chemical composition of our blood stream and well-being, there is the equally visceral awareness of enclosure, protection (therefore relaxation), light and sound, contemplation (of interior *and* exterior views) as well as the many layers of color and texture. So it was, that with the help of her teahouse, my grandmother arrested time, at least for me.

Since her gazebo was long since demolished, I did some research and found it had been grander than most, purpose-built in the joiner's shop of the family business, J. Wimpenny & Co. But in the 1920s and 30s, you could order a much more modest one and in kit form, from a company called Boulton & Paul. One such order was shipped out to the writer, George Bernard Shaw, and you can still visit it as a museum piece of the National Trust at the bottom of his garden in Hertfordshire, England. Shaw named it "London" so that his wife could honestly report (to those phoning the main house) where her husband was without fibbing.

Aesthetics aside, both gazebo and writing hut are good examples of sustainable architecture. Touching the land lightly, they make judicious use of renewable resources and employ other materials such as glass with considered economy. With no rigid connections and no need for drainage, they can spin, turning their backs against inclement weather and making passive use of solar gain. Furthermore, they can rotate when summer shade is needed and achieve cross ventilation simply by propping open a small window opposite the entrance door. Being self sufficient and distant enough (particularly from the busy comings and goings of a Victorian household) made the garden pavilion an ideal retreat. Here one could ruminate over a favorite cuppa whether it be in the quiet isolation of editing a manuscript or with an intimate gathering for high tea. All this with the simplest of shed design!

The Japanese take a ritual and cultural stride much further with their 'chashitsu' (teahouses). Purposefully simple (as our hut and gazebo examples above), visual distraction is avoided by stripping away any pretense, emphasizing simplicity and form of the architectural frame, which becomes an element within the garden and encourages a quiet reflection of the manicured tableau. The goal here is not to impress with any grandiose or monumental building but provide the host with an ideal setting to contemplate the art of living and exist along with his guests in harmony with the surrounding nature.

For the host, the approach to the chashitsu is of crucial concern, for it is this that prepares the guests for the upcoming event, the 'chanoyu' (tea ceremony). The first stone pavers of the 'soto-roji' (lower path) lead them through the outer garden to the 'machiai' (a waiting place), where they are greeted by the host with an 'aisatsu' (greeting); he offers them water at his tsukubai' (a paved area around a pool or water basin), in order that they can wash their hands and

Bernard Shaw's Rotating House Is an Aid to Health

George Bernard Shaw revolving his workshop.

A REVOLVING turntable is one of the factors in the splendid health of George Bernard Shaw, famous English author. At the age of 72, he is in the prime of physical condition and attributes it partially to his appreciation of sunlight. Mr. Shaw has a plan to keep the sun shining on him constantly while he works. He has constructed a small hut on his grounds that is built on a turntable. When the morning sun shifts, he merely places his shoulder against the side of the hut and gives it a push so that the warming beams fall through his window at the correct angle.

Mr. Shaw's plan to keep the sun shining on him is a simple health measure, and not a wanton eccentricity.

The house is not a new idea. Several years ago such a building was constructed in France. It was built with glass walls and was equipped with a motor that moved it at the touch of an electric button. The original model cost $50,000. Mr. Shaw's cost much less than $1,000.

The author has spent most of his life out of doors, but when he moved to London he didn't get as much sun as he thought he needed. Hence the hut.

From *Modern Mechanix* magazine, August 1929.

rinse their mouths (a gesture symbolic of leaving the dust of the real world behind). After an invitation to pass through a simple bamboo gate, they are led along the 'uchi-roji' (inner garden path) to their final destination, the host's 'chashitsu'.

The whole idea of this progression along the 'roji', similar in our western culture to the incline and final steps up to the Parthenon, represents a journey in preparation for a spiritual event, which in their case is the 'Cha-e' (tea ceremony). Without going into the details of the tea ritual itself (which I am *not at all* qualified to relate), I would like to stress the rigid symmetry and formality of the architecture and the interior space embracing it. Every post, every lintel, every tatami mat has its place. Architectural form is uncompromising; even the 'nijiriguchi' (entrance door) is built so low that it forces all guests, no matter what their rank, to crawl through on hands and knees. Order and tradition rule; nothing should perplex or puzzle the onlooker, who is to be honored with his own defined space, which will allow quiet meditation of the tea ceremony: the ebb and flow of flickering sunlight and framed views of nature outside. The ideal environment has been prepared purely for the guests' solace and to embolden contemplation on the calm stillness of the enclosure, the manicured man-made garden contrasting with the capricious vagaries of nature—sounds and rhythms of water, sky and vegetation, upturned leaves or swaying branches caused by the silent breeze outside.

If architecture is the container of stories and tradition, it is most successful when it meets the criteria of our cultural expectations, then registers them as memories of record. Be it Japanese tea ceremony or the formality of my grandmother's "high tea," we must respect the moment and stop the clock. As my grandmother was fond of saying, when it is high time for tea, "time must stand still".

Likewise, architecture stands still when it achieves a balance of Platonic perfection, for example, Bramante's Tempietto in Rome, or the Parthenon in Athens. In recent times we can see it when the ideas of the Modern Movement were introduced from the German Bauhaus into the United States. Mies Van der Rohe's Farnsworth House is the archetypal example.

"Here, the purity of the cage is undisturbed," wrote Philip Johnson of its structure. "Neither steel columns from which it is suspended, nor the independent floating terrace, break the taut skin." Like the Japanese teahouse, the surrounding grounds are an integral part of Van Der Rohe's concept—a floating glass pavilion, a single geometric form dominating the landscape. In this temple-like atmosphere, the owner may sit and enjoy Nature without ever having to remove his silk shoes.

This need for Platonic balance in architecture continues with recent work such as that of the Italian architect Renzo Piano. Witness the calm stillness of his projects, such as the Beyeler Foundation Gallery in Basle Switzerland, or his extension to the Morgan Library in New York City. Yet as of late, architecture has turned in an opposing direction and opened the Euclidian box to release a genie that is the very antipathy of the quiet, calm spirit of tea.

With a restless recognition of computer power (and thus the burgeoning possibilities of building information modeling), the geometries of the Modern Movement have recently been shattered in a petulant conniption. High on an espresso buzz, the architect touts his model to feed a public craving for status symbols and branding: the more bizarre or unusual, the better. For the Center for the Performing Arts at Bard College, New York, Frank Gehry disguised a more than mundane concrete frame by wrapping it in tinfoil and calling it art. Tom Mayne asked us to adjust one's mindset of the student campus, and when Cornell proposed to turn Roosevelt Island, NY into a version of Silicon Valley, his academic buildings took a radical turn.

There is no hierarchy in Mayne's ivory tower, no gathering round a central quad. Instead, we zip along cavernous, flowing spaces as they interweave and interconnect, and we are left searching for our cafe latte and somewhere to sit. "The principle is not so different from preschool", wrote Justin Davidson in New York Magazine, "where children gather on the reading rug, migrate to the costume center, cluster at the art table, or go off in a corner to sulk."

The United States is not unique to this trend. In 2008 in England, when Gordon Brown's minister of State for Culture Media and Sports suggested that libraries should "look beyond the bookcase and be a place for families and joy and chatter," there was an uproar. Victoria Coren wrote: "My brain is struggling with the philosophical question (like that of the tree falling in the empty forest): if there is nothing inside but people eating burgers and playing the Sims, is it actually a library? Isn't it just an internet café?" And referencing the line about looking beyond the bookcase, "Why? Why must they? They're libraries. The bookcase is exactly where they should be looking. For God's sake, someone should be. I can eat and make phone calls at home."

If our last forced space of disconnection is the shower, then we need to escape the continual distractions of our ultra connected world, create an antidote to what Jon Kabat-Zinn calls our modern-day 'full catastrophe living'. It's not that I'm a luddite or despise city life, far from it; it's just that I believe our souls sometimes need a quiet place to sit and think.

Although the odd exhibition can sometimes draw a weekend crowd (something I naturally avoid), my chosen refuge is off 37th Street, a few steps away from the thrum and throng of Madison Avenue. The street entrance is in itself unprepossessing (a seemingly industrial façade linking a jumble of older Beaux Arts buildings, contrasting sharply with this recent intervention under a cloak of Palladian grandeur), but the architect Renzo Piano takes this screen-of-steel aesthetic in his stride, and with his deft sleight of hand, prepares us for a treat.

The doors close behind us, and Madison Avenue is hushed as we enter into a New York gem known as the Morgan Library. Immediately, we sense the nuances of filtered light, streaming and shimmering around us as we marvel at the engineering of this cathedral-like glass sanctuary. High above us, a cantilevered platform punctures the space with an elevator shaft beside it. We begin to notice a passenger or two, appearing like monks or library cognoscenti, quietly appearing then drifting off-stage with their preconceived agendas to the vault-like rooms surrounding us. There is no clatter, for the wood floor has silenced their tread, adding a sense of luxury to an atmosphere already heavy (at least for one imagined moment!) with the perfumed zephyr of leather and parchment scrolls.

There is one corner of this place that I have made my own. For it is here where I take my cup, settle into the chair by the corner table, warming both hands before taking a fragrant sip of tea to enjoy a moment of peace within.

Jonathan Wimpenny was born in Yorkshire, England and trained as an architect. He now lives and practices in New York City. President of the Royal Institute of British Architects USA, he is also a member of the American Institute of Architects

Workers harvest young tea leaves in Malaysia, Photography © Ahmad
Faizal Yahya.

Part III

THE FUTURE
OF TEA

Chapter 15

TEA DRINKING AND MEDITATION
CAN EITHER PRACTICE PAVE THE PATH TO ENLIGHTENMENT?

Genevieve Price

What do tea and meditation have in common? To put it simply, tea time is 'me' time. Tea time transcends the ticking clock that is dictated by the relentless pace of modern life. In making a space in our day to pause and indulge in the simple pleasure of sipping a cup of quality tea, we give ourselves the gift of time. The ritual of drinking tea with full awareness draws our senses to the present moment, and creates a space of connection to the graceful rhythm of nature and by extension, our most authentic selves. When we make it a daily practice to pause and enjoy a cup of tea, we actively create a space of remembrance of who we really are. Drinking tea without distraction cultivates a sense of groundedness that is similarly cultivated during meditation, a practice that roots us to the earth—body, mind, and spirit. This sense of groundedness enables us to confront life after the cup with a renewed sense of clarity, creativity, and connection to the world around us.

Meditation, particularly of the Zen tradition, is a grounding practice because it enables us to face our present reality by focusing our senses inward. Drinking a cup of tea with intention gives our senses a hook on which to latch, simplifying the experience of the moment. The feel of the warm porcelain in one's palm and fingers, the bitter yet smooth taste, the earthy smell, the image of steam dispelling from a cup, and the sound of running water—these comforting sensual pleasures connect us to our body and to a feeling of home. In evoking all of our senses, tea provides a spiritual comfort, as the practice empties the conceptual mind and helps us to concentrate better while connecting us to our bodies. We are what we consume, and *how* we consume affects how we feel. The "how" behind our rituals, or the manner in which our bodies move about those daily routines, is the primary determinant of the quality of our mental states.

Anthropologist Clifford Geertz elucidates the effect of ritual on the body in describing it as a practice " . . . which acts to establish powerful, pervasive, and long-lasting moods and motivations by formulating conceptions of a general order of existence."[1] Geertz's conception of the role of ritual in mundane life as establishing a particular set of sensibilities rings true in my own experience of habitually drinking tea. I find that drinking a cup of tea first thing in the morning establishes a sense of order to start my day. On days when I lack the time or resources to access a cup of tea upon waking, I realize that a vital part of my daily routine has been stripped away, and this lack sets a precedent for the entire day. I start my day feeling a slight sense of disorientation and disconnectedness between my body and mind. Just as group rituals act as a bind laced in the fabric of society, personal rituals provide a sense of coherence so that we feel at home in our bodies. Everyone has their morning rituals, and for me, a cup of tea is just as important brushing my teeth. My day has not begun in earnest until I have had a cup of tea.

Drinking tea throughout the day, or taking "tea breaks", serves as a way of resetting my body and mind. It is a way of checking in and taking a conscious pause so that I can face the present moment instead of spending my entire day chasing after myself, completing

---

1. Herbert Plutschow, "An Anthropological Perspective on the Japanese Tea Ceremony". University of California at Los Angeles, 1999. <http://www.anthropoetics.ucla.edu/ap0501/tea.htm>

THE SOUL & SPIRIT OF TEA

one task just to meet a new obligation. When I take a tea break, the only task at hand is to savor my cup of tea. This ritual is an ultimate expression of self-care. Like setting aside ten minutes to sit and meditate and "just be", the purpose of a wholesome cup of tea is to let go of expectation, anticipation, and the need to accomplish. In a way, a tea break is an escape from the pressure to perform that dictates the demands of daily life; however, it is only a temporary escape that enables me to practically face the rest of my day with more clarity and awareness. Some people smoke a cigarette, some people take coffee, and some take tea, like me.

However, the overall aesthetic of tea differs from that of a cigarette or coffee. Smoking a cigarette offers a chance to pause but is a blatantly unhealthy means of coping with stress, while coffee is a symbol of productivity—it sends a subliminal message to our body and mind to "speed up" and "do more". Tea, on the other hand, is a symbol of health and well-being, and slows down the body and mind in order to make us more aware and conscious.

Historically, tea drinking is a sacred practice. Chan Buddhism, the root of Zen meditation as practiced in the modern Western world, influenced the creation of the traditional tea ceremony of Japan. The habit of drinking tea was brought to Japan from China in the 8th century by Zen monks, who used it to stay awake during long meditations. Tea was able to relax them as well as enhance their concentration, making their minds fresh and alert. The philosophy of Zen teaches that everyone can achieve enlightenment, but that mundane ruminations stifle it and detract one from accepting the true nature of reality. Enlightenment can thus be found in the midst of everyday activities, such as the simple act of drinking tea. The Japanese tea ceremony, which the Japanese call "cha-no-yu", emphasizes the concept of attitude. The focused mindset in which participants approach the ceremony is absolutely essential to performing the ritual. The aesthetics of the "cha-no-yu" room help to cultivate this sense of focus. The Japanese tea room is small, simple, and minimally adorned, providing a quiet, uncluttered space in which a state of deep meditation can be accessed. In providing this physical space for a special ritual to be performed, the tea ceremony unlocks a portal to go beyond this world and enter a mental and spiritual realm apart. Tea ceremonies are still practiced today in Zen monasteries.

A Buddhist abbot named Shuko was the first to formulate the tea ceremony as a sort of sacrament, a "Way" in 1473. He attained enlightenment one day when it occurred to him that filling an ordinary tea bowl with hot water also expresses the Law of the Universe.[2] The path to *satori* involves cultivating cognizance of the triviality of worldly vanity. Japanese tea master Sen-no Rikyu (1521-91) undertook Zen meditation training and purified and codified the Japanese tea ceremony during the Muromachi period. This was a time in Japanese history characterized by civil strife and feudal warfare amongst rival clans. Rikyu saw the Way of Tea, or *chado*, as a way of being that stood in contrast to the chaos of the social landscape which he inhabited. Acceptance of the chaos is the primary ideal of the Way of Tea, which is given form through the tea ceremony, a simple yet purposeful ritual.[3] The Japanese tea ceremony thus provides a unique space to simplify one's life to a single activity. While the external world can be overstimulating, the tea room is a quiet, uncluttered space to live with intention and in turn find clarity within the noise of the conceptual mind and the chaos of the sensual world. Kakuzo Okakura, trained within the strict moral code of a Japanese samurai, wrote in *The Book of Tea* in 1906, "Tea . . . is a religion of the art of life . . . all movements to be performed simply and naturally."[4] The Way of Tea promotes a sense of ease that is obtained by a careful balance between actively living by an intention and willfully accepting the present moment. This is a primary tenet of meditation as well—relaxation does not give way to passivity. Rather, it lends itself to a greater ease of focus.

While the mind may resist the discomfort of the present and seek a source of distraction by ruminating on the past or fantasizing about the future, the wandering mind leads us astray from reality. Reality

---

2. James Norwood Pratt, *Tea Lover's Treasury*. Tea Society, San Francisco: 2009. p. 17.
3. Ibid, p. 18.
4. Ibid, p. 20.

in its absolute honesty comprises both the suffering and the bliss of life—respectively the *dukha* and the *sukha*, the Sanskrit terms alluded to in yoga philosophy. The ego's vices of craving, aversion and delusion which Patanjali addressed in his *Yoga Sutras* are the same as that which the Buddha taught in the *Dhammapada*. Actively practicing acceptance of life *as is* is the path to imagining the ideal of what life could be like if we were to see reality as the gods do. This can be accomplished by transcending the dualism of the conceptual mind, the fragment of our psyche that compels us to label aspects of the sensual world as "good" or "bad". Ultimately, these labels are bounded by the ego's incomplete realm of understanding, and thus limit our consciousness. Yoga, a constant practice within my life, provides a unique space for me to evaluate how my mind reacts to certain sensations in my body as I flow through different poses. In drawing attention to the precise movements of specific muscle groups, it is a practice that grounds me in my body, and in so doing, exposes the ordinary limitations and misconceptions of my ego. In providing a space to simply be, drinking tea similarly frees my mind so that I can approach life with a lesser degree of delusion and greater degree of clarity, and perhaps many lifetimes away grasp the universal.

However, there is a distinction to be made between certain purposeful spiritual activities such as yoga or tai-chi, and the Way of Tea. Drinking tea is a ritual act of consumption, whereby the intention of mindfulness assimilates directly into our bodies through the process of digestion. The Japanese tea ceremony shares similarities with the Holy Eucharist, a ritual act of consumption that I was exposed to as a raised Roman Catholic. Fittingly, the Japanese adopted the host aspect of mass from Portuguese Roman Catholic priests in the 17th century and incorporated it into to Japanese *chado* tea ceremony.[5] In the Eucharistic sacrament, the Host, symbolizing the Body of Christ, is carefully prepared before it is given to guests in a mass service. The priest prepares the Host with such careful deliberation on the altar in front of the congregation of parishioners,

---

5. Okakura Kakuzo, *The Book of Tea;* Introduction by Liza Dalby, Boston : Tuttle Pub., 2000.

who later are offered a piece of the Host. The Eucharistic sacrament connects the members of a congregation together "under one body" through this ritual act of consumption of the Body of Christ. This ritual symbolizes what is perhaps the primary tenet of Catholicism: the Transfiguration that Christ is entirely human and entirely divine at the same time. In communally consuming Christ's body, members of the faith absorb a piece of the divine, and are united, cultivating a sense of connectedness to an entity beyond the limited scope of the individual. The Japanese tea ceremony is a similar ritual that unites the host with his or her guests through the carefully deliberated procedures comprising the ceremony.

Beyond the communal aspect, drinking a cup of tea even in solitude unites one with a more expansive consciousness. The tea leaves themselves connect us with the earth and the natural forces at play that are beyond our control. Fundamentally, this is the purpose of meditation as well; it is a practice in the art of surrender so we can gradually become more graceful and efficient in maneuvering the waves of the Dao. The finest tea leaves are acquired only through such careful prodding and tending to quality soil. The leaves embody this thoughtfulness, which we in turn consume when we sip a cup several steps down the preparation process. Tea provides us with a sense of balance and connects us with our true nature in the same way that meditation does.

Although the tea ceremony stemmed from Chan Buddhism, it is categorically a secular practice in which the object of devotion is the guest. Philosophically, the Way of Tea embodies a spirit of four basic principles which promote a reverence towards the sacred. These are harmony, respect, purity and tranquility (wa, kei, sei, jaku), virtues similarly cultivated during meditation practice.[6] Harmony brings us in touch with nature, respect provides a reverence for life, purity imbues us with clarity and selflessness of purpose, and tranquility offers a sense of acceptance of life as is. These philosophical principles

---

6. Sheila Fling, "Psychological Aspects of the Way of Tea". *Japan Studies Association Journal*, Vol. 2, pp.29-36.

THE SOUL & SPIRIT OF TEA

provide the practical foundation to live with a sense of intention and connection to the world around us.

The precision and intricacies of the cha-no-yu tea ceremony reflect these four principles. Through this ritual, the process of drinking tea becomes an aesthetic act rather than a mere form of consumption. The full ceremony demands a very specific etiquette and the viewpoint of the guest is always taken into consideration, with careful placement of utensils and conscientious deliberation of pacing and tone in conversation. Tea is prepared in silence for guests, so as to focus the host, or *Teishu*, on each step of the preparation process. The *Teishu* must pay careful attention to which hand he or she is using to hold utensils and napkins. This directs one to focus on the precise movements of the body. Each utensil has a specific purpose; for example, small chopsticks, called *Kuromoji*, are used specifically to pick up sweets, or *Omogashi*. The folding of napkins and orientation towards the guest are also specified. Every movement has an intent and purpose in relation to the guest, reinforcing this sentiment of respect, or *kei*, for the other.

In focusing fully on a ritual that revolves around this sense of otherness, a participant in the ceremony is given a space to transcend the egocentrism of the conceptual mind. The teleological goal of enlightenment through the practice of Zen meditation is to rise above the conceptual mind by reuniting with the universal Self, a self-identification that transcends the gap between subject and object, between self and other.[7] *Chado*, The Way of Tea, reflects a similar aesthetic through its principles of harmony and respect, which cultivate a sense of oneness with the universe that exists beyond the sphere of the individual mind.

How does one find a sense of ease and acceptance in a ceremony that is so stringent? The specificities of the ceremony demand one's total focus, and in so doing, evoke a state of flow where one can be fully present. A mental state of flow empties the mind of its ruminations and mental chatter that results from a lack of attention to the

7. Wallace A (1999) The Buddhist tradition of Samatha: methods for refining and examining consciousness. *J Conscious Stud*, 6:175–187.

movements and considerations of the present moment. The concept of undistracted attention is central to both the cha-no-yu ceremony and to meditation practice. Mental states of flow and their role in overall life satisfaction has been explored in the budding field of positive psychology.[8] The more we are engaged in mental states of flow in day-to-day life, whether it be in our careers, our social life, or our hobbies, the more likely we are to reflect on our lives with an overall sense of contentment. Naturally, activities that are of more interest to us evoke our full attention and we are thus happier overall when we pursue them. Furthermore, when we are able to moderate our attention as we see fit, we can more finely control our consciousness. In turn, we are able to control the quality of our experience and be happier as individuals. Although the average tea enthusiast does not regularly take part in esoteric Japanese tea ceremonies, we can all invariably benefit from drinking our tea with the same intention of focus and consideration as the most experienced of the Japanese tea masters.

While the consumption of tea predisposes one to engage fully in the practice and thus cultivate a mindset of meditation, the physiological effects on the body and mind illustrate these attentional effects as well. The concept of attention has been investigated extensively in neuroscience research, and specific experiments have been conducted to study the effect of tea on attention as well as the effect of meditation on attention. In investigating these effects, it is important to distinguish between the two different categories of attention as they relate to meditation: open monitoring attention and focused attention.[9] Mindfulness meditation is associated with open monitoring attention, which cultivates a sense of passive observance and acceptance of reality to achieve clarity and integrity in the everyday. We exercise open monitoring attention when we are in a state of non-judgmental reflection. Zen meditation strengthens focused attention on a fixed object such as the breath or a mantra to reach a

---

8. Csikszentmihalyi M., Flow: The Psychology of Optimal Experience. *Harper* p.5
9. Raffone, A. & Srinivasan, N. (2010) The exploration of meditation in the neuroscience of attention and consciousness. *Cogn Process*, 11, 1-7.

THE SOUL & SPIRIT OF TEA

meditative state. In the tea ceremony, this object is the ritual itself. Drinking a cup of tea in the morning to clear the mind and cultivate a positive intention for the day can be associated with open monitoring attention. Depending on our consciousness and intention when we drink it, tea can have different attentional effects.

Theoretically and practically, tea has been used to cultivate the level of attention necessary to achieve higher states of consciousness. Specific research has been done exploring the anti-anxiety effects of the Camellia sinensis tea leaf through its major amino acid, L-theanine. Results show that L-theanine enhances long-term attention through its modulation of alpha band activity, an electrical signal in the brain with a specific frequency of 8-12 Hz that is implicated in relaxation and prolonged attention.[10] Research on meditation similarly affects alpha-band signals.[11] Based on these two separate avenues of research on L-theanine and meditation, one can infer that drinking tea with mindfulness would fortify the attentional effects of L-theanine. Further research is yet to be done exploring the effects of drinking tea the *"chado"* Way. This research would rest on the gap between mind and brain, exploring the compound effects of mindfulness and L-theanine on brain physiology. Drinking tea as if one is meditating would capture the attentional effects of meditation as well as L-theanine, further enhancing alpha band activity. Undoubtedly, *how* we drink our tea alters our consciousness just as much if not more than the raw materials of the leaf itself. The intention that we set when drinking a cup of tea alters our perception of the experience, and in so doing, affects the hardware of our brain. Approaching simple, mundane life experiences such as walking in the park with a mindset of devotion and consciousness brings a sense of joy and peace to our lives. Drinking a cup of tea uniquely reminds me of the sanctity of the everyday by providing a space to

10. Kelly, S.P., Gomez-Ramirez, M., Montesi, J.L. & Foxe, J.J. (2008) L-theanine and caffeine in combination affect human cognition as evidenced by oscillatory alpha-band activity and attention task performance. *J Nutr*, 138, 1572S.

11. Aftanas, L.I. & Golocheikine, S.A. (2001) Human anterior and frontal midline theta and lower alpha reflect emotionally positive state and internalized attention: high-resolution EEG investigation of meditation. *Neurosci Lett*, 310, 57.

cultivate gratitude and acceptance towards the simplicity of life as is. After thoroughly enjoying a quality cup, I am infused with a sense of contentment, a sense that I have been provided with all that I need, despite the demands of the day that await me. This has been the role of tea throughout history—to make the seemingly mundane act of sipping a bowl of tea a sacred practice that expands our consciousness by creating a sense of being in a world apart.

Genevieve Price is an avid tea drinker and tea enthusiast. She graduated with a degree in Neuroscience from Barnard College of Columbia University in New York and is moving to San Diego in September of 2013 to study Naturopathic Medicine at Bastyr University. She seeks to learn alternative healing modalities such as botanical medicine, homeopathy, and mind-body-spirit medicine. She is a world traveler and seeks to learn diverse cross-cultural approaches to healing.

Chapter 16

BLESSED BY BIG ISLAND TEA

Eliah Halpenny and Cam Muir

I stepped off the plane onto American soil four days after 9/11. I flew on one of the first flights leaving Canada, my home, my family, friends and career. My husband Cam had promised me a charmed existence on the Big Island, and he had relocated to Hawai'i two years before. That ominous world catastrophe was not a sign of assurance as I left all that I had ever known for fifty years. Star spangled flags were everywhere, patriotism pulsing with the unified grief of a nation.

As a Canadian, I did not have the freedom shared by citizens of this country. Cam's employment status at the University of Hawaii-Hilo enabled both of us to be welcomed aliens, but I was not allowed employment in the USA. I was considered a parenthesis of Cam. My personal employment restriction handed me an empty canvas to recreate Eliah in a new country. What was I going to do with myself?

I brought my tools. I had been a backyard horticulturist most of my adult life, creating colorful flower garden extravaganzas that people would walk out of their way to enjoy. As a young woman I had been employed as a gardener. Later, a soil surveying summer job convinced me that I was on the wrong path studying Landscape

Architecture at the University of British Columbia. Learning about plant and soil science was valuable knowledge, but I wanted dirt under my nails. Sitting at a drafting table was not going to satisfy the hidden farm girl in me. How could I have known where I was being lead, magnetized by the symbiotic relationship between plants and soil? After all, I was a city girl.

Stepping onto Hawaiian soil, I faced an opportunity to realize a dream, to create a Garden of Eden, a flower farm. I projected ahead. Once I had my green card, I could sell my flowers year round to Canada, a giant palette of potential! Winters in Canada were long and cold. Driven inside during those harsh months, I made art, another self-expression for my love of color, but I was merely biding my time, waiting for spring when I could once again root around in the earth. My sister used to say that she would see me lose my leaves every fall, becoming melancholy with the approach of winter. No more! Hawaii was now my home. I could play outside 365 days of the year! How perfect for my soul!

Another set of tools packed for my new life was my career experience in advertising sales and marketing. I had spent eleven years marketing another's product, and now I wanted to create my own. I had witnessed the rise of so many health products, items appealing to Baby Boomers. I lived in Vancouver during the '70s, where I watched a neighborhood hippie health food store, "Lifestream," expand into a mega product success. It grew with the demand of people wanting good health. This was a large set of people, the Baby Boomers. Boomers were willing to pay for products that offered the promise of longevity. Could I not grow something targeting that demographic group?

My cogs were turning. I decided to learn more about growing an organic product to appeal to that market. But first, I had to learn about farming—and as I soon discovered, gardening is not farming.

I started reading about and researching permaculture. I lived with an excellent educational resource, my husband Cam. Cam had moved to Hawaii to study the ecology and evolution of high elevation cloud forests. Together, we decided to take an orchid growing class offered through the university and to start an orchid farm. Many others were already running successful operations on the Big Island, so I imagined we could join an existing industry. Wrong! I learned that pesticides were almost a mandate in growing orchids commercially, but I was unwilling to poison the insects on my plants, nor hire anyone else to do the nasty deed.

Long ago, when I had made one of my first backyard veggie gardens, I had added some "non-organic" fertilizer to my prepared plot. Much to my horror, as the fertilizer was watered into the soil, the earthworms came screaming out—I was hurting the worms, friends of plants and soil alike. It was a sad lesson. It left an indelible reminder, soils are alive and must be handled with the respect we give all living things.

At this point I will add that I am a practicing Tibetan Buddhist, how could I deliberately harm another? I realized I was not going to become an orchid farmer, so I continued my personal research looking for a farming niche, something to grab my passion and give me purpose in paradise, a crop that did not require poisoning our soil, critters or plants.

Two months later, I was given a gem, a wish-fulfilling gem in the form of a newspaper article about the optimistic findings of research being done on Camellia sinensis by a local arm of the USDA. Hawaiian grown tea appeared to have few natural predators and was thriving in the volcanic soil and climate. Three experimental tea gardens had been set up, one garden right in my neighborhood, just a few miles from where Cam was doing research in a cloud forest.

I nearly jumped out of my seat reading that article. I was so excited. I felt that I had found gold. I telephoned the researcher and asked to be sent some seeds, and when those nine seeds arrived, I put them straight into the ground. Then waited. And waited. Boy did they take a long time to germinate! After 6 weeks of my eyes pleading for sprouting evidence (a normal length of time as it turns out), my seedlings broke the soil surface. Yippee! I knew I could grow tea! Both of my green thumbs were pointed up, and I was keen to start immediately. This was an opportunity I did not want to miss.

Back in the mid '70s, my geologist boyfriend and I came up with what we thought was a brilliant idea. He was working for the Geological Survey of Canada in the coastal mountains of northern British Columbia. Dropped from a helicopter in that pristine environment, we could scoop the water out of any stream and drink it . . . what if we bottled it and sold it to California? This was years before bottled water glutted the market, but we were young and did not act on our plan. We missed an opportunity.

When we had children together, another brilliant idea popped up. I was making herbal teas, diluting them with fruit juice and feeding them to our toddlers. We called it "juicy tea". What if we bottled herbal tea with juice to replace soda? It was another golden opportunity missed, because again we did not act ahead of the bottled juice/tea craze that subsequently flooded the market. I share these anecdotes to give the history of my not acting on potentially successful· ideas. When I thought about growing tea, I knew it was a great opportunity. The timing was perfect.

I had already noticed that research on the health benefits of tea was being published in magazines, newspapers and broadcasted on news reports. Tea had become the darling of the media, and I felt certain it was appealing to health-minded individuals. Drinking green tea was the new panacea. Since the media was doing all of the heavy lifting by educating the public, or so I thought at the time, I just had to take my green thumbs and get planting! The spiritual connection I felt with tea was similar to the historical connection between the Buddhist monks and early tea cultivation. My marketing acumen was leading me to the spiritual journey of a tea plantation, and what a journey it was to become.

Cam and I wanted to grow a tea with an exquisite taste. After speaking with a tea purveyor in Honolulu, Byron Goo of the Tea Chest, his advice pointed us to producing an ultra-high-end loose-leaf tea. He told us that whole leaf tea was the fastest growing segment in retail tea sales and if we were just getting started, we should target that niche market. I met another tea connoisseur/purveyor from Taiwan who laughed at my audacity when I told him that I was growing tea in Hawaii. He said, and I quote, "You can't grow tea! How can you grow tea?" I replied, "Because I am." I hold dear his lingering caution, "Always be humble with tea!"

Armed with this sage advice, we moved ahead. The focus on a high value product was consistent with our goal to employ workers at a level that they could afford to raise families. We also wanted to make sure that our crop was sustainably grown. Sustainability has a very specific meaning taken from the UN definition (development that does not hinder the ability of future generations to also develop). In Hawaii we often see on t-shirts and posters: "Sust-aina-bility". This plays on the Hawaiian word 'aina commonly used to describe "the land". A fuller translation of the word 'aina is "that which feeds us". We are fed by our culture, community, economics and environment. Therefore, our tea project, which we named Big Island Tea, needed to be culturally, socially, economically, and environmentally sustainable in order to be completely sustainable. That is our mission statement.

We searched for two years to find the perfect location with the right elevation with plenty of fertile soil. We purchased a rundown lettuce farm on the slope of Mauna Loa volcano. We systematically tore down eight 40 x100 foot dilapidated greenhouses (with the help of several furious uninvited tropical storms I might add) and prepared the ground for planting. To acquire the 6,000 tea plants that now make up our small-scale tea farm involved patience. These plants could not readily be acquired in Hawaii, so I turned to the World Wide Web.

I searched for months until one day, I found myself in a tea chatroom. I read an entry from a person looking for tea seeds. Satyam Pradhan, owner of Himalayan Orchid Exports in Kalimpong, India answered that inquiry. I immediately jumped in and requested seeds too. My random internet search resulted in the acquisition of seeds needed to set up our farm. Seven years later, I traveled to Kalimpong to be a guest in Satyam's home. His kind and generous family welcomed me open-heartedly and we are now lifelong friends.

One of the family's senior members, Kamal Pradhan, taught me the secret to making heavenly black tea. Kamal had managed a tea estate in the 1980s, and at that time his Darjeeling tea sold for the highest bidding price in history. I am forever grateful to have met Satyam and his entire family and so thankful for Kamal's advice. I consider it a blessing to have learned a secret to processing exquisite black tea. Although Kamal passed away before I could share the results of his mentoring, I consider him a vital reason why our tea is now being sold at Harrods in London, England at a price unimaginable when we first planted our seeds.

Kamal's guidance, matched with my overly exaggerated sense of smell and the diligent recording of every experimental batch of tea processed over nine years, have led to the creation of a green and black tea expressing Hawai'i's distinct flavor. We believe the loving attention given to growing our plants is the ethereal ingredient to our tea. Next to parenting my daughters, I have never put more love into a creative project. Working with the plants daily, I imagine that they are infused with my wish that the drinkers of our finished tea will enjoy a feeling of wellbeing, even for a few moments. When I harvest the leaves and hand-roll our tea, I say mantras wishing that all beings be happy and free from suffering. This sacred attitude is the motivation behind our labor of love.

We started our tea project with no working capital. The acronym for Big Island Tea is BIT. Bit by bit, a fortuitous manifestation of labor and resources has trickled into our project. Whenever I get fatigued or feel despair, an email or enquiry appears and once again I am rejuvenated by a new opportunity for Big Island Tea.

The year of our first commercial harvest, a mere two kilograms of finished tea, we were approached by a rare tea wholesaler, Lalani and Co. Jameel Lalani found our website, was attracted to our agro-ecological farming techniques and requested a sampling of tea. Months later we were able to send him some green and black tea. After tasting those samples, he said we were setting a new bar for tea quality!

Who knew? Cam and I were stunned by this feedback. We had wanted to produce an exquisite tea but were isolated on the farm without the expertise to judge our own product. Jameel took our tea to Harrods and the East India Company, and they both wanted exclusive rights to sell it. The taster from the East India Company asked if we had added rose oil to our black tea? Not at all! He was tasting the unique taste of Hawai'i grown tea. It seemed incredible to us! Jameel had found a rare tea niche for our first harvest. We could not be more grateful to him. How could we have magnetized such interest to our product? We believe it is the spirit of tea showering us with blessings.

Cam and I have asked ourselves, how do we measure our success? It means that we can offer good employment to our neighbors while rebuilding a native forest and producing an exquisite tea. We measure our success by our ability to attract others to the noble profession of farming. Since Big Island Tea's inception, I have called it a success-in-the-making. It is not economic wealth that makes our project a success but rather our ability to help our community, to share our culture and to rebuild our environment. We hope over the next few years to also realize the fiscal reward of working hard to create a sustainable high value crop in a re-forested mid-elevation cloud forest on the slope of Mauna Loa volcano.

Another jewel in the crown of our success is meeting Jesse Potter, a graduate from the University of Hawaii-Hilo's agriculture program. We consider it a privilege to be working to improve soil damaged by decades of unsustainable agricultural practices. Jesse has helped us rehabilitate our farm. Jesse grew up on the Big Island, and we are training him to become our farm manager. One of our goals is to train young farmers in growing a high value crop to help the revitalization of agriculture in Hawai'i, which crashed following the end of the sugar cane industry in the '90s. There are two advantages to hiring local youth: they can work and live near their families so they are happier employees, and they can help develop sustainable remote small-scale agricultural communities.

We have had many aspiring farmers approach us for help in starting their own tea estates. Presently we have attracted a small "hui" (group) of tea farmers who are willing to use agro-ecological farming methods. The agro-ecological approach requires that a farm be created as a complete ecosystem, of which the crop species are members. This perspective acknowledges that a diverse collection of complimentary organisms require little intervention; forests don't need fertilizer and are naturally pest resistant. Cam's experience as an ecological geneticist helped us understand that creating a forest would invite birds, cast shade, and blunt the harsh effects of the tor-rential rains as well as conserve water and maintain humidity during dryer times.

Tea is a perfect understory crop. Not only does it thrive in the shade, shade growth enhances some of the leaf chemistry respon-sible for tea's health benefits. When we first moved onto the farm, we began to plant native trees and plants. We have dug ponds and seeded them with Asian catfish and koi to enrich the water with ni-trogen, which we use to irrigate and nourish our tea. We have never added petroleum-based fertilizers, herbicides or pesticides. After nine years, we have large koa trees (nitrogen fixing trees), whose canopy is housing the return of wildlife, including birds. One of the reasons we endeavor to re-forest our farm is to create a demonstra-tion project. We want to educate new farmers that it is not necessary to clear-cut one's land in order to establish a high value crop; instead, farmers can help reverse the loss of native forest in Hawai'i.

Currently, we are growing 40,000 tea seedlings for a statewide agriculture grant. These seedlings will be distributed for free to ear-nest farmers keen to start a farm or to expand their own plant stock. Our in-kind donation to grow the seedlings at an 80% loss is given with the intent to help the Hawai'i tea industry expand. Part of the grant mandate is to educate new farmers and to encourage farm sus-tainability.

Cam and I started our tea farm with obstacles galore, but now it is starting to hum. We literally live in the clouds in a forest that we have built one seed at a time. It is our monastery! Our friends tell us that we have a charmed existence, and we both agree. How blessed to be tea farmers living in Hawai'i, working assiduously to be worthy of this service. Are we successful? I say the proof is in the tasting, tea truly is the Drink of Gods.

Eliah and **Cam** are the co-owners of Big Island Tea, one of Hawai'i's pioneer tea gardens located on the northeast slope of Mauna Loa volcano. They hand pick, hand fire, and hand roll all of their tea in small batches.

Chapter 17

THE DAWN OF TRUTH FOR SUSTAINABLE TEA

Rajah Banerjee

After the initial euphoria of mega crop increases in the 1960s and '70s ushered in by the rampant use of chemicals, Darjeeling tea began to decline in all aspects. The choice to use such chemicals brought this magical area to the brink of chaos and collapse. At the Makaibari Tea Estate, this trend has not only been reversed by bio-dynamic practices; it has become an inspirational cornerstone. Our success has positioned the Kurseong sub-district of Darjeeling with the greatest number of organic tea estates, which has soared to seventy, the greatest number in the country today.

When asked why we take the time and trouble to promote bio-dynamic tea farming, I like to say that it awakens both the farmer and the consumer to the realization that agricultural practices are determined by the earth's evolution. There is great beauty to this vision and to this practice. The earth is a cosmic creation; hence, our thinking is determined by the natural forces of the universe. We have the ability to create machines, but all floras, including tea, grow by the natural laws of the cosmos, which means we must stay in accord with them.

The beauty—and the problem—with machines is that they are independent of time and season, whereas all agriculture is dependent on the rhythms of nature. Understanding these forces and working in harmony with them evolves and fulfills all concerned with it. Natural forces are holistic in production and reproduction, whereas machines are not. For instance, a tea bush yields tea leaves, and when its productive life is over it offers up a seed for its own replacement. On the other hand, machines wear out and have to be replaced. This is the fundamental difference between social order based on dead thoughts and one that stems from natural laws.

Today, society's stress on economics, especially the emphasis on greed that often accompanies it, have shifted our focus from living in a social order guided by sustainable forces to a confusing, destructive social scenario dictated by machines. The times we are living through are frenetic. The pace of life has been dictated by the explosive development of technology. The growth of hi-tech over the past hundred years has made the technological advances of the previous five thousand years seem pedestrian. The upsurge in technological marvels, which stems from our intellect and reason, has brought about tremendous advances, but has also fostered its attendant downside, which is that we have drifted further and further away from natural laws and practices.

It's time for all to step aside to a neutral corner and assess the gains and losses dispassionately. These often awe-inspiring advances of technology have created a complexity of social issues that are extremely difficult to comprehend. To understand them, all one needs to do is wander out into nature, such as the vast tea fields here at the Makaibari Tea Estate. When one does, a sense of peace soon prevails, an immediate relief from the confusion of our daily grind. Tuning our antennae, we realize the wisdom of nature and her simplicity through observation and a commitment to the natural rhythms of planting, nurturing, and harvesting.

This voyage at Makaibari has created awareness and built its attendant capacity slowly and steadily over four decades. Using the tea plantation, which occupies half the forest area, the resident communities in seven villages have evolved to be a rhythm of nature, to be certified community forest management (CFM) status. It's the only tea estate community that knows that monocultural tea only plays a small role, as an extension of the forests. Thus to have harmony, one needs to realize the core values that foster this wisdom, irrespective of our location.

For instance, if we are to travel from Darjeeling to Delhi, the social implications of travel and execution of work at the Delhi end is indeed very complicated. We would be focused on our own agenda, primarily the execution of the job, which enables us to prioritize and cope with only a handful of manageable issues, with nary a thought on the social implications. However, the moment we take a little time out to mull over the social ramifications, we are confounded by the enormity of the impulses that assail us. It is simply bewildering in its myriad permutations and combinations just to make this flight across the ancient land of India. All problems of humanity are those of harmony. Hence, Makaibari's holistic agricultural practices in tea have become an inspirational window for the nine hundred million marginalized farmers of the sub-continent and abroad.

THE SOCIAL RAMIFICATIONS OF TEA

Let us consider the gamut of logistics necessary to make this 2,000-mile flight happen almost painlessly. The breakdown reveals a chauffeured car ride from the garden to the airport on a cement road. One enters the infrastructure of the airport, through security and check in. There are personnel involved at every step, on the ground, in-flight, on arrival, check out, the transfers at the Delhi end, the hotel end. What has gone into making the car, licensing the chauffeur and pilot, building the roads, airplanes, airports and the entire personnel are all taken for granted today. Hence, to make even a short flight possible, the social implications are enormously complex. Even an individual bestowed with intelligence and education is inadequately equipped to understand the concepts of our social situation. This is an urban phenomenon in India, which is rapidly spreading to suburbia, with industrialization and rapid improvement in all communication systems.

Mercifully, the rural scenario, where the majority of people reside, is relatively unspoiled, and this is largely because of our deep commitment to maintain an organic and natural way of growing tea on our estate. The surplus of Makaibari's agriculture is tea. Cereals, vegetables, fruits and meat are raised and used within the commune. It's a tad more than a high-end, single estate organic Darjeeling tea. In reality, it's a magical, mystical Himalayan herb, possessing the spirit of Makaibari. It's a fact that the ideal elixir for all urbanites in the global village is to sip a cup of tea, de-stress and earn instant bliss through the ultimate balm in a Makaibari tea cup.

THE INDUSTRIALIZATION OF AGRICULTURE

When and how did the industrialization of agriculture occur and catalyze in the West? When did we begin to jeopardize our own foods and grains—and teas? Prior to World War II, the majority of farmlands globally were organic. Farmers relied on nature for their harvest, manure from their farmyard and farm livestock, and human labor to gather in the seasonal bounty. It was a hard, intense life, lived close to the land, a life that had evolved over thousands of years from deep attention and reverence to the ebb and flow of the natural rhythms of the world. World War II dramatically altered the farm scenario in the Western World. One of those ill-fated and rarely regarded influences was the desperate need for naptha, which helped make the explosives needed for armaments. Naptha is a long chain carbon compound, which is a by-product of the petroleum industry. Naptha was copiously used in the atom bombs that were dropped over Nagasaki and Hiroshima. The adjacent tea areas around Nagasaki and Hiroshima were all abandoned, and it was only after many decades that tea areas like Yame, near Nagasaki, were revived to health. The death and devastation in naptha's wake swiftly brought the war to an end. General Dwight. D. Eisenhower, or "Big Ike", as he was popularly mandated for his election campaign post Second

World War, was the supreme leader of the Allied Forces, and he became the President Elect following his successful campaign.

After the cessation of the horrific hostilities of the war, the U.S. armament manufacturers were sitting on huge stocks of naptha. The manufacturers looked up to "Big Ike" to compensate them for their deadly naptha stocks, which were no longer needed for the manufacture of explosives. That is when they turned to farmers around the world and argued something along the lines of, "We helped you win the war, please reward us by lifting this naptha burden off our noble shoulders." Scientists were complicit in inventing both the greatest bombs the world had ever seen and the illusion of a magical wand for farmers: agro chemicals, which are all naptha-based. The use of chemical fertilizers, pesticides, weedicides, fungicides, acaracides, and herbicides catalyzed the industrialization of agriculture. Bumper yields resulted with a tenth of the effort. Effectively, all farmers happily created their myriad tiny Nagasakis and Hiroshimas, by bombing their farmlands with indiscriminate chemical applications.

This was touted as the Green Revolution until 1957 when Rachel Carson shook the farming community with her groundbreaking publication *Silent Spring*. This courageous and visionary book spawned an awareness, which took seed with the organic/biodynamic movement, and eventually came to be used with Makabarai Tea Estates. Her book helped usher in alternative, sustainable synergies as a counter to the unabated, conventionally oriented agricultural practices that had industrialized farming, aided and abetted by the all-powerful petroleum lobby. To overcome the Petroleum lobby's agenda needs superhuman effort and commitment. Hence, it is an immense challenge, particularly in the West, which has had a very small percentage of its population of farmers switch to the sustainable farming method.

Today, most developed nations have around five percent of their population directly involved in farming. In the Indian sub-continent, eighty percent of the inhabitants are farmers, and seventy-five percent of their produce is rain-dependent, so per se, it's organic. However, these marginalized farmers are so poor that they have no access or affordability for certification, and no opportunity whatsoever to market their produce for a fair price. There are 16,000 registered tea estates in India, and the tea areas, by contrast, are organized farmlands that are affluent with a host of statuary benefits for the garden residents. The pioneering efforts at Makaibari have already converted seventy percent of Darjeeling tea estates to organic farming methods, and this trend is now snowballing to the Assam, Terai, Dooars, and South Indian tea as well. This is an excellent augury that bodes well for the marginalized farmers in their respective regions who go organic. Hence, as awareness dawns that eco-agriculture is economically viable, the lead adopted by the regional tea estates will have a far greater impact in neutralizing the effects of global warming.

WHY IS THE COW HOLY?

The cow holds the key for all agriculture in India, even for our beloved tea. The cow is revered in the majority of villages in India. No farmer has any qualms of getting their hands mucky with cow dung. All are aware that well-managed cow dung isn't just the best fertilizer for farmland; it's the best healer for the land. Nothing goes to waste: even the cow's urine is extensively used as an insect repellent.

Where did this knowledge stem from? Why are biodynamic practices appealing to the marginalized Indian farmer? The bridge was Rudolph Steiner's high esteem for the ancient wisdom of India. Rudolph Steiner was a philosopher, scientist, psychic and seer. He appreciated the nuances of the Bhagavad Gita—a sacred book that is the manifesto of Krishna for mankind—for its grand depth and beauty. For whatever was achievable on the spiritual path of knowledge is achieved with highest perfection through Krishna for the individual soul. Christ, on the other hand, ushers in revelation for the community. This is the polarity between East and West, but it's not an antagonistic relationship. Both complement each other, like two faces of a coin.

The great philosopher, through the will of his cognition, embraced the Karmic laws as propounded by the enlightened Rishis of Vedic times. The sages who wrote the Vedic scriptures were the founders of Ayurvedic herbals for improving human health. The vast majority of the herbal preparations had their origin from the Himalayas, particularly from either side of the Himalayas, now known as Darjeeling and Tibet. Vastusastra—the science of aerodynamic airflow as applied to buildings, landmasses and individual positions—together with Ayurvedic herbals and Buddhism, were exported to China over three thousand years ago. It would not be extravagant to guess that one of the herbs was tea, which gained momentum as a magical cure-all in Chinese culture 1400 years ago. Viewed from this assumed perspective, tea has been a healer for more than five thousand years.

The human spirit is immortal, being present before birth and continuing after death, going inexorably towards its development via many incarnations. The spirit is allowed to process the results of its former life in the long interim between incarnations, in preparation for the next life. Steiner's belief in the Karmic laws resulted in pedagogic therapy, still practiced in many countries today for treatment and education of developmentally delayed children. Steiner's lectures on the Bhagavad Gita in the last week of 1912 and the talks on Occult fundaments in the Bhagavad Gita in the summer of 1913 are the most important attempts to understand and explain the equity between East and West, with no superiority of any side. The poles of the world were created to complement each other, to join hands in order to overcome the prevailing materialism that is rampant in all societies today.

It's not surprising that the Goetheanum, the Steiner Center at Dornach, Switzerland, represented the alternative solutions to the threefold formation of the social organism—as man consists of body, mind and spirit. Likewise, society had to be conscious of three functional aspects. Legal life-guaranteeing equality for all, economic life fostering brotherhood, and cultural life to provide the conduit for freedom and liberation became a target for the opposition, who destroyed the Goetheanum on New Year's Eve 1924. Edifices are destroyed, but the spirit never. Hence the universal genius of Rudolph Steiner's spirit continues to influence more powerfully all corners of the globe holistically today, and the tangible proof is the Goetheanum—a sphinx risen from the ashes to project his vision to a heightened firmament.

Why did Steiner appreciate the Bhagavad Gita? He opines that anyone concerned with the spiritual life of his own times had in reality to study the period of a thousand years pre-Christian, and two thousand years of post-Christianity. In the pre-Christian Chaldean/Egyptian era, there existed a spiritual stream of continuity—a connected spiritual life with no outstanding individual personalities. It was only during the Greeks' pursuit of spiritual life, did the vibrant personalities surface: Plato, Aristotle, Socrates, Phidias, etc. This trend continues to this day, for people seek the spiritual path separately as individuals, to find hope, peace and inner comfort.

Whatever happened to spiritual pursuits prior to three thousand years ago? The revelation occurred when the magnificence of the Bhagavad Gita was exposed to the European world in the 19th century. This is the great spiritual song that sounds forth from the primeval holy times of Indian antiquity. Three distinct streams of spiritual thoughts emerged from this era: the Vedas, the Sankhya philosophy, and Yoga. The Bhagavad Gita is a harmonious interpenetration of these three distinct spiritual streams, three parts flowing harmoniously into one organism. The greatness of Bhagavad Gita lies in assimilating the tributaries of the Vedas, the Sankhya philosophy, and the Yoga of Patanjali into a comprehensive whole. The Veda philosophy is clairvoyant knowledge—inspiration given by grace from above for self-realization, to attain Sachitananda or cosmic consciousness. Sankhya philosophy is knowledge sought for just as we seek now-a-days—but sought for by people to whom clairvoyance was accessible. It is a contemplation of the sheaths with which the soul impresses or covers itself, a study of Satva, Rajas & Tamas. Yoga is the guidance of the soul to the higher stages of inner awakening, the higher forces of the soul, which unlock the doors to even higher and higher stages of existence. This is the path to the spiritual worlds.

In this era, we are called upon once again to unite these three spiritual streams, by bringing them to the surface befittingly for our epoch from the sub-soil of our soul and the depths of the cosmos. The revelations of Krishna to his pupil Arjuna in the battlefield of Kurukshetra were threefold: of the world (Vedas), of the law (Sankhya), and of reverent devotion to the spirit (Yoga). These are the streams by which the soul carries out its development in this terrestrial infirma. The Trinity of the Vedas, Sankhya and Yoga were the redness of the dawn of this civilization, which rose as the sun later.

The wisdom of the Bhagvad Gita in essence is that a conscious balance must be established between that which the present seeks to acquire and that which stretches back to the depths of Indian antiquity. How does one build this bridge? All problems of existence are essentially those of harmony, but where does one find harmony today? Nature, of course. Nature builds a crystal-filled wisdom. This crystal-filled wisdom can enchant us when we wander out in nature. The light that reaches us from the sun, quickening our hearts, is also everywhere in nature as divine light, and our souls must be able to feel and find it there. It was on one of these walks through the primary forests of Makaibari tea estates in 1971 that the realization dawned on me that the topsoils in the forests were never depleted. It was an ever-evolving process of upgradation. The layers of falling leaves created a mulch, preventing erosion from heavy rains. The mulch or decay created humus, which is the gauge for soil fertility and real wealth. This paved the way for adopting Steiner's methods of biodynamic practices, in which practices enhanced by permaculture were further enhanced by permaculture, and in which tea was part of a six-tiered structure of permanent and temporary species of vegetation that continuously upgraded the soil by replicating the forest mulch.

These biodynamic practices were the diamond in the crown that turned Makaibari to an ever-evolving dynamic organism. Sustainable agriculture leads one to realize that the essence of sustainability is to work in harmony with nature and not against it. Biodynamic practices epitomize and catalyze this realization. The Makaibari community has evolved to community forest management (CFM) status, fusing bio dynamics and stakeholder participation addressing Agenda 21. This is a working window of global rural living styles in this millennium. This is the forerunner that offers a route—a return to sustainable ways.

Why, one may ask, should we be so concerned with sustainability? In the vast majority of villages in India, there still exists a different social system yet untrammeled by industrialization. The place of worship or temple is the source of inspiration, where the community gathers. Time-tested spiritual insights of the trinity, handed down from primeval times of antiquity, are still followed and practiced in social life. The magic mantras nurtured by the Brahmins or priests touch the soul of the people, and social activities are based on this morality. The relaying of the message from the tip of the pyramid to the base is reflected by the work on the land—the foundational base—the base for holistic sustainable agriculture. The work on the land is a streaming down of cosmic forces and their effective conversion for diverse life forms, from below the earth, to offerings from crops, fruits and other resources. It's a complete social unity. Civilization evolves one to a clarity of thought processes, and logical thinking emerges out of this intellectual development. Technical sciences are a fallout of this logic. Scientific thought is localized to the physical world and hence, this thinking is dead. In this era, this thinking is dominant.

This thinking creates machines and industry, which divide human labor, regulating production and hence the economy. The social unity is lost in the jostle for one-upmanship, as egos are fanned and titillated for needless competition. Biodynamic agriculture offers a positive solution to reverse this trend, regain lost ground and put one back on course for a positive evolution. Conventional agriculture does create temporary surpluses—but at what cost? Chemicals are all tools of short-term gain and long-term destruction.

THE MAKAIBARI TEA PROCESS

The process at Makaibari Tea Estate has been initiated by an honest attempt to liberate ourselves from the bondage of industrialization. We have endeavored to translate and transform the truth on the land, its environment and air: we have limited water resources; we revere and preserve by copious mulching. The mulch takes the impact of the monsoonal rains, preventing erosion and topsoil loss. It stymies weed growth but does not kill, saving weeding costs. In its decay and decomposition it creates hospitable conditions for soil microorganisms, which translates to soil health and fertility. Respecting all life forms and treating the tea as a part of an evolutionary system help to obviate false egoism. The focus is on the subtropical rain forests, which occupy twice the tea area. The tea is broken down in five more stages of permanent and temporary legumes: alternative trees (fruit/medicinal), the recycling of pruned tea litter and the ground vegetation interspersed with a variety of clover—indigenous and imported. The mulch generated from this floral diversity has created a soil that is totally unique.

The icing on the cake is man's positive intervention. All villagers are enthusiastically involved in creating biodynamic compost from animal waste, primarily cows. This awareness has been created by intense interaction between individuals, groups and villages over a period of time. Man can be a creator or destroyer with equal intensity, and biodynamics evolves man to be the medium to transform the earth dynamically, utilizing the cosmic forces in a harmonious, tranquil way. It's not domination, as domination creates self, imposing shackles. It's mutually beneficial upliftment that liberates. In the ultimate analysis, the creature that wins against the environment destroys itself.

CONCLUSION

One cannot be an island of prosperity in a sea of unhappiness. The holistic initiatives at Makaibari—which has pioneered organics to global tea producers since 1987 (there are over seventy countries globally growing tea), biodynamics to tropical agriculture since 1993, and Fair Trade to the global tea producers since 1993—have inspired many new initiatives, far beyond her boundaries. Organic Ekta, established with over three hundred small growers in the region, is a cynosure of Agenda 21 for the eco-sensitive Himalayan hills, and now an inspiration for all mountain farmers globally. Makaibari's holistic tea initiatives in the hills of Meghalaya and the Nilgiris (Blue Mountains) in Southern India are all evolving dynamically. These initiatives unleash holistic agricultural practices, empower women, and implement the use of alternative non-polluting renewable energy with bio-gas that benefits the environment.

We believe that this is paving the way for the creation of a self-respecting grassroots entrepreneurial community. Exchanges of Makaibari's practicing agricultural philosophy with like-minded organizations and research institutes in France, Switzerland, Japan, Germany, UK, U.S., Italy and China are fostering bridge-building. The bridges are firmly grouted in two pillars: one of technology and the other of holistic sustainable synergy. The goal is to create the connecter for all, to walk into a new era of Peace, Prosperity and Radiance. The new mantra is: Partnerships not Ownership. It is the cornerstone of the sustainable global village that we have become today.

ACKNOWLEDGMENTS

1. Mr. H. Koeps & Mr. M. Klent—*Tomorrow's Agriculture*.
2. J. Smillie—*Soul of Soil*.
3. Rudolph Steiner—*Occult Science*.

Mr. Swaraj Kumar (Rajah) Banerjee is the owner of the Makaibari Tea Estates, Kurseong, India and also the author of the book *The Rajah of Darjeeling Organic Tea: Makaibari*.

Chapter 18

TEA AS PEACEMAKER

Arun Gandhi

Tea, a modest plant that grows abundantly in tropical climes, is known to have caused many conflicts—the American Revolution, for one—and, contrarily, many moments of calm for those troubled by the day's events. Tea is as addictive a drink as any other, and those who are firmly in its grip will testify to their inability to perform efficiently without ingesting what the British call a "cuppa"! Even the most vaunted British game of cricket, played throughout its erstwhile empire and stretching over a period of three or five days, has a tea break, which is important not just to be refreshed but often to tranquilize a well-entrenched batsman so he can get out within seconds and resume the game. This stimulating cup of tea has made or marred many careers in the game of cricket. The game is perhaps the only one in the world that is played between nations, so winning or losing becomes a matter of national pride or prejudice, as the case may be. Millions in both opposing countries sit for seven to eight hours, watching and cheering their players while sipping that wonderful elixir called TEA!

Important transactions in world history were negotiated over a cup of tea, until coffee and golf came onto the scene. Tea has long been a staple in Indian homes, and the first thing offered to guests is a nice cup of tea. This tradition has carried itself into Indian and British politics too. Whenever a meeting takes place, a tea service precedes all discussions. Now, of course, because of American influence, a guest is asked to choose between tea and coffee. One can do no more than wonder what the outcome would have been if the British Prime Minister, Neville Chamberlain, who went to Germany to talk with Hitler, had instead invited Hitler to England and treated him to a delicious cup of tea. While coffee is energizing, tea is soothing. There is something about tea that can put one in a good frame of mind!! Perhaps, who knows, Hitler may have seen the wisdom in peaceful solutions rather than violent aggression.

Then there is the famous photograph of my grandfather, Mohandas K. Gandhi, sitting on the porch of the palatial Viceroy's residence (now the Presidential Palace), surrounded by the exquisite Mughal garden, with Lord and Lady Mountbatten, the last Viceroy of British India, discussing the future of India over a cup of tea. Of course, by 1946, grandfather had given up tea drinking, with a host of other foods and drinks, because he believed human beings must refrain from any food or drink that is addictive. Gandhi was an avid tea-drinker as a young man. But when he realized in South Africa that his life was going to be spent mostly in prison for opposing discrimination, he gave up tea with determination. There is a myth spread on the internet that he quietly drank tea when no one was watching, but Gandhi was convinced that anyone seeking to sacrifice for justice had to be free of all addictions. If one is addicted to anything, one becomes a slave to injustice. I believe he spoke from experience, because in his younger days he consumed several cups of piping hot tea made the Indian way called chai.

There are many facts and fantasies about tea. The Indian brew, chai, has now become an international drink and has been found to be very stimulating. Chai is made with equal parts water and milk and boiled with some cardamom, cinnamon, sugar to taste, and a couple of cloves. One usually adds more water and milk, because the longer it boils with the tea leaves, the better the taste. In a country with so many millions living in poverty, becoming a mobile chai vendor is lucrative. Films have been made about the legendry Chai-wallah—or the chai vendor. On Indian trains and in train stations, bus stations and, in fact, on every street corner, there is always someone, either in a little hut or just by the wayside, with a large canister full of boiling hot tea. His singsong call "Chai-wallah" can be heard far and wide. They even sign contracts with surrounding shops and offices to supply them with cups of tea on demand. They have become masters at brewing tea, which is as it should be because the Indian tea-drinker is quite a connoisseur. To cater to the milder western tea drinker, they have now concocted what they call the dip-dip tea. They serve the customer with a hot cup of water and milk mixture and a tea bag that you dip in the liquid to make a mild cup of tea.

I escort a group of Americans on a "Gandhian Legacy Tour" to India and we travel by train to most places. They are always confused when the vendor asks if they would like "dip-dip" tea or chai. Once they drink the chai most of them are hooked on it. They always buy the ready-made tea masala (spices) so that they can make chai when they return home.

Sometimes, even a veteran tea-drinker like me is foxed by the evolution in the tea business. In December of 2012, I was on a road trip around North India. On the highways, there are no rest stops like we have in the U.S. Usually, at strategic distances there are small complexes of tea and snack stalls and a restaurant serving a full meal catering to the needs of truckers and motorists. Often the many unemployed become more imaginative. They put up modest little mud and bamboo structures and cook tea (yes, the tea is cooked) and snacks. I stopped at one of these stalls to get an enervating cup of tea.

"How many miles?" the vendor asked.

I was puzzled. What on earth did he mean? What could miles have to do with a cup of tea? I asked him to explain.

"Oh!" he said with the air of someone more knowledgeable than a city bumpkin. "How many miles do you want to stay awake? One hundred, two hundred, or three hundred?"

Apparently, this is how they measure the strength of the brew. It is guaranteed to keep you awake for that many miles.

Speaking of keeping awake, I have met people who drink tea to keep awake and several who drink tea to go to sleep. I am one of those phenoms who can make it work both ways. In another lifetime when I was a journalist for the *Times of India* and had to do night duty every second week, I drank many cups of tea to keep me awake. Now I find that a mild cup of soothing tea calms me to such an extent that I feel the need for a power-nap after a "cuppa".

Historically, tea goes back several centuries to when the un-named leaves were brewed to make a tasty drink. The drink was known as an elixir. In fact, tea and spices were the reason that the British and several other European countries colonized India. The British developed the industry and called the leaves tea. Large tea estates were planted, and the world was introduced to a drink that has grown in popularity over the centuries.

Today, the tea plantations are confined mainly to the South Asian countries, and tea is now one of their biggest exports to the world. There are probably a thousand varieties of tea, but there is only one chai, the one that is guaranteed to make one sleep soundly. Although the tea industry is a legacy of British Rule, it is not seen as an "evil" legacy. In fact, the British have left behind them many good institutions, infrastructure and, yes, memories. It is the beauty of a nonviolent revolution that instead of parting with bitterness and enmity, the two countries parted as friends. The Indians forgave the British for their colonial sins, built a strong bond of friendship, and continue to collaborate on many mutually beneficial issues. In fact, English is one of the umpteen official languages of the country. To this day, high tea at four p.m. is an institution in the elite sections of Indian society, and you will hear women chattering in chaste English and reciting Milton and Shakespeare.

What is strange is that although many of the tea estates are in the southern parts of India, the true tea drinkers are the people of the rest of India. In the south, they still swear by their coffee, also brewed like tea with some spices. Why the southerners have not taken to tea is unfathomable. It could be due to the persistent North-South ideological divide that seems to affect all nations of the world. The southerners eat more rice because they grow more rice, while the northerners eat more wheat products because they grow more wheat. But, for some mysterious reason, that is not true for tea. The southerners grow tea and export to the north and the rest of the world.

Arun Gandhi is the fifth grandson of India's legendary leader, Mohandas K. "Mahatma" Gandhi. Growing up under the discriminatory apartheid laws of South Africa, he was beaten by "white" South Africans for being too black and "black" South Africans for being too white; so, Arun sought eye-for-an-eye justice. However, he learned from his parents and grandparents that justice does not mean revenge, it means transforming the opponent through love and suffering.

Grandfather taught Arun to understand nonviolence through understanding violence. "If we know how much passive violence we perpetrate against one another we will understand why there is so much physical violence plaguing societies and the world," Gandhi said. Through daily lessons, Arun says, he learned about violence and about anger.

Arun shares these lessons all around the world. For the past five years, he has participated in the Renaissance Weekend deliberations with President Clinton and other well-respected Rhodes Scholars. This year, some of his engagements included speaking at the Chicago Children's Museum and the Women's Justice Center in Ann Arbor, Michigan. He also delivered talks at the Young President's Organization in Mexico, the Trade Union Leaders' Meeting in Milan, Italy, as well as the Peace and Justice Center in St. Louis,

Missouri. Sometimes, his journeys take him even further. Arun has spoken in Croatia, France, Ireland, Holland, Lithuania, Nicaragua, China, Scotland and Japan. Also, he is a very popular speaker on college campuses. In the past year, he spoke at, North Dakota State University, Concordia College, Baker University, Morehouse College, Marquette University, and the University of San Diego.

Arun is very involved in social programs and writing, as well. Shortly after Arun married his wife Sunanda, they were informed the South African government would not allow her to accompany him there. Sunanda and Arun decided to live in India, and Arun worked for 30 years as a journalist for *The Times* of India. Together, Arun and Sunanda started projects for the social and economic uplifting of the oppressed using constructive programs, the backbone of Gandhi's philosophy of nonviolence. The programs changed the lives of more than half a million people in over 300 villages and they still continue to grow. Sunanda died in February of 2007 and the family is working to establish a school in poorest rural India in her name.

Arun is the author of several books. The first, *A Patch of White* (1949), is about life in prejudiced South Africa; then, he wrote two books on poverty and politics in India; followed by a compilation of M.K. Gandhi's *Wit & Wisdom*. He also edited a book of essays on *World Without Violence: Can Gandhi's Vision Become Reality?* And, more recently, wrote *The Forgotten Woman: The Untold Story of Kastur, the Wife of Mahatma Gandhi*, jointly with his late wife Sunanda.

Chapter 19

SLOWLY WAKING UP TO TEA

Jen Ahlstrom

"Bring tea for the Tillerman
Steak for the sun . . . "
—CAT STEVENS, "TEA FOR THE TILLERMAN"

What can be said about the connection between tea and music? Leonard Cohen, Sting, and the Beatles were all avid tea drinkers. What do musicians get from tea they might not from other drinks? Can tea influence music itself? Does it stimulate creativity? We know that tea ceremony is often enhanced by traditional music. We know that both tea and music can be shared or enjoyed alone, that each can inspire friendship, provide a sense of companionship, enjoyment, escape, and calm. The intimacy of two people sitting down for tea can be likened to two people sitting at the piano, a sense of convening, a shared secret, a sense of wonderment, two people leaning in, smiling with anticipation. We also know tea is associated with Zen Buddhism. Buddhist monks drink tea to enhance focus, mindfulness, and concentration. The goal is to reach mushin, "no-mind". Are these the same qualities of tea that musicians rely on? Can tea help stimulate creativity? Can the energy you get from tea infuse a song with spirit? Or does the soul of tea help establish a connection to the source, the place where ideas come from, where you might feel a spark? Can tea be a muse?

In 2010 Yoko Ono wrote an article for the New York Times describing a scene with three cats in the kitchen, middle of the night, and John making tea for two. She remembers how they cracked up about the proper way to make tea, and how this was one of her fondest memories of the two of them. One moment, frozen in time. Ichigo ichie is a Japanese cultural concept associated with the tea master Sen no Rikyu, which infers that in this lifetime, you and I may only meet once, and so each moment, each meeting, is unique. Live and die in each moment. This was the way John Lennon lived his life, and one of the many reasons why he is still the most beloved songwriter of all time. He believed in truth, and the path he took to finding his truth was fascinating to us all. When Lennon went to India, what was he looking for? When he practiced scream therapy, what was he trying to purge himself of? What do his songs do for people? What role does music play in life? In truth?

Most musicians don't just sit down and pop out a song. Much time is spent waiting, thinking, writing and rewriting lyrics. It is incredibly time consuming. The performance of a five-minute song (or listening to it on the radio) does not even remotely reflect the amount of time that went into crafting that song. Or the amount of time spent waiting for an idea that would stick. The amount of patience it took to sew the pieces together into a coherent whole. The late nights layering track after track of parts that the average listener won't even hear. The compression on a drumbeat. The equalization of the guitar. I think many people like to think of songwriting as a purging, a burst of creativity. But it's a process. It can be a painful one. It can be frustrating. It can fill you with feelings of crushing inadequacy. You will feel like giving up. You will feel you're not worthy. You will constantly question yourself and your worth as an artist. A Facebook friend recently wrote, "The tricky thing about aspiring to get good at something is that you have to allow yourself to be re-

       THE SOUL & SPIRIT OF TEA

ally bad at it first, for an indefinite period of time. And the more you learn, the farther you can see you have to go."

I can't speak for other musicians, but as a songwriter I have drawn immense inspiration from the mystic poet Rumi. His words have soothed me in times of loneliness and self-doubt. I always wonder how words written by someone in the 13th century could speak so directly to my sense of feeling lost, and point me back in the direction of meaning. Rumi tends to use many images of water, which is particularly appropriate in this exploration of tea and creativity. For these reasons, I'm treating Rumi's words as I would song lyrics, since he not only embodies the spirit of tea, but because his poems, like tea and like music, transcend language and culture. Over seven hundred years ago, he wrote, in Coleman Bark's marvelous translation:

"Today, like every other day, we wake up empty and frightened. Don't open the door to the study and begin reading. Take down a musical instrument."

I have to admit that even though I know it is important to create time for reflection, I struggle with this in the modern world. First, the world we live in today is accelerating at a terrifying pace. My life is a matrix of competing demands. I struggle to find the time for creativity. I fail to prioritize alone time. I am easily distracted. The high-tech society that we live in only increases these demands. It increases the demands on our concentration and decreases our ability to focus. Twitter only lets you have 140 characters. Boop. Beep. Thought fragments. How can you write something meaningful in 140 characters? Are we even able to form whole thoughts anymore? Rumi struggled with the same questions and wrote:

"There is a way between voice and presence
where information flows.
In disciplined silence it opens.
With wandering talk it closes."
—Coleman Barks, *The Essential Rumi*

I've come to expect constant stimulation. Billboards, magazines, advertisements, commercials, blinking screens everywhere. Who can focus with constant stimuli flashing at us all the time (even at the doctor's office)? Living in New York for the last five years only exacerbated my feelings of being bombarded. Even watching TV does not relax or regenerate me anymore. It does not recharge my battery. In addition, our networks have grown. People have so many acquaintances nowadays that the human bond has been cheapened. It's been spread out too thin. Everything is shorter. People read phones. They tweet. They text. Communication has become instant. There are almost no barriers. It doesn't take time to send a message. Nobody sits down to write a letter anymore. When the main prerogative is being fast, is there any reason to devote time to activities that are slow? In Janis Ian's song "Tea & Sympathy," she reveals that she wants to slow down, get off the "milk train" of life, go to bed earlier and wake up at dawn, have normal meals. All she asks is for:

"The comfort of a few old friends long past their prime
Pass the tea & sympathy
for the good old days long gone"

I've always thought that my generation should be called the "something for nothing" generation. We want success. In fact, we expect it. But we don't want to have to work hard for it. We want instant success. We want the story fed to us since childhood by television and books and all the glorification of American celebrity. Overnight success. You can buy hardboiled eggs in a bag from Trader Joe's. Fast food. Go-gurt. With all of these shortcuts, we are losing our connection not only to other human beings, but to the earth, and most importantly to ourselves. Wikipedia says, "It is approximated that roughly 40 million American adults ages 18 and older (18.1%) have an anxiety disorder."

"Instant Karma's gonna get you
Gonna look you right in the face
You better get yourself together darling

THE SOUL & SPIRIT OF TEA

Join the human race"

—John Lennon

Whether it's eating disorders, prescription medication, or just constant activity, people are increasingly drawn to find ways to escape from dealing with the anxiety of the fast life, to avoid facing the emptiness. And it seems that artists are particularly unstable and therefore vulnerable to these vices. So as much as I want to claim a correlation between musicians and tea, the musicians that I admire most have a much higher correlation between music and alcohol. Music and drugs. Music and recklessness. Oblivion. Destruction. Once again we can turn to Rumi, who was concerned about the same things in Konya, Turkey, during his lifetime:

> "The tavern is a kind of glorious hell that human beings enjoy and suffer and then push off from in their search for truth."

—Coleman Barks, The Essential Rumi

Rumi says that music and language are possible only because we're empty. I believe that tea can provide a space, a channel for this inspiration to pass through. For me the place of meaning has been music. In 2008, a friend named Scott Hoyt gave me a tremendous gift. Like many people in this modern communication age, I met Scott indirectly through an ad placed online for a post-production assistant for a documentary film about tea. After I had worked on the film for a few months, we came up with the idea for another project. We would produce an album of original music. Over the next few months, up against a real deadline of scheduled studio time in San Francisco, I started to painstakingly assemble the tiny fragments of inspiration that would come to me over extended periods of sitting at the piano. I told myself, you can't just be a singer. You can't be that woman. You need to be Jimi Hendrix. You need to be John Lennon. You must be skilled at your instrument and not somebody's object of desire, some doll. If you take away the instrument, the focus becomes your body. And I definitely did not want that. You will sit here and put in the hours. You will someday match the playing ability of the guys you know who have been playing since they're ten.

Yeah right.

So after a summer of listening to Stevie Wonder (high hopes indeed), I sat down in August and put my hands on the keys. The project was to be recorded in October. I had to write at least six songs. To my great surprise, the tedium was unbearable. I had to force myself to sit there. It was as if I didn't even know my own hands. They were like someone else's hands, moving jerkily on the keyboard, wrong notes, disjointed rhythms, and seemingly no communication between fingers. I was filled with feelings of crushing inadequacy. So I did what anyone would do, I went into the kitchen to get a glass of wine. Here, this will help me loosen my inhibitions. This will help relax me. Now the music will really start flowing. For that moment, all was well. I felt comfortable and safe until the next morning when I had to start the process all over again. And then it hit me. There are no shortcuts. I would have to stay sitting on that piano bench for hours just to get one shred of one line of one verse. (For whatever reason, songs come very slowly for me. I might spend five hours at the piano and walk away with one usable verse.) So the only thing to do was to spend every spare moment sitting at that piano. Compared to the glory of rockstardom, nothing could be more anticlimactic. I guess at that point I realized I wanted something more. Something less temporary. Something better. Something more fulfilling. And I realized that wanting to get there is not the same as getting there. Getting there takes work. Awareness takes work. It takes patience. I would have to try to sweep the cobwebs out of my brain. I realized I had been asleep. I was slowly waking up to Rumi's wisdom:

"If the soundbox is stuffed full of anything, no music".
                    —Coleman Barks, *The Essential Rumi*

This is when I first reached out to tea. Tea is the only thing I've found that both soothes and energizes me. It's a work in progress. It's a pause, to paraphrase Stevie Wonder, "in the key of life." Tea does not burn you with unfulfilled promises, 5-hour energy. Tea does not turn you into a mindless babbling idiot. It does not become the justification for doing something you'll regret. Tea allows me to sit still and let the ideas flow through me. When I drink too much tea, I feel euphoric. It's subtle but I know I'm in a fantastic mood. When I drink too much coffee, I can't breathe. I feel anxious. I feel a spike of energy but then I feel frantic when that energy wears off. If I drink coffee too late in the afternoon, I can't sleep. Tea is safe for morning and night. Tea is soothing. Tea is water flowing, it's music washing over you, it's harmony between body and mind, between spirit and earth. To this effect, Rumi wrote:

"Your old life was a frantic running from silence. / The speechless full moon comes out now."
—Coleman Barks, *The Essential Rumi*

I used to think that inspiration came from pain, but now I know it comes from patience. Only when we become empty and open can we receive messages from the source. It can't be forced. Sometimes I sit at the piano for hours and still nothing comes. But the sitting and waiting is just as important as the act of creation itself. The distractions are always calling out to me. The real work is the commitment it takes to wait. Many pieces of inspiration come, and only some stick. Tea is the only drink I've found that lets me dial into the music without any jagged edges or backlash. Sound comes from silence. Creativity comes from emptiness. We are only seeking what's already there. Tea expands your ability to love and feel peace. Again, in Barks' translation Rumi writes:

"When you do things from your soul, / the river itself moves through you. / Freshness and a deep joy are signs of the current."
—Coleman Barks, *The Essential Rumi*

After years of sitting at the piano, I finally realized that my left hand could move independently of my right hand, instead of just playing octaves (two of the same note twelve keys apart). Years! That's something that a five year old could learn in just a couple months of piano lessons. But despite my slow going, it felt like it was a huge breakthrough. I had logged hundreds of hours before I got to this point, but I was building something inside myself that no one could take away. I knew that every time I sat down at the piano, it was one more drop in the well. But it was something. And all those tiny somethings had finally added up to something miraculous. That devotion had helped me to feel whole again.

Even if you're not artistically inclined, you might think of this creativity as a constant moral reckoning. The opening of tea leaves can be likened to the unfurling of ideas. Let those ideas marinate. Life requires an incessant movement of becoming, it is a continuous process of self-creation. Each individual must take responsibility for freely forming his own selfhood. I think that tea can bring you back to earth while at the same time elevating you to cosmic revelation. Young people tend to think that tea is boring. It's for grandmas. But tea is just time. It's acknowledging time and existing within the moment. No expectations, no demands, just you and maybe a friend. There. Existing. Enjoying. Relaxing. Living. Nothing is any different than it has ever been. You're okay. I'm okay. We're here.

"Don't let your throat tighten with fear," wrote Rumi, "Take sips of breath all day and night, before death closes your mouth."

It started to occur to me that technology is not the problem. It's a distraction, and it's a proliferation of wanting. But the search for meaning is timeless. It goes back much further. Rumi felt it. John Lennon and Yoko Ono felt it. Artists throughout the ages felt it. So at the end of the day, tea is just a drink. But it's a drink that can create a space. If you can bring yourself to be still, tea has a song. So rather than try to pinpoint the exact relationship between tea and music, I'll settle for the correlation. There is something about tea and music. The spirit infused in the leaves and the energy that comes into us as we place our hands around the warm cup. The reassurance we get from a quiet moment, the ideas that flow through time. Next time you're there, try putting pen to paper. The soul is liberated through this small act of creation. Think of tea as a friend who will be with you during these times. There is a tie between tea and music. There

THE SOUL & SPIRIT OF TEA

is a relationship between emptiness and art. Tea is the harmony that weaves them together.

And for Yoko, was a lifetime of loneliness assuaged by her memories of this tea time moment with John? She said that on the day he was assassinated, it was the image of that night in the kitchen that came into her mind. Yoko and John cracking up over tea. A whole lifetime condensed into one moment.

Jen Ahlstrom is a musician living in Los Angeles, California. Her first album, *Self Help Hotel* by Rabbi & the Popes, will be released in July 2013. She would like to thank Coleman Barks profusely for his generosity in allowing her to draw from *The Essential Rumi*, the magnificent work from which she has drawn endless inspiration.

Chapter 20

BOOTLEG TEA

James Norwood Pratt

Tea had become England's national drink by 1800 and she was importing an average of twenty-four million pounds a year, it is said. It is now time for me to admit that all figures relating to earlier tea consumption in England are merely official, which is to say, misleading. The English drank vastly more tea than any John Company records before 1784 reveal, thanks to a nationwide network of "free traders" or-from the government's viewpoint-smugglers.

About a decade after the Company began importing tea on a regular basis, the Crown slapped a duty of five shillings on each pound irrespective of quality. This did not much affect the price of the most expensive teas, but it served to knock the cheap right out of the market, or rather, to create a black market for it. The cheapest sort one could legally buy then cost seven shillings a pound-almost a laborer's whole week's wages-while just across the Channel or across the North Sea in Holland tea of this same quality could be had for two shillings. With a 350 percent profit to play with, "free traders" were not long in multiplying along the whole length of England's coastline. Mr. J.M. Scott, to whose grand book The Great Tea Venture these pages are much indebted, has written: "The trouble and talk which resulted publicized tea as nothing else could have done, and as the illegal industry spread and prospered it carried the new commodity to every door. It was calculated that at the height of this illegal campaign two-thirds of the tea drunk in England had been smuggled."

Many a fine old home near the English coast was built on the proceeds of a venturer, one who put up the smuggling capital but kept well in the background, leaving the risks to the captain and the lander. The captain purchased his goods quite legally abroad and then waited for a dark night to run them across to one of several spots the lander might arrange. The lander arranged with the local farmhands for transport, with the local parson, perhaps, for storage in the church, and for eventual sales. Besides the venturer, very often the only principal in the whole business who could read and write was the quill driver, the man who kept the accounts. Eternal vigilance is, to be sure, the price of law breaking if it is to be successful for long, and this is but one of the ways tea smuggling was carried on from 1680, the year of the tax, until 1784, the year of its repeal. In 1733, no less than fifty-four thousand pounds of bootleg tea were seized; present-day American consumption of illegally imported drugs can give us some idea of how much was not.

The smugglers succeeded mainly because they had the sympathy of the whole countryside. On the Isle of Man they often unloaded as much tea and brandy as a hundred horses could carry, and stored their contraband in large caves no revenue man ever managed to discover because, as a pious old Manxman said, "Who'd ever be so wicked as to tell them?" The free traders knew every time a coast guard craft went into drydock, or when a riding officer had the gout or planned a raid. The country folks dealt with the smugglers less for the sake of getting luxuries cheap than of getting them at all. But the larger the band, the more contra-band, and the more overawed the revenuers and the populace. The day of the small-scale free trader had passed well before the mid-1700s. And as the business grew, as rich men found it profit-able to own three or four sloops engaged in illegal traffic, it be-came the part of wisdom to know nothing of what went on.

Without regard for secrecy, smugglers boldly stole their car-goes back from government customs houses more than once. Long caval-cades of horses loaded with tea were led quite openly through Kent; it is said six tons a week were run from France through Sussex. "The best that can be said of this period," ob-serves J.M. Scott, "is that it was the beginning of yacht racing-revenue cutters chasing smugglers who almost invariably won the cup of tea." There were, of course, occasional casualties on both sides. One of the famous "Wiltshire Moonrakers," who used the old church in Kingstone as their hiding place, is buried in its churchyard under this epitaph:

> To the memory of Robert Trotman, late of Rowd, in the
> county of Wilts, who was barbarously murdered on the
> shore near Poole, the 24th of March, 1765: A little tea;
> one leaf I did not steal. For guiltless bloodshed I to God
> appeal. Put tea in one scale, human blood in t'other,
> And think what 'tis to slay a harmless brother.

Stripped of their glamour, most smuggling gangs must have been rather like the one Daphne du Maurier depicted in her novel Jamaica Inn: bloodthirsty and wholly out for themselves. Still, in a time when inland communications were unimaginably bad, when most roads in England were tracks, dangerous at night and unusable part of the year, when most of the populace was illiterate, living and dying within ten or twenty miles of their birthplaces, smugglers undertook a nationwide sales campaign of an expensive novelty-and succeeded. They were only put out of business entirely after Waterloo, when the country finally had spare troops enough to enforce the laws. But the large-scale smuggling of tea had ended in 1784, when the gov-ernment finally repealed the tea tax at the behest of Richard Twin-ing, chairman of the dealers of tea.

For most Britishers, it was the first intelligent act of government in living memory, coming as it did three years after their American colonists had ended another dispute over tea by compelling the surrender of Lord Cornwallis at Yorktown.

James Norwood Pratt is the author of *The Wine Bibber's Bible* (1971), *The Tea Lover's Treasury* (1982), *The Tea Lover's Companion* (1995), and the whimsical *Reading Tea Leaves* (1996) authored as "by a Highland Seer." He was named Honorary Director of Imperial Tea Court, America's first traditional Chinese teahouse, which opened in 1993 in San Francisco.

Chapter 21

HOW THE DUCKS CAME TO THE POND

AN EYEWITNESS ACCOUNT OF AMERICA'S TEA RENAISSANCE

James Norwood Pratt

The United States is rapidly becoming a tea-consuming society—something we have not been before now, just as the U.S. only started becoming a wine-consuming society in the 1960s. As of 2010, the U.S. was importing more tea than the U.K. The only country importing more tea than the U.S. these days is the Russian Federation, they of the samovar, and we are unlikely to ever surpass their thirst. The producing countries China and India may always remain the foremost tea consumers, but in terms of per capita consumption, Americans have now overtaken the Japanese. The adoption of tea as a routine part of daily American life is a social and cultural development fully as significant as acceptance of same sex marriage rights and marijuana. The tealeaf confers both spiritual and bodily blessings, benefits that cannot be calculated much less documented, but are sure to help us become a happier, healthier and less quarrelsome people in consequence. In 2010, our cash registers rang up roughly 10 billion dollars in retail tea sales, which is almost as much as was spent on guns. All these figures are portents of a cultural shift. But while guns are a gross fact of American life and culture, tea is a quiet, almost imperceptible comfort to body and spirit for many millions of people every day. Tea is liquid sunshine, a form of energy, which has very gradually become humanity's favorite drink. Its slow and irresistible triumph is due to the simple fact that tea always makes us feel a bit better. It lifts up the heart, whether in company or in solitude. Who could do without it? Here follows my testimony as an eyewitness to how tea came to be embraced among us who were strangers to it, and the importance of honoring those who brought it.

THE ARCHIVIST & AFTER

William Harrison Ukers was the founding father of business journalism. He was a New York City businessman in the Gilded Age of the Vanderbilts, Morgans and Whitneys and like them he made his mark, founding the Audit Board of Circulation among other accomplishments. But his monument was his love child, *The Tea & Coffee Trade Journal*, which he founded in 1899 at a time when tea and coffee were still the most actively traded international commodities, accounting for about one-third of all ocean-borne cargo during the nineteenth century. By the 1930s Japan and its colonial possession Taiwan supplied about 40 percent of America's tea. This was mostly green or oolong distributed by firms like the Jewel Tea Company of Chicago, which eventually employed almost 1,500 sales people who serviced almost a million households door-to-door. Good tea was big business, as evidenced by the country's leading supermarket chain: Great Atlantic & Pacific Tea Company. No tea enterprise from Tokyo to Timbuktu escaped Mr. Ukers's notice, and for thirty-five years he collected richly detailed material on the trade. He compiled his discoveries into two massive volumes aptly entitled *All About Tea*, published in 1935 with an initial run of only 600 copies. Before they were finally reprinted in the 1990s, these rare volumes sold for over a thousand dollars for the set, and still remain an indispensable sourcebook on tea history today.

THE RACE TO THE BOTTOM

World War II changed the worldwide tea trade in every respect. In the West, traditions over 300 years in the making were ruined and never revived. In the new beginning was the teabag—ubiquitously accepted throughout postwar America and Great Britain in the name of "modern convenience." It rather quickly became difficult to find tea that was not packaged in teabags anywhere outside the tea-producing countries.

Here and there, a few elderly and aristocratic firms continued to cater to the carriage trade in American cities—Mark T. Wendell in Boston, Simpson & Vail in New York, John Wagner & Sons in Philadelphia, Freed Teller Freed in San Francisco—but very few tea businesses of any other kind survived. Tea was as mass-merchandized as a supermarket loss leader, an anonymous brown beverage confusingly called "black tea." Teabags became almost identical in content and "convenience" with brands like Tetley, Lipton, Red Rose and White Rose, and they lost whatever differences may have once existed between them. Consumers simply shopped for the cheapest teabag—and the race to the bottom began.

Tea packers learned to economize on quality by substituting mechanically harvested and manufactured teas from new tea lands, notably Kenya and Argentina. As long as the tea was strong and dark, flavor mattered only slightly more than leaf appearance, which mattered not at all since the powder-like leaf was concealed inside its shroud. Teas such as poets once praised—*Hyson, congou, bohea / And a few lesser divinities*—altogether disappeared from the market. Tea had been drained of all romance.

This situation, which had prevailed since the 1940s, persisted in 1980, when I undertook my first tea book. I found the tea trade was not just sleepy, it was comatose, except for a very few exceptional individuals.

THE HAPPY FEW
G.S. Haly Co., Grace Rare Teas, Bigelow

The first of these I met was the leading U.S. importer of fine teas, Michael Spillane of San Francisco's venerable G.S. Haly Company. From age nine, he had learned tasting at his mother's knee after

Marie Spillane was widowed and left to run her husband's tea-importing business. Her husband's colleagues in the trade made sure the business did not fail while she learned—and she learned fast and taught her son. After college, he went into the business full-time and inherited not simply contacts but relationships around the world with firms and families that had been dealing with G.S. Haly Co. for many years. Michael taught me the rudiments of tasting and the language of the trade. For instance, he taught that Formosa oolong exhibits "no peaks, no bites." One did not say "Taiwan" in those days, and Japan sencha was called "spider leg." But the new flavored teas Mike was importing from Germany produced most of G. S. Haly's profits.

Also exceptional was Richard Sanders, owner of Grace Rare Teas. Grace, which sold only loose leaf teas by the half pound, had been the top-quality U.S. tea brand since its founding in 1954 by Dick's former roommate at Harvard. Like Dick, the company and the teas were unapologetically elegant and old school, while the U.S. trade was all teabags all the time. Such firms and individuals were condescendingly dismissed by the Tea Association of the U.S. as being dealers in "specialty tea." In fact, they constituted almost the whole of the U.S. "specialty tea" business, at most 1 or 2 percent of the total. About the only other "specialty tea" came from Bigelow, the U.S. firm famous for "Constant Comment," and imported British lines like Twinings, Jacksons and Fortnum & Mason.

NEW BLOOD & NEW BUSINESS
Harney & Sons, Snapple, Upton Tea Imports, International Tea Importers

John Harney, then new owner of a minuscule company he re-named Harney & Sons Fine Teas, claims that America's Tea Renaissance began with the publication of my own book, *The Tea Lover's Treasury*, and a letter to the editor of the *New York Times* from Mrs. Elaine Cogan of Portland, Oregon. Mrs. Cogan wrote that she could not get a decent cup of tea anywhere in New York City, because the quality of the tea was so poor and nobody knew how to prepare it properly. In October of 1983, the editor decried this gasping for tea, along with pretensions to superior coffee from Mrs. Cogan's native Northwest, with an editorial entitled "Tea Snobs and Coffee Bigots," but he included these still-too-true sentiments: "Mrs. Cogan is exactly right about the soggy, grim feeling that overcomes a tea drinker when served a cup of hot water and a tea bag. Besides, in restaurants like that, the water is usually lukewarm. The only thing worse is take-out tea, a styrofoam cup containing a stewed tea bag bobbing in warm iodine." Armed with Mrs. Cogan's indictment and with my book for credibility, John Harney landed the Waldorf-Astoria as his first hotel account and began the climb to the eminence his firm presently occupies.

The media took serious notice of tea starting only with the success story of Snapple. Snapple was the first "ready-to-drink" (RTD) tea to catch on nation-wide, but the tea itself was secondary to the story of how profitable the company quickly became. It was soon sold for over a billion dollars, back when that was still an impressive figure. At the time of Snapple's debut the entire U.S. tea market was estimated at 1.3 billion dollars a year.

It sounded pretentious to even speak of a "U.S. tea market" before the 1990s. As a herald, Upton Tea Imports was established in 1989 near Boston as a mail-order retailer. Tom Eck had traveled the world in his previous profession as a software engineer and discovered fine tea available everywhere he went except back in the U.S. He decided to fill this lack, convinced he was not the only American enamored of "specialty tea." The easy part was his expert's understanding of how to design and operate systems and enterprises, but Tom also had all the aptitudes and passion needed to become a tea man. *Upton Tea Quarterly* has been from its first issue the mother of all mail order tea catalogs, making hundreds of selections representing almost all types of tea available to isolated and far-flung customers. Next onto the scene came Devan Shah, exceptional even among the exceptional few. Devan's school vacations were spent in India's cool Nilgiri mountains on the tea estate managed by his eldest sister's husband. After he took his college degree in business he dutifully but swiftly climbed the rungs of the tea profession, starting as an assistant to a South India tea broker. Like many Indian professionals in his mid-twenties, he emigrated to the U.S., where he became an electronics importer. The money was good but it was not the right livelihood for a born tea man. Disregarding warnings from friends and family that Americans simply don't drink tea, Devan launched India Tea Importers with the conviction he could convert them. He stored the first six chests he imported in his father-in-law's garage and set about creating markets for tea where there were no markets previously. For instance, no RTD chai existed in the U.S. before Devan;. again and again he has played a decisive role in developing America's tastes in tea.

THE PACE QUICKENS
Republic of Tea, Oregon Chai, Chez Panisse, Tea Magazine, Elmwood Inn Fine Teas, T Salon, Dushanbe, Teacup, Chado, Ching-Ching Cha, Teaism

In 1992, the Republic of Tea was brought into being by young Zentrepreneur Will Rosenzweig, with coaching and investment from his fellow tea lover Mel Ziegler of Banana Republic clothiers. Their story came out as a book, *The Republic of Tea: The Story of the Creation of a Business, as Told Through the Personal Letters of Its Founders*, published at the same time their line of teas first appeared. It's a story that speaks to the true reasons for tea's popularity and appeal—that it is an agricultural product that can become a work of art. Rosenzweig and Ziegler realized tea is not a commodity like oatmeal or salt but an artisan product like wine and should be valued and sold accordingly, with the romance of tea as the sizzle. They proceeded to disregard all price ceilings and charge what their teas were worth. *The Republic of Tea* proved an overnight success

Oregon Chai was another innovation that found a ready market. Returning to Portland from an extended stay in India, Heather Mac-Millan brought home an unappeasable craving for India's national drink, then unheard of in the U.S. She gave birth to Oregon Chai in her mother's kitchen and quickly won a local following. Her chai got its authentic taste from the Nilgiri tea Devan Shah supplied. She got her first national exposure exhibiting in his booth at a New York Fancy Food Show, where she was spotted by *Newsweek*. Heather's example inspired chai makers in Colorado and eventually across the country: another milepost.

Tea commerce and tea culture are inseparable twins and as the specialty tea business grew in the U.S., so did the cult of tea. It was aided, in some measure, at least, by *The Tea Lover's Treasury*, which is now widely considered to be the first "serious" investigation of tea since Ukers. Despite an introduction by M.F.K. Fisher, the book was a commercial disappointment, grudgingly kept in print and selling barely over 20,000 copies in its first decade. My readers proved influential out of all proportion to their numbers, however, and made their presence felt within the broader "foodie" trend of the times. Helen Gustafson of Chez Panisse became a beacon in our embryonic cult of tea as it gradually became conscious of itself. Pearl Dexter launched *Tea: A Magazine*, and newsletters by Diana Rosen in California and Linda Ashley Leamer appreared in Minnesota. We were soon nodes in a sort of underground tea network and were besieged with requests for information or introductions. Another milepost was the first "Harney Tea Summit," held in 1994 in an effort to educate the press about the joys and varieties of tea, though none of them cared anything about tea until a year or two later when the health benefits of tea drinking became a running story. Untold millions of Americans who had never given tea a thought were suddenly giving it a try and the "specialty tea" business began to boom. Harney Tea Summits in subsequent years focused on teaching attendees how to enter the trade.

Because Americans are simply giddy over good health, it took a parade of scientific proofs that tea is good for the human body to make sales soar. This factor, which is almost entirely to the credit of the Tea Association of the U.S.A., cannot be over-estimated. But it was not the only factor. Aging Baby Boomers began discovering that

coffee is no friend of over-50s the way tea can be. Even while Starbucks' growth still seemed inexorable, a Coffee Recovery Movement
of sorts was also growing. But successful trends need to be fun, and
for this, tea had to escape what I secretly thought of as the "Doily
Ghetto," a cultural artifact inherited from other times and places,
chiefly British, and beloved by generations of grandmothers who believed in a proper way of doing things, tea most of all. Their image of
a tearoom was decidedly feminine, with more attention to hats and
linens than to the tea itself. Picture: *The Importance of Being Ernest.* Tea
was only an after-thought at haute-"Doily Ghetto" temples like the
Palm Court at the Plaza in New York, where poor preparation guaranteed terrible tea even after John Harney created their signature
Palm Court blend. Nobody in the Doily Ghetto really cared about
the tea, in contrast to pioneer entrepreneurs like Bruce and Shelley
Richardson of Elmwood Inn in Perryville, Kentucky, Miriam Novalle
at Manhattan's T Salon at the SoHo Guggenheim, and others at Dushanbe Teahouse in Boulder, Teacup in Seattle, Lisa's Tea Treasures
in Northern Calfornia, Chado in Los Angeles, or Ching-Ching Cha
and Teaism in Washington, DC. These early establishments were
responsible for *beaucoup* buzz in the press and a serious raising of tea
consciousness in and outside our small but growing cult of tea.

PERSONAL JOURNEYS
Imperial Tea Court, Silk Road Teas, Q-Trade, ABC Taiwan
Teahouse, Brian Keating's Sage Group Reports, APTI.
SerendipiTea, Barnes & Watson, East Indies

My own tea education throughout the early 90s was principally influenced by Devan Shah, Roy Fong and one or two others with a
vocation for tea the way some have vocations for teaching or the
priesthood. It was through them I discovered tea to be my vocation
also, and I feel quite fortunate to be one of their numbers. When
the student is ready, the teacher appears, sometimes right down the
street. So it was in July 1993 when the very first traditional Chinese
tea house in the U.S. appeared, just two steep blocks down San Fran-

cisco's Russian Hill from my front door. I saw the sign and tried the door, was told they were not open (but was not told to leave), and have never been the same since that hour. There were China's Ten Most Famous Teas and dozens of more exotic ones that I'd never expected to see outside China. For their part, my hosts Grace and Roy Fong had never expected to see a "round-eye" who had even heard of their teas. A Taoist priest as well as a budding tea merchant, Roy gradually initiated me into the ancient tea culture of the homeland of tea. He eventually even named me Honorary Director of Imperial Tea Court, in recognition of my efforts to become the Apostle of China Tea to my fellow round-eyes. How could I not wish to spread the good news about *guywans* and *gongfu* and wonders like Fujian White Tea or Yunnan Royal Gold? At first, I even thought to handle mail order for Roy, but we soon realized that business is not for writers.

Just before Roy appeared, David Lee Hoffman, recently back from a tea-buying trip to China, introduced me to Pu-Erh tea, which he sold at a flea market across the Golden Gate in Marin under his brand Silk Road Teas. Helen Gustafson and I invited David and every other tea lover we knew near San Francisco to a reception at Imperial Tea Court to meet the founder of London's Bramah Tea Museum, the notoriously grumpy Edward Bramah. David fell into conversation with Roy, and I heard someone say, "Those two are discussing teas the rest of us have never heard of." Only then did I realize that Roy, David, Helen and I were the only devotees of classic China teas in the room, or perhaps in the entire country. I was a keen student of all tea, of course, and fortunate in my teachers. Before extremists targeted his family in Sri Lanka, where he held the rank of army colonel, Manik Jayakumar was director in charge of five classic Uva estates, one of which he transformed into the world's first organic tea estate. Manik spent time in Indonesia and Japan before establishing himself as an importer of fine teas in California. I met Gabriella Karsch, the first to import tea (or anything else) from Vietnam, and Thomas Shu of Taiwan's first family of tea, who soon opened ABC Teahouse in Los Angeles. The amazing Nat Litt became a friend. He had been an architect trained and employed by Frank Lloyd Wright, but he abandoned that career to join Ringling Brothers Circus as a clown, which he also gave up in order to become a pastry chef trained in the cordon-bleu academy in Paris. Then Nat discovered his true calling, and as a fourth career, he established the House of Tea in Philadelphia. During this time, all of us burned with zeal for tea and succeeded in conveying our enthusiasm to many another.

As Helen wrote in *The Agony of the Leaves*, about our tasting rare and legendary China teas together, ". . . I made a little covenant with myself: I will get behind these teas. I will get Chez Panisse to serve these teas. I will spread the word. I will bear witness! I will put a fire under Alice, I *will*." I kept my holy feeling to myself that afternoon, but I called her the next morning, striding around my kitchen and roaring into the phone. She reassured me, yes, yes, we would start. Some have passions for boats and sailing and others for horses or cars; we were mad for tea and could not keep our enthusiasm to ourselves. I no longer felt like a solitary eccentric but was now an acknowledged member of a cult. It was not really my choice; you might say the spirit inhabiting the tea plant had chosen me, just as it had the others. But at that time a love of tea still seemed exotic, and none of us could have envisioned the U.S. becoming a tea-consuming society.

The U.S. tea community was just beginning to wake up to our needs as an identifiable group in 1995. Tea had for several years constituted the fastest-growing business category at the semi-annual, bi-coastal Fancy Food Shows. Start-up companies needed information for sourcing, business plans, bank loans, etc., and data for such purposes was first made available in the 1995 "Tea Is Hot" Report, which relieved newcomers of the need to locate the phone numbers of insiders and beg them for help. Brian Keating, who owned Tea-cup Tea House in Seattle and was a veteran of the nutriceutical, or health supplement industry, recognized that tea was a new national trend in the making, with a need for start-up data all its own. Business data is no substitute for tea education, however, and this had also become a crying need. "What's the difference between green and black?" and other basic questions from newcomers required endlessly time-consuming one-on-one, start-from-the-beginning tea education. More than consumer education, our first need was an apprenticeship program for on-going education within the burgeoning trade. The American Premium Tea Institute (APTI) was established in 1996 under the leadership of Mike Spillane to fill this and other needs of "specialty tea." Our model was the California Wine Institute, which championed industry-wide standards and consumer education. Up to this point The Tea Association of the U.S. had been no help, perhaps because the teabag companies it represented realized, however dimly, that every supermarket tea customer who discovered premium, i.e. "specialty" tea, was lost to them forever. This began to change when Joe Simrany was hired as Executive Director of the Association and promptly proposed the Board should embrace the concept of specialty tea. The Specialty Tea Registry was finally launched four years later, about the same time as APTI.

If the Tea Renaissance has an Honor Role, APTI's founders and all-volunteer Board of Directors rank high on it: Eliot Jordan of Peets' Coffee & Tea, August Techeira of Freeds, Michael Harney of Harney & Sons, Ken Rudee of Barnes & Watson, Tomaslav Podreka of SerendipiTea, Thomas Shu of ABC Teahouse and Ron Rubin of Republic of Tea among them, not to mention Mim Enck, Ric Rinehardt, Richard Gazaukas, and others. In San Francisco in 1996, the organization staged the first national tea symposium open to consumers as well as professionals. They envisioned the courses and credentialing which have now been developed, but most of all they managed to establish an ethos of collegiality and welcome to everybody joining: America's tea community. Their valiant efforts jolted the Tea Association into creating a similar entity, with which APTI merged in 2002 to form today's STI, or Specialty Tea Institute. Tea, which must be learned, requires teaching, and in the absence of Old World Style apprenticeship programs, STI is filling this need for basic training.

The second half of the 1990's witnessed world historical changes in the international tea trade, any one of which deserves a chapter. The transformations due to global airfreight and internet connections began amidst many endings. Widely publicized but actually inconsequential was the termination in 1996 of the U.S. Tea Board of Experts and position of Tea Examiner. These official functions were mandated by the oldest consumer protection law on the national books, the Tea Act of 1897, which had been enacted at the request of the U.S. tea trade to deny entry to defective or adulterated teas. The Act spared importers lengthy disputes, saving them insurance and litigation costs at no cost whatever to the government, since the trade voluntarily paid an assessment to cover the cost of the program. It was ended amidst loud and false claims of saving tax dollars. The only actual public benefit was the "legalization" of Pu-Erh, an immense category of China tea denied legal entry for a century because U.S. Tea Examiners deemed it "musty"—as it undeniably and often is. No Chinatown ever went without its Pu-Erh, admittedly, but at last it could be imported within the law. A more fitting symbol for the end of previous eras was Jardine Matheson's 1997 termination of its tea division. The canny Scotsmen who gave the firm their names in 1832 grew wealthy in the tea-and-opium trade. They deserved principal credit for fomenting the Opium War of 1840-42, which ruined China but left the firm practically owning Hong Kong and a good deal else. William Jardine's life story was thinly fictionalized in James Clavell's novel *Taipan*. The effects of his firm's depredations will remain unto the seventh generation, but its exit from the tea trade, which it once dominated, was a non-event.

Another ending: the last London Tea Auction was held on June 29, 1998, over three centuries after the first in 1679. These were quarterly events until the demise of the East India Company's monopoly in 1834, when tea became a "free trade" commodity in Britain. The London auctions were then moved to Mincing Lane, which quickly became what "Wall Street" is to finance, the address of the world tea trade. These auctions were held monthly, then weekly, then daily, by country of origin until the 1950s when fully one-third of all the world's tea was bought and sold in London. After independence, most colonial countries had established their own auctions. However, the telephone and internet would soon finish off a world just recently lost but already half forgotten, the Old Order.

HEALTH & HAPPINESS

The Tea News of the 1990's was not that the Old Order changeth, it was that Tea is Good for Health, common knowledge in China since the time of Christ but now blessed, as if by Him, in the name of Science. Clinical research began to document various benefits from various teas, and health-obsessed Americans obediently drank whatever the latest health bulletin prescribed. This started with green tea, the national drink in Japan, where the earliest tea-related health research was done.

As its cancer-preventing properties became known in the early 1990s, America's consumption of green tea soared. Ten years later the pattern was repeated with white tea, practically unheard of in the U.S. until pop star Britney Spears divulged that her personal trainer recommended it as containing even more antioxidants than green tea. Since then, and not undeservedly, oolong has enjoyed a mini-boom among weight watchers, and Pu-Erh has won a reputation as something of a panacea. The largest single reason U.S. tea sales climbed throughout the 1990s was the constant barrage of proof of tea's health benefits. Yet, what began as health fads became permanent patterns in an over-all trend toward increased tea consumption. Health claims for tea were widely and effectively publicized in the popular press. In 1998, the Second International Scientific Symposium on Tea and Human Health—sponsored by the Tea Council of the U.S.A., together with numerous medical societies—was held in the FDA auditorium in Washington, DC, and it created such an impression it helped make research into tea and health a growth industry in itself. Over 110 papers a year were produced between the Third Symposium in 2003 and the Fourth in 2007. This abundant scientific testimony helped immeasurably to make tea the drink of health-conscious Americans. Myriads kept hearing how good tea was for them and tried it, then stuck to it because they found it simply good. America's *new tea lover* had arrived and green, white and the other teas had come to stay.

Before 1990, it was pretentious to even speak of a U.S. "tea market," with its annual net under two billion dollars at best. By 2000, that figure was five times bigger and worth discussing. But beyond any dollar value, our emerging Tea Renaissance also signified an enormous cultural shift, as Americans turned to tea for reasons other than health. In tea many "took refuge," as the Buddhists say, seeking respite from a society that demanded more and more from them and delivered less and less. Whether as a simple pleasure or as a spiritual refreshment, tea became a daily necessity for millions of Americans who have embraced, in varying degree, all the world's various tea traditions, from Scottish scones in the afternoon to Japanese tea ceremonies, Russian samovars, China green and Pu-Erh and Indian chai, to mention only the obvious. These new tea lovers owe no allegiance to any one way of tea. Moroccans drink only Moroccan tea, which is never served in Ostfriesland on the North Sea coast of Germany where one drinks Ostfriesen tea only, just as India only knows chai, and so forth. America's new tea lovers do not come to tea from any family or ethnic tradition, but happily welcome all the world's tea traditions and feel free to enjoy their various pleasures. It was to this new cultural breed that I dedicated my *NEW Tea Lover's Treasury* at the end of 1999, the year of Tazo and Adagio.

BRANCHING STREAMS
Tazo, Adagio, Rishi, MEM, Honest Tea, World Tea Expo

As the cult of tea gathered steam, the market for tea continued to grow in all directions. Like the Second Coming, "the Starbucks of Tea" had been predicted for years by 1999, when Starbucks made its tea move and acquired Tazo and the creative energy of Tazo founder Steve Smith. As its tea buyer, Steve Smith had brought such success and distinction to Stash that the "hippie" company was bought by the Japanese tea behemoth Yamamoto-yama in 1993. A year later he launched Tazo, and then sold his new baby when it was barely five years old, suddenly making Starbucks a major player in the U.S. tea business, or so it seemed. In actual fact, his impact on Starbucks proved slight: corporate politics is unkind to passions, for tea or anything else, and they gained only a profitable brand and the matcha latte. Instead, the new direction in U.S. tea sales came not from Starbucks, but Adagio, started the same year Tazo was acquired. Michael Cramer, fresh from the Peace Corps, was asked by his Russian Jewish mother if he thought she could make a living in a tea business.

After investigation Michael could foresee not just a livelihood, but a potential for wealth beyond the dreams of avarice, in Dr. Johnson's words. He persuaded his brother Ilya to leave Goldman Sachs and add his computer mastery to Michael's growing tea expertise. Together, they have made Adagio the leading tea retailer on the web, a huge and growing market to which they supply first-rate and affordable teas and wares of every description. Adagio, which now has brick-and-mortar outlets also, is not only a monument to their vision and intelligence. In many ways, Michael and Ilya represent the wave of new tea lovers turned tea entrepreneurs who have created America's Tea Renaissance—people crazy about tea, but not too crazy to make it a profitable business. Second to none of these is Caroline Cahan, who has made Southern Season in Chapel Hill, N.C. the nation's leading tea retail store, with honorable mentions to Tealuxe of Harvard Square and Winnie Yu's Teance in Berkeley. Importer/explorer Joshua Kaiser has made his firm Rishi a major source of fine quality loose-leaf teas, like the herbals from Mark Mooradian's MEM Tea Imports or the RTD's from Seth Goldman's Honest Tea.

These examples must be multiplied many-fold to account for the proliferation of tea enterprises that have sprung up around the country. San Francisco now has three Samovar Tea Lounges and Los Angeles four Chados. America's new tea lovers and their businesses were numerous enough by 2003 to support the first World Tea Expo (then called Take Me2Tea). Everything old was new again as the once-tired U.S. tea trade descended on Las Vegas to party with visitors from around the world, eager to get in on our action. Its infancy and childhood past, our Tea Renaissance had arrived at adolescence, and it has continued to mature with each annual World Tea Expo.

For some years now, America's Tea Renaissance has been driving changes in the worldwide trade. Tea is increasingly used in alcoholic drinks, not to mention cosmetics, cooking, and sundry soaps and potions. Paper sacks have replaced wooden chests for transport, bio-degradable pyramid teabags have become commonplace, and U.S. supermarket blends and food service tea equipment have been considerably up-graded. We have led the way in making organic tea a major growth category and even taken up foreign fads like Bubble Tea and *matcha* drinks of all sorts. Our appetite for green and white tea has induced otherwise sensible estate managers in Darjeeling, Sri Lanka and elsewhere to create new tea types like green Darjeeling and silver and golden Ceylons, sometimes with stunning success. Our new tea lovers have even conveyed some of our enthusiasm to Britain, where tea consumption was stagnating, and even to France and India. In the U.S., our tribe has increased to the point that perhaps 100 million Americans make tea a routine part of daily life and spend about ten billion a year on it. We are now approaching a tipping point. Economically speaking, few prospects for small business in the U.S. are brighter than our future tea trade—and maybe big business too.

In 2012, the Teavana company, with well over 300 outlets, was acquired by Starbucks for over half a billion dollars, suggesting that our new breed of tea lover represents not simply a new market but a major cultural shift. Just as we have, within living memory, become a wine consuming nation—something we were not before—the U.S. is on its way to becoming a tea consuming nation. Today, good wine at fair prices is available pretty much everywhere, and it is a part of daily life for millions. A society that can pronounce "cabernet sauvignon" can learn to say *"Da hong pao."*

Historically, tea always enters a society almost imperceptibly at first, but by the slow and irresistible efforts of its devotees and its own obvious virtues, it eventually triumphs, as each one teaches another how to enjoy it. Tea is a face-to-face transmission, as the Buddhists would say, and this is part of its power. It proves hard to resist and impossible to dislodge, because tea is not simply enjoyed for itself; it is a form of energy and a key to love and laughter with friends, the enjoyment of food, beauty and humor, and art and music. Its rewards are far beyond its cost.

THE SOUL & SPIRIT OF TEA

ALL ONE MIND AND TEA

Tea is a gift to the world. As Queen Victoria's Prime Minister William Gladstone told her, "If you are cold, tea will warm you; if you are heated it will cool you; if you are depressed it will cheer you; if you are excited it will calm you." In Asia, tea has always been recognized as a Way—that is, a Path that leads to the peace and poetry of life—which we all seek, sometimes desperately.

"I'll give you everything I got for a little peace of mind," sang the great Beatle, John Lennon, quite as great a tea lover as any Victorian. Tea lovers know that tea is quiet and takes you to a quiet place inside, where you can "Turn off your mind, relax and float downstream," as another Beatle, George Harrison, sang in "Within and Without You."

Most of us, most of the time, swim against the current of the River Tao and grow weary. Tea offers a way out of our spiritual energy crisis. It is a Wayless Way that requires no disciplines, exercises, retreats, or sacrifices. It leads to a world of harmony, to which we can also take our friends. It quietly asks, "Do you always have to be in such a rush?" It's not something *more* we really need, but something *beyond*. Tea offers an escape from Planet Egomania and that vague and terrible emptiness that prosperity has brought upon us.

One great gift of tea is this: tea can teach you how to be alone with yourself in a small room and like the company you keep. Another great gift: nothing contributes more to our enjoyment of leisure, friendship, sociability and conversation than sharing tea with others. We become not One and not Two, but feel ourselves transformed into Togetherness by the Holy Spirit that inhabits the leaf. This greatest gift of tea is a face-to-face transmission of peace and pleasure. Tea teaches that as the Beatles also sang in "I am the Walrus":

"I am you as you are me
as we are we
as we are all one
mind and tea
is here to help us see
that this is true,
Goo Goo Ga Choo."

Two-thousand-year-old Roman "tea table" used by Sir Arthur Evans, at his home at the ancient Minoan site of Knossus, Crete. Photography © Phil Cousineau, 2012.

Appendices

Appendix A

HEALTH BENEFITS OF TEA (CAMELLIA SINENSIS)

A Review of Recent Clinical & Epidemiological Research, with Emphasis on Green Tea

Mark Blumenthal

INTRODUCTION

Aside from its long history of use and it being the world's second most widely consumed beverage, tea is also one of the healthiest beverages known to mankind. This chapter is intended as a relatively comprehensive yet selective review of the clinical and epidemiological literature published since 2007 and through 2013 on the health benefits of green tea, oolong tea, and black tea, with primary emphasis on green tea. (For the purpose of this chapter, green tea will be abbreviated as GT, while green tea extract—of various formulations and chemical profiles—will be abbreviated GTE.)

Although comprehensive but certainly not exhaustive, with the increase of scientific and clinical research in the health effects of tea in the past decade, this chapter will summarize some of the cardiovascular and cancer-prevention benefits of drinking tea (mainly, but not always, green tea) as well as tea extracts in solid dosage form (i.e., dietary supplements).

Increase in Scientific & Clinical Research on Tea in Past 10–20 Years

Scientific and clinical research on herbs, medicinal plants, and phytomedicinal preparations in general has increased dramatically in the past thirty years. In 2010, English researchers published a review of all published articles on herbal medicine appearing between 1977 and 2007 in any language in the U.S. National Library of Medicine's Medline PubMed database. They discovered that over a thirty-year study period, the amount of herbal medicine-related articles published rose from 739 in 1977 to 6,364 in 2007. The largest numbers of articles were review articles and randomized controlled clinical trials. [Hung SK, Ernst E.; Herbal medicine: an overview of the literature from three decades. *J Diet Suppl.* 2010;7(3):217–226.] While this author has not located a similar article showing metrics for the numbers of tea-related research, a review of PubMed as well as the HerbClip and HerbMedPro databases at the nonprofit American Botanical Council indicates a significant increase in scientific and clinical research on tea (all types, particularly green tea) in the period from 1995 to 2012, as shown in Tables A.1 and A.2.

Table A.1 Green Tea Clinical Publications (Clinical Trials, Reviews, Systematic Reviews, and Meta-analyses)* Cited in PubMed at the US National Library of Medicine (up to May 30, 2012)

Search Term	Number of Citations (Hits)
"Green Tea"	240
"Camellia sinensis"	49
"epigallocatechingallate"	93
"EGCG"	55

* Not including chemical studies & in vitro & in vivo pharmacological & toxicological research.

Table A.2 Green Tea & Related Tea Article Summaries in the American Botanical Council's HerbClipTM Database

Key Word	Hit Results, Nov 30, 2012
Green Tea	ca 251 HCs
Camellia sinensis	ca 283 HCs
EGCG	ca 104 HCs

Further evidence of the growth of tea-related scientific and clinical research publications is available by viewing the Tea Record on ABC's HerbMedProTM Database. As of August 31, 2012 this unique database contained abstracts on a total of 1796 scientific and clinical trials, including 161 clinical trials on Tea (C. sinensis). This total number of papers included human clinical trials (161), epidemiological studies, review papers, traditional and folk use, pharmacology (pharmacokinetic, pharmacodynamic, etc.), toxicology and adverse effects, botany, geographical distribution of tea, etc., as shown in Table 1.3. Listings in the HerbMedPro database include one-sentence summaries of each published article with direct links to scientific abstracts on each publication, linked to PubMed, Cochrane Database, or other free-access databases. (From 2009 through 2011 the Tea record in the HerbMedPro database was compiled and maintained via a grant to ABC from Tea Dragon Films.)

Table A.3 Tea Research in American Botanical Council's HerbMedPro Database

Evidence for Efficacy (Human Data)

Clinical Trials (161)
Observational Studies/Case Reports (103)
Traditional and Folk Use (29)

Safety Data

Adverse Effects & Toxicity (61)
Interactions (9)
Contraindications (1)

Evidence of Activity

Animal Studies (355)
Pharmacodynamics (781)
Analytical Chemistry (207)
Pharmacokinetics (ADME) (35)
Genetics & Molecular Biology (83)

Formulas/Blends

Modern Methods of Preparation (73)
Patents (3)

Other Information

Pictures & Distribution Maps (5)
Cultivation, Conservation & Ecology (72)
Related Links (12)

---

* http://cms.herbalgram.org/herbmedpro/overview.html. Numbers in parentheses indicate total number of the type of study.

Table A.4 Abbreviations Used in this Chapter

Abbreviation	Meaning
CHD	Coronary Heart Disease
CVD	Cardiovascular Disease
ECGC	Epigallocatechin gallate
GT	Green Tea

CARDIOVASCULAR BENEFITS OF GREEN TEA

Based on a growing body of research, the consumption of tea (all kinds) results in cardiovascular, chemopreventive (anti-cancer), and neurological health benefits, aids in various weight loss regimens, and has salubrious effects on hepatic (liver) function, iron absorption, oral health, bone density, etc. Externally, green tea extracts in various types of topical preparations have been shown to be beneficial for treating genital warts (see below) and as an antioxidant to help reduce various aging factors on skin.

A 2009 review at Tufts University encompassed the results of then-recent observational studies and clinical trials showing the probable relationship of tea and tea catechins to a wide variety of health parameters; these include body weight control and energy metabolism, impaired glucose tolerance and diabetes, cardiovascular disease (CVD), bone mineral density, cognitive function and neurodegenerative disease, and various types of cancer. The review concluded that the evidence for efficacy and potency of tea and tea extracts in benefiting these outcomes ranges from compelling for CVD to equivocal at best for some forms of cancer. [Bolling BW, Chen CY, Blumberg JB. Tea and health: preventive and therapeutic usefulness in the elderly? *Curr Opin Clin Nutr Metab Care.* 2009 Jan;12(1):42–48.] This publication stated that although randomized controlled trials (RCTs) of tea have generally been of short duration and with small sample sizes, together with experimental and epidemiological studies (i.e., long-term observational studies on large populations), the totality of data suggests a role for tea in health promotion as a beverage absent in calories and rich in phytochemicals. As is often the case in such scientific reviews, the authors conclude that further scientific and clinical research is warranted on the putative benefits of tea and the potential for synergy among its constituent flavonoids, L-theanine, and caffeine.

One of the most comprehensive and frequently-cited scientific publications on the general health benefits of tea is called the Ohsaki study, published in the Journal of the American Medical Association in 2006. The objective of this study was to investigate associations between the consumption of green tea (GT) and all-cause vs. cause-specific mortality. This study, officially referred to as the Ohsaki National Health Insurance Cohort Study, is a population-based, prospective cohort study initiated in 1994 among 40,530 Japanese adults (40–79 yrs of age) with no history of stroke, coronary heart disease (CHD), or cancer at baseline (i.e., at the beginning of the study when they were assessed). These people were tracked and monitored for various outcomes for up to 11 years (from 1995 to 2005) for all-cause mortality and for up to 7 years (1995–2001) for cause-specific mortality (i.e., death associated with a particular cause). The main outcomes measured were mortality due to CVD, cancer, and all causes. The researchers concluded that GT consumption "is associated with reduced mortality due to all causes and due to cardiovascular disease but not with reduced mortality due to cancer." [Kuriyama S, Shimazu T, Ohmori K, et al. Green tea consumption and mortality due to cardiovascular disease, cancer, and all causes in Japan. The Ohsaki study. *JAMA.* 2006;296(10):1255–1265.]

Green tea has been shown in numerous controlled human clinical trials to have a variety of beneficial effects on the cardiovascular system. While this is not intended to be an exhaustive review of this subject, the following studies provide a reasonably comprehensive view of these cardiovascular effects.

Green Tea & Endothelial Function

One of the areas where green tea consumption has shown to provide health benefits is in its ability to enhance the function of the endothelium, the inner lining of arteries and veins that has the constricting/dilating capacity to increase/decrease blood pressure. Numerous human clinical trials have demonstrated GT's ability to provide increased vasodilation, thereby improving blood pressure by slightly lowering it, especially in mildly hypertensive individuals.

- Flow-mediated dilatation (FMD) of the brachial artery is related to coronary endothelial function and it is an independent predictor of cardiovascular risk.
- N = 14 healthy adults, no prior CVD (except 50% = smokers)
- Dose: (a) 6 g of green tea, (b) 125 mg of caffeine (= 6 g GT), or (c) hot water on 3 occasions.
- Resting & hyperemic brachial artery diameter did not change w/ GT or caffeine.
- FMD increased significantly w/ GT (by 3.69%), whereas it did not change significantly w/ caffeine.

- Conclusion: GT consumption has an acute beneficial effect on endothelial function, assessed by FMD of brachial artery in healthy individuals. This may be involved in beneficial effect of GT on CV risk.

Alexopoulos N, Vlachopoulos C, Aznaouridis K, Baou K, Vasiliadou C, Pietri P, Xaplanteris P, Stefanadi E, Stefanadis C. The acute effect of green tea consumption on endothelial function in healthy individuals. *Eur J Cardiovasc Prev Rehabil.* 2008 Jun;15(3):300–5.

GT Lowers CV Risk

- R, DB, PC, n = 111 healthy adults (21–70 yrs)
- Standardized capsule of decaffeinated GT compounds 2x/d.
- In as soon as 3 weeks, GT capsule was effective for decreasing BP, LDL cholesterol, oxidative stress, & a marker of chronic inflammation—all independent CV risk factors.

Nantz MP, Rowe CA, Bukowski JF, Percival SS. Standardized capsule of Camellia sinensis lowers cardiovascular risk factors in a randomized, double-blind, placebo-controlled study. *Nutrition* 2009 Feb;25(2):147–154.

Effect of Green Tea on Glucose Abnormalities in Japanese Adults

- N = 60 subjects, 32–73 yrs (49 males, 11 females)
- Crossover: packet of GTE (containing 544 mg polyphenols; 456 mg catechins) daily for 1st 2 months & then 2–month nonintervention period.
- Daily supplementary intake of GT extract powder lowered hemoglobin A1c level in individuals with borderline diabetes—an indicator of glucose levels of 2–3 month period.

Fukino Y, Ikeda A, Maruyama K, Aoki N, Okubo T, Iso H. Randomized controlled trial for an effect of green tea-extract powder supplementation on glucose abnormalities. *Eur J Clin Nutr.* 2008;62: 953–960.

Green Tea: Fat Oxidation & Glucose Tolerance–1

- OBJECTIVE: Investigated effects of acute ingestion of green tea extract (GTE) on glucose tolerance & fat oxidation during moderate-intensity exercise in humans.
- DESIGN: 2 studies performed, both counter-balanced crossover design.
- Study A: 12 healthy men performed 30–min cycling exercise at 60% of maximal O2 consumption before & after supplementation.

- Study B: 11 healthy men took an oral-glucose-tolerance test (GTT) before & after supplementation.
- 24 hours before experimental trials, men took 3 capsules containing either GTE (total: 890 +/- 13 mg polyphenols and 366 +/- 5 mg EGCG) or corn-flour placebo.

Venables MC, Hulston CJ, Cox HR, Jeukendrup AE. Green tea extract ingestion, fat oxidation, and glucose tolerance in healthy humans. *Am J Clin Nutr.* 2008 Mar;87(3):778–84. Human Performance Laboratory, School of Sport & Exercise Sciences, Univ of Birmingham, Birmingham, UK

Green Tea: Fat Oxidation & Glucose Tolerance—2

- RESULTS: Avg fat oxidation rates = 17% higher after GTE ingestion than after ingestion of P (P < 0.05).
- The contribution of fat oxidation to total energy expenditure was also significantly higher, by a similar %, after GTE supplementation.
- CONCLUSION: Acute GTE ingestion can increase fat oxidation during moderate-intensity exercise and can improve insulin sensitivity & glucose tolerance in healthy young men.

Venables MC, Hulston CJ, Cox HR, Jeukendrup AE. Green tea extract ingestion, fat oxidation, and glucose tolerance in healthy humans. *Am J Clin Nutr.* 2008 Mar;87(3):778–84. Human Performance Laboratory, School of Sport & Exercise Sciences, Univ of Birmingham, Birmingham, UK

Black & Green Tea Extract: No effect on Type 2 Diabetics –1

- Evidence shows that tea has a hypoglycemic effect.
- Tested ability of extract of green & black tea to improve glucose control over 3 months
- R, DB, PC, multiple-dose (0, 375, or 750 mg/day for 3 months)
- N = 49 (completed) adults w/ type 2 diabetes not taking insulin
- Predominantly white w/ avg 65 yrs & median duration of diabetes of 6 yrs
- 80% of them reported using Rx hypoglycemic medication.
- Primary end-point = change in glycosylated hemoglobin (GH) at 3 months

Mackenzie T, Leary L, Brooks WB. The effect of an extract of green and black tea on glucose control in adults with type 2 diabetes mellitus: double-blind randomized study. 1: *Metabolism.* 2007 Oct;56(10):1340–4. Dept Community & Family Medicine, Dartmouth Med School

Black & Green Tea Extract: No effect on Type 2 diabetics –2

- After 3 months, mean changes in GH were not significantly different between study arms.
- We did not find a hypoglycemic effect of extract of GT & BT in adults w/ type 2 diabetes mellitus.

Mackenzie T, Leary L, Brooks WB. The effect of an extract of green and black tea on glucose control in adults with type 2 diabetes mellitus: double-blind randomized study. 1: *Metabolism*. 2007 Oct;56(10):1340–4. Dept Community & Family Medicine, Dartmouth Med School

Long-term Tea Intake Is Associated with a Reduced Risk of Type 2 Diabetes in the Elderly

- Mediterranean Islands Study (MEDIS)—health & nutrition survey to evaluate bio-clinical, lifestyle, behavioral, & dietary characteristics of 1190 elderly men & women living in the Mediterranean islands.
- Ca. 50% participants reported they consumed tea at least once weekly (mean intake: 1.6 ± 1.1 cups/day) for at least past 30 yrs.
- Green & black tea were predominantly consumed (98%).
- Moderate tea consumption (1–2 cups/d) assoc. w/ 70% reduced risk of diabetes, regardless of age, sex, body mass, smoking status, physical activity, & dietary habits.
- Results suggest that long-term moderate tea consumption is assoc. w/ decrease in fasting plasma glucose concentrations & lower prevalence of type 2 diabetes in elderly persons living in Mediterranean islands.

Panagiotakos DB, Lionis C, Zeimbekis A, et al. Long-term tea intake is associated with reduced prevalence of (type 2) diabetes mellitus among elderly people from Mediterranean Islands: MEDIS Epidemiological Study. *Yonsei Med J*. 2009;50(1): 31–38.

Pilot Trial: Black Tea Has Little Effect on CVD Risk Factors—1

- BACKGROUND: Effects of black tea (BT) use on CV risk factors have been inconsistent in previous RCTs, all of which have been limited to a few weeks.
- METHODS: Pilot parallel-design RCT
- N= 31 adults aged 55+ yrs w/ either diabetes or 2 other CV risk factors but no established clinical CVD.

- Participants randomized to drink 3 glasses daily of either a standardized BT or H20 for 6 months, CV risk factors measured at beginning & end of study.

Mukamal KJ, MacDermott K, Vinson JA, Oyama N, Manning WJ, Mittleman MA. A 6–month randomized pilot study of black tea and cardiovascular risk factors. *Am Heart J.* 2007 Oct;154(4):724.e1–6. Dept Medicine, Beth Israel Deaconess Medical Center, Harvard Medical School]

Pilot Trial: Black Tea Has Little Effect on CVD Risk Factors—2

- RESULTS: 3 dropouts, leaving 14 assigned to tea and 14 assigned to H20 eligible for analyses.
- We found no statistically significant effects of BT on CV biomarkers, (e.g., lipids, inflammatory markers, hemoglobin, adhesion molecules, prothrombotic & fibrinolytic parameters, and lipoprotein oxidizability).
- Assignment to BT did not appreciably influence BP
- HR among participants assigned to BT was marginally higher than among control participants at 3 months ($P = .07$) but not 6 months.
- CONCLUSIONS: BT did not appreciably influence any traditional or novel biomarkers of CV risk.
- Longer randomized trials needed to verify inverse assn of tea w/ risk of CVD seen in cohort studies & i.d. potential candidate mechanisms for such an assn.

Mukamal KJ, MacDermott K, Vinson JA, Oyama N, Manning WJ, Mittleman MA. A 6–month randomized pilot study of black tea and cardiovascular risk factors. *Am Heart J.* 2007 Oct;154(4):724.e1–6. Dept Medicine, Beth Israel Deaconess Medical Center, Harvard Medical School

Meta-analysis: Cocoa: Yes; Tea: No Effect on BP –1

- BACKGROUND: Epidemiological evidence suggests BP-lowering effects of cocoa & tea. Researchers conducted an m-a of RCTs to determine changes in systolic & diastolic BP due to ingestion of cocoa products or black & green tea.
- METHODS: 4 databases were searched from 1966–Oct 2006 for studies in parallel group or CO design w/ 10+ adults in whom BP was assessed before & after receiving cocoa products or black or green tea for 7+ days.

Taubert D, Roesen R, Schömig E. Effect of cocoa and tea intake on blood pressure: a meta-analysis. *Arch Intern Med.* 2007 Apr 9;167(7):626–34. Dept Pharmacol, Univ Hospital of Cologne, Cologne, Germany.

- RESULTS: 5 RCTs of cocoa administration involving total 173 subjects w/ median duration of 2 wks were included. After the cocoa diets, the pooled mean systolic and diastolic BP were -4.7 mm Hg (P = .002) and -2.8 mm Hg (P = .006) lower, respectively, compared w/ cocoa-free controls.
- 5 RCTs of tea consumption involving n= 343 w/ median duration of 4 wks were selected. The tea intake had no significant effects on BP. The estimated pooled changes were 0.4 mm Hg (95% CI, -1.3 to 2.2 mm Hg; P = .63) in systolic and -0.6 mm Hg (95% CI, -1.5 to 0.4 mm Hg; P = .38) in diastolic blood pressure compared with controls.
- CONCLUSION: Current randomized dietary studies indicate that consumption of foods rich in cocoa may reduce BP, while tea intake appears to have no effect.

Taubert D, Roesen R, Schömig E. Effect of cocoa and tea intake on blood pressure: a meta-analysis. *Arch Intern Med*. 2007 Apr 9;167(7):626–34. Dept Pharmacol, Univ Hospital of Cologne, Cologne, Germany.

Black Tea Reduces CRP & Inflammation −1

- BACKGROUND: Tea drinking appears to protect against the development of coronary heart disease (CHD), but the mediating pathways are uncertain. We studied the effects of 6 wks of black tea, or P, on platelet activation, C-reactive protein (CRP), total antioxidant status, and soluble (s) P-Selectin in a randomized double-blind trial.
- METHODS: 75 healthy non-smoking men (18–55 yrs) were randomized to black tea (N=37) or placebo (N=38) following a 4–week washout period during which they drank no tea, coffee or caffeinated beverages, but consumed caffeinated placebo tea.
- Bloods drawn after 6 weeks of treatment.

Steptoe A, Gibson EL, Vuononvirta R, Hamer M, Wardle J, Rycroft JA, Martin JF, Erusalimsky JD. The effects of chronic tea intake on platelet activation and inflammation: a double-blind placebo controlled trial. *Atherosclerosis*. 2007 Aug;193(2):277–82. Epub 2006 Sep 29. Dept of Epidemiology & Public Health, Univ College London, London, UK.

Black Tea Reduces CRP & Inflammation—2

RESULTS: Following treatment, tea group had fewer monocyte-platelet aggregates, neutrophil-platelet aggregates, total leukocyte-platelet aggregates, and lower plasma CRP than P group. There were no differences in total AO status or soluble P-Selectin.

CONCLUSIONS:
- Chronic tea consumption reduces platelet activation & plasma CRP in healthy men.
- Effects cannot be attributed to observer bias or lifestyle confounders.
- These effects of tea may contribute to sustained CV health.

Steptoe A, Gibson EL, Vuononvirta R, Hamer M, Wardle J, Rycroft JA, Martin JF, Erusalimsky JD. The effects of chronic tea intake on platelet activation and inflammation: a double-blind placebo controlled trial. *Atherosclerosis*. 2007 Aug;193(2):277–82. Epub 2006 Sep 29. Dept of Epidemiology & Public Health, Univ College London, London, UK.

Vascular Benefits of Green Tea Consumption: A Review

In addition to endothelial function, green tea catechins have an impact on CVD risk by lowering cholesterol & increasing insulin sensitivity.

ABSTRACT: The health benefits of green tea (Camellia sinensis) catechins are becoming increasingly recognized. Amongst the proposed benefits are the maintenance of endothelial function and vascular homeostasis and an associated reduction in atherogenesis and CVD risk. The mounting evidence for the influential effect of green tea catechins on vascular function from epidemiological, human intervention and animal studies is subject to review, together with exploration of the potential mechanistic pathways involved. Epigallocatechin-3–gallate, one of the most abundant and widely studied catechins found in green tea, will be prominent in the present review. Since there is a substantial inconsistency in the published data with regards to the impact of green tea catechins on vascular function, evaluation and interpretation of the inter- and intra-study variability is included. In conclusion, a positive effect of green tea catechins on vascular function is becoming apparent. Further studies in animal and cell models using physiological concentrations of catechins and their metabolites are warranted in order to gain some insight into the physiology and molecular basis of the observed beneficial effects.

Br J Nutr. 2009 Dec;102(12):1790–802. doi: 10.1017/S0007114509991218. Green tea (Camellia sinensis) catechins and vascular function. Moore RJ, Jackson KG, Minihane AM. Source: Department of Food Biosciences, University of Reading, Whiteknights, Reading, UK.

Antiatherosclerotic Effect

In a small randomized, placebo-controlled, double-blind clinical trial on 30 healthy male smokers, Japanese researchers gave groups of 10 men the following doses of green tea catechins (extracted from green tea): 0 mg (control group), 80 mg (medium-dose group), or 580 mg (high-dose group) for 2 weeks. Endothelial-dependent & independent vasodilatation (expanding of blood vessels) was investigated by measuring forearm blood flow (FBF)

- FBF response to acetylcholine significantly increased at 2 h & 1 & 2 wks after GTC intake in high-dose group, but no increase was observed in other groups. FBF responses to sodium nitroprusside did not alter in any group at any time point.
- A significant increase in plasma nitric oxide (NO) & decrease in asymmetrical dimethylarginine, malondealdehyde and 4–hydroxynonenal, C-reactive protein, monocyte chemotactic protein-1, and soluble CD40 ligand levels were detected after chronic consumption of high-dose GTC.
- CONCLUSIONS: GTC have antiatherosclerotic effects on dysfunctional vessels in smokers through increasing level of NO & reducing oxidative stress.

Oyama J, Maeda T, Kouzuma K, et al. Green tea catechins improve human forearm endothelial dysfunction and have antiatherosclerotic effects in smokers. Circ J. 2010 Feb 4:1–11.

Potential Chemopreventive (Anticancer) Effects of Green Tea

To date, pharmacological, clinical and epidemiological research has shown that the consumption of green tea, particularly long term, appears to have a risk-reducing effect on the following types of cancers: gastrointestinal (GI), oral, breast, prostate, liver, lung, and others. The discussion below provides the various levels of supporting evidence.

Review: Insufficient Evidence to Support GT Consumption for Cancer Prevention

- 675 articles retrieved from lit searches:
- 51 studies met criteria for this review:
- 1 RCT
- 23 prospective cohort studies
- 27 retrospective case-control studies
- The 51 studies included 1,236,687 participants from 5 countries & were published from 1985 to 2008.

- Conclusion: consumption of GT appears to be safe at moderate, regular, & habitual use & can be seen as a healthy addition to the human diet.
- However, "there is insufficient and conflicting evidence to give any firm recommendations regarding green tea consumption for cancer prevention."

Boehm K, Borrelli F, Ernst E, et al. Green tea (Camellia sinensis) for the prevention of cancer (review). Cochrane Database Syst Rev. 2009, Issue 3. Art. No.: CD005004. DOI: 10.1002/14651858.CD005004.pub2.

EGCG & GT Catechins: "United They Work, Divided They Fall"

- Polyphenon E® (Poly E; Polyphenon Pharma; New York, New York) = a pharmaceutical-grade form of GT made of at least 5 catechins (epicatechin, gallocatechin gallate, epigallocatechin, epicatechin gallate, & EGCG).
- Poly E is being used in clinical trials at NCI to evaluate benefits of GT consumption in humans.
- Clinical evidence suggests that Poly E is more bioavailable than is EGCG alone & that combinations of chemopreventive agents, such as Poly E, "may be superior to such agents used singly."

Bode AM, Dong ZA. Epigallocatechin 3–gallate and green tea catechins: united they work, divided they fall. *Cancer Prev Res.* Jun 2009. 2(6):514–517. Perspective on Fu et al. 2009

Green Tea & Cancer Prevention Systematic Review

- 48 clinical studies (1984–2008): incl 42 epidemiological studies, 1 Phase 1 trial, 4RCTs, & 1 M-A.
- 60% judged good; 40% fair.
- Cancer types: gastrointestinal (incl. oral, esophageal, stomach, pancreatic, liver, biliary duct & colorectal), reproductive (incl. breast, prostate, endometrial, & ovarian), lung, urinary, & leukemia.
- 58% studies suggested l-t consumption of GT may reduce risk of certain cancers, esp. most GI cancers.
- Women may benefit more than men from GT drinking but beneficial effects are not consistent across all studies.
- No severe adverse effects reported.

- While some epidemiological studies demonstrated protective effects of GT consumption, these findings were not confirmed by other studies covered in this review.

Liu J, Xing J, Fei Y. Green tea (Camellia sinensis) and cancer prevention: a systematic review of randomized trials and epidemiological studies. *Chinese Med.* 2008; 3:12–18.

Mayo EGCG Anticancer Review—1

- Derivatives of green tea (GT), particularly EGCG, have been proposed to have anticarcinogenic properties based on preclinical, observational, & clinical trial data.
- To summarize, clarify, & extend current knowledge, Mayo conducted comprehensive search of databases regarding chemopreventive potential of EGCG
- EGCG functions as an AO, preventing oxidative damage in healthy cells, but also as an antiangiogenic agent, preventing tumors from developing a blood supply needed to grow larger.
- Furthermore, EGCG may stimulate apoptosis in cancerous cells by negatively regulating the cell cycle to prevent continued division.
- Finally, EGCG exhibits antibacterial activity, which may be implicated in prevention of gastric cancer.

Carlson JR, Bauer BA, Vincent A, Limburg PJ, Wilson T. Reading the tea leaves: anticarcinogenic properties of (-)-epigallocatechin-3–gallate. *Mayo Clin Proc.* Jun 2007;82(6):725–732.

Mayo EGCG Anticancer Review—2

- Although in vitro research of anticancer properties of EGCG seems promising, many diverse & unknown factors may influence its in vivo activity in animals & humans.
- Some epidemiological studies suggest that GT compounds could protect against cancer, but existing data is inconsistent, & limitations in study design hinder full interpretation and generalizability of the published observational findings.
- Several RCTs w/ GT derivatives are ongoing, & further research should help to clarify the clinical potential of EGCG for chemoprevention and/ or chemotherapy applications.

Carlson JR, Bauer BA, Vincent A, Limburg PJ, Wilson T. Reading the tea leaves: anticarcinogenic properties of (-)-epigallocatechin-3–gallate. *Mayo Clin Proc.* Jun 2007;82(6):725–732.

THE SOUL & SPIRIT OF TEA

Green Tea Consumption May Decrease the Risk of Gastric Cancer in Women [Pooled Analysis of 6 Cohort Studies]

- Total of 3,577 gastric cancer cases (2,495 men; 1,082 women) were diagnosed in a total of 219,080 subjects (100,479 men; 118,601 women) over 2,285,968 person-years of follow-up.
- Pooled analysis showed significant decrease in gastric cancer risk only in women in highest category of GT consumption (at least 5 cups / day).
- This decreased risk was also observed in non-smokers or those that never smoked and for distal gastric cancer.

Inoue M, Sasazuki S, Wakai K, et al. Green tea consumption and gastric cancer in Japanese: a pooled analysis of six cohort studies. *Gut.* 2009 Oct;58(10): 1323–1332

Meta-Analysis: Green Tea & Stomach Cancer

- 13 epidemiologic studies
- In M-A of case-control studies, GT was shown to have a preventive effect on stomach cancer using adjusted data.
- In M-A of recent cohort studies, highest GT consumption was shown to significantly increase stomach cancer risk using crude data, but no significant assn b/t them was seen when using the adjusted data.
- Unlike case-control studies, no preventive effect on stomach cancer was seen for highest GT consumption in M-A of recent cohort studies.

Myung SK, Bae WK, Oh SM, et al. Green tea consumption and risk of stomach cancer: a meta-analysis of epidemiologic studies. *Int J Cancer.* 2009;124:670–677.

GT Catechins in Lung Cancer

- Rat trial using aerolized Polyphenon E mixture from GT.
- Reduced rate of tumorigenesis in mice w/ lung cancer.

Fu H, He J, Mei F, et al. Anti-lung cancer effect of epigallocatechin-3–gallate is dependent on its presence in a complex mixture (polyphenon E). *Cancer Prev Res.* 2009;2:531–537.

Green Tea & Lung Cancer

- In summary, there is only ltd evidence from epidemiological studies that GT is protective against lung cancer among smokers.

- In most of epidemiol studies, GT exposure was w/in 5 yrs of interview or follow-up, which would coincide w/ the induction period & latent period of lung cancer.
- CONCLUSION: The review suggests that regular intake of GT at high levels (>3 cups/d) may offer protection against tobacco carcinogens for smokers, provided that the duration of GT consumption is sufficiently long to cover the smoking period.
- For epidemiol studies, improvement in measuring GT intake is required to confirm the chemopreventive effect of GT observed in in vitro, animal, and human trials.

Liang W, Binns C, Jian L, Lee A. Does the consumption of green tea reduce the risk of lung cancer among smokers?. *eCAM*. 2007;4(1):17–22.

Green Tea Reduces Death Risk from Pneumonia in Japanese Women

- Design: Population-based cohort study, w/ follow-up from 1995 to 2006.
- Participants were National Health Insurance beneficiaries in Japan (19,079 men & 21,493 women aged 40–79 yrs).
- Results: Over 12 yrs of follow-up, we documented 406 deaths from pneumonia.
- In women, the multivariate hazard ratios of death from pneumonia that were associated w/ different frequencies of GT consumption were 1.00 (reference) for <1 cup/d, 0.59 for 1–2 cups/d, 0.55 for 3–4 cups/d, and 0.53 for 5 cups/d, respectively (P for trend: 0.008).
- In men, no significant association was observed.
- Conclusion: GT consumption was associated w/ lower risk of death from pneumonia in Japanese women.

Ikue Watanabe, Shinichi Kuriyama, Masako Kakizaki, Toshimasa Sone, Kaori Ohmori-Matsuda, Naoki Nakaya, Atsushi Hozawa and Ichiro Tsuji Green tea and death from pneumonia in Japan: the Ohsaki cohort study. *Am J Clin Nutr.* 2009;90(3):672–679. doi:10.3945/ajcn.2009.27599

GTE May Improve Short-term Outcomes in Persons w/ Oral Premalignant Lesions

- Persons w/ oral cancer have an overall 5–year survival rate of less than 50%.
- Overall, ca 2–3% of oral premalignant lesions (OPLs) develop into oral cancer but 17.5% of dysplastic & high-risk OPLs develop into cancer.
- R, DB, PC, n= 41 (39 completed), 12 wks

- GTE caps (THEA-FLAN 30 ARG) supplied by Ito En Ltd at 500 mg, 750 mg, 1000mg
- At 750 & 1000mg findings suggests that "potential GTE preventive activity may be linked mechanistically to the inhibition of angiogenesis, which is believed to promote carcinogenesis in premalignant conditions.
- Findings "support future trials of GTE monotherapy given for a longer period of time or in combination with a targeted agent such as an epidermal growth factor receptor inhibitor."

Tsao AS, Liu D, Martin J, et al. Phase II randomized, placebo-controlled trial of green tea extract in patients with high-risk oral premalignant lesions. *Cancer Prev Res.* 2009;2(11): 931–941.

Does Green Tea Prevent Oral Cancer?—1

- There have been no previous prospective epidemiologic studies of GT & oral cancer (OC).
- Researchers sought to prospectively examine relationship b/t GT consumption & the risk of OC by analyzing data from Japan Collaborative Cohort Study for Evaluation of Cancer Risk, a nationwide large-scale cohort study.
- 24 institutions in 45 areas of Japan
- 65,184 subjects (26,464 m; 38,720 f) studied to i.d. incidence of cancer.
- During mean 10.3 yr follow-up period, 37 OC cases were identified (22 = tongue; 15 = oral cavity). Of these 37, 20 subjects died (13 from OC & 7 from other causes).

Ide R, Fujino Y, Hoshiyama Y, et al. A prospective study of green tea consumption and oral cancer incidence in Japan. *Ann Epidemiol.* 2007 Oct;17(10):821–826.

Does Green Tea Prevent Oral Cancer?—2

- Subjects who consumed 5+ cups/d had a reduced risk of OC compared w/ those who consumed >1 c/d.
- Overall, authors propose that GT consumption may prevent OC thru prevention of caries & periodontal disease.
- Present findings must be confirmed by larger scale studies, & additional epidemiol studies are needed to evaluate the assn b/t GT consumption & OC in Japan.

Ide R, Fujino Y, Hoshiyama Y, et al. A prospective study of green tea consumption and oral cancer incidence in Japan. *Ann Epidemiol.* 2007 Oct;17(10):821–826.

Review of EGCG in Colon Cancer Chemoprevention

- Green tea polyphenols, eg, EGCG, inhibit mutagenesis & proliferation.
- GTPs are relatively non-toxic, are low cost & can be taken orally or as a part of the daily diet.
- Epidemiol & laboratory studies have identified EGCG in GT as the most potent chemopreventive agent that can induce apoptosis & suppress the formation & growth of human cancers including colorectal cancers (CRC).

Kumar N, Shibata D, Helm J, Coppola D, Malafa M. Green tea polyphenols in the prevention of colon cancer. *Front Biosci.* 2007 Jan 1;12:2309–15. Div of Health Outcomes & Behavior, H. Lee Moffitt Cancer Center & Research Inst., Univ. So. Florida Coll Med, Tampa, FL

Meta-Analysis: GT Intake Assoc w/ Reduced Risk for Gynecologic Cancers

- PubMed search (from 1962 to Dec 2010) for English-language articles (with 1 exception) on epidemiologic studies evaluating tea intake & cancers of the ovary, endometrium, cervix, vagina, &/or vulva in humans.
- 17 epidemiologic studies have evaluated tea & ovarian cancer risk.
- Overall, authors report that in their critical review & M-A of published studies from observational data, GT intake is assoc. w/ decreases of 32% for ovarian cancer risk & 23% for endometrial cancer risk.
- The strong experimental evidence for the antitumor, antiviral, & immunomodulatory effects of GT catechins on HPV-positive cells & tumors supports an underlying mechanism for GT & protection against genital cancers.

Butler LM, Wu AH. Green and black tea in relation to gynecologic cancers. *Mol Nutr Food Res.* 2011 Jun;55(6):931–940.

Green Tea May Be Useful at Preventing Prostate Cancer

- It has become evident over time that standardized GT polyphenols should be used, as opposed to GT infusions, for interventional purposes to ensure the content of polyphenols being investigated.
- Evidence collected thus far on effects of GT polyphenols on PC prevention & treatment "suggests that green tea may be a promising agent for PC chemoprevention and further clinical trials of participants at risk of PC or early stage PC are warranted."

Johnson JJ, Bailey HH, Mukhtar H. Green tea polyphenols for prostate cancer chemoprevention: a translational perspective. *Phytomed.* 2010;17: 3–13.

Green Tea is Associated with Lower Risk of Advanced Prostate Cancer –1

- The incidence of prostate cancer (PC) is much lower in Asian than Western populations. Since environmental factors such as dietary habits may play a major role in the causation of PC & the high consumption of GT in Asian populations, this low incidence may be partly due to effects of GT.
- The JPHC Study (Japan Public Health Center-based Prospective Study) was established in 1990 for cohort I and in 1993 for cohort II.
- N= 49,920 men (40–69 yrs) who completed a questionnaire that included their GT consumption habit at baseline & were followed until the end of 2004.
- During this time, 404 men were newly diagnosed with PC, of whom 114 had advanced cases, 271 were localized, and 19 were of an undetermined stage.

Kurahashi N, Sasazuki S, Iwasaki M, Inoue M, Tsugane S; JPHC Study Group. Green tea consumption and prostate cancer risk in Japanese men: a prospectivstudy. *Am J Epidemiol*. 2008 Jan 1;167(1):71–7. Epub 2007 Sep 29. Epidemiol & Prevention Div, Research Center for Cancer Prevention & Screening, National Cancer Center, Tokyo, Japan

Green Tea is Associated with Lower Risk of Advanced Prostate Cancer—2

- Green tea was not associated with localized PC.
- However, GT consumption was associated with a dose-dependent decrease in the risk of advanced PC. The multivariate relative risk was 0.52 for men drinking 5+ cups/day compared with less than 1 cup/day (= 0.01).
- GT may be associated with a decreased risk of advanced prostate cancer.

Kurahashi N, Sasazuki S, Iwasaki M, Inoue M, Tsugane S; JPHC Study Group. Green tea consumption and prostate cancer risk in Japanese men: a prospectivstudy. *Am J Epidemiol*. 2008 Jan 1;167(1):71–7. Epub 2007 Sep 29. Epidemiol & Prevention Div, Research Center for Cancer Prevention & Screening, National Cancer Center, Tokyo, Japan

Green Tea & Lycopene Protect Against Prostate Cancer—1

- First epidemiological study examining the joint effects of tea drinking & lycopene (L) intake on prostate cancer (PC) risk.

- Prostate cancer patients (n = 130 men, 45+ years) & controls (n = 274 men w/ no history of cancer) recruited from Zhejiang Province area of China between 2001–2002.
- A comprehensive food-frequency questionnaire determined habitual frequencies & quantities of food consumed, etc.
- Compared with the controls, PC patients tended to have higher body mass indices, a greater family history of prostate cancer, drink less tea, and eat fewer fruits & vegetables.

Jian L, Lee AH, Binns CW. Tea and lycopene protect against prostate cancer. *Asia Pac J Clin Nutr.* 2007;16(suppl 1):453–457.

Green Tea & Lycopene Protect Against Prostate Cancer—2

- PC risk decreased w/ increasing intakes of GT; similar effects were observed w/ increasing intakes of L.
- Protective effect of L & GT combined was synergistic (P < 0.01).
- No significant differences in physical activity were found between the cases and the controls.

Jian L, Lee AH, Binns CW. Tea and lycopene protect against prostate cancer. *Asia Pac J Clin Nutr.* 2007;16(suppl 1):453–457.

GT does not lower risks of pancreatic cancer

- 292 pancreatic cancer deaths reviewed after baseline 13 yrs prior
- In men & women combined, the relative risk was 1.23 for participants who consumed 7 or more cups of GT/d compared w/ those who consumed less than 1 cup/d
- No significant trend in risk reduction was noted with increasing consumption of GT.
- We found no inverse association between cups of GT consumed per day & risk of pancreatic cancer in either men or women.

Lin Y, Kikuchi S, Tamakoshi A, Green tea consumption and the risk of pancreatic cancer in Japanese adults. *Pancreas.* 2008 Jul;37(1):25–30.

Japanese Study Demonstrates Inverse Correlation between Green Tea Consumption and Hematologic Malignancies

- Based on Ohsaki study 2006
- During 326,012 person-years of follow-up (154,348 person-years for men; 171,664 person-years for women).

- 157 hematologic malignancies documented (88 men, 69 women)
- 119 cases of lymphoid neoplasms
- 36 cases of myeloid neoplasms (bone marrow, spine, or white blood cells).
- Authors found a significant inverse association b/t GT tea consumption & risk of hematologic malignancies.
- GT consumption associated w/ lower risk of hematologic malignancies.
- Since the lower risk was obvious only in group consuming 5 or more cups of GT/d, "the preventive effect of green tea consumption against hematologic malignancies seems to have a threshold effect rather than a dose-response effect."

Naganuma T, Kuriyama S, Kakizaki M, et al. Green tea consumption and hematologic malignancies in Japan. The Ohsaki Study. *Am J Epidemiol.* 2009;170(6): 730–738.

COGNITIVE AND OTHER MISCELLANEOUS BENEFITS OF GREEN TEA

Tea Consumption May Be Associated with Lowering Cognitive Impairment Risk

- Review of Chinese tea drinkers, mostly drinking black or oolong, some green tea.
- 55 yrs or older
- 2–yr study
- Regularly drinking tea, particularly black or oolong tea, is associated with a lower risk of cognitive impairment & decline.

Ng TP, Feng L, Niti M, Kua EH, Yap KB. Tea consumption and cognitive impairment and decline in older Chinese adults. *Am J Clin Nutr.* Jul 2008;88(1): 224–231.

Caffeine & Black Tea Reduce Parkinson's Disease Incidence?—1

- Data from Singapore Chinese Health Study, a population-based cohort Apr 1993–Dec 1998.
- Cohort = 63,257 ethnic Chinese, 45–75 yrs, residing in government-built housing estates.
- Participants completed food frequency questionnaire listing 165 food items or groups of commonly-consumed Chinese foods.
- Authors developed a food-nutrient database providing nutrient levels of 96 components/ 100g of cooked food & beverages.
- Mean daily intake of caffeine & other nutrients for each subject was computed.

- Cigarette smoking also assessed.
- Subjects reported new cases of Parkinson's disease.
- Approximately 50% of the subjects drank tea at least once/wk, w/ approx.1/3rd drinking only GT, 1/3rd drinking only BT, & 1/3rd both types of tea.

Tan LC, Koh W-P, Yuan J-M, et al. Differential effects of black versus green tea on risk of Parkinson's disease in the Singapore Chinese Health Study. *Am J Epidemiol.* March 1, 2008;167(5):553–560.

Caffeine & Black Tea Reduce Parkinson's Disease Incidence?—2

- But, in this cohort coffee = main source of caffeine exposure, with 70% of the population drinking coffee on a daily basis. Total caffeine intake exhibited a significant, dose-dependent inverse association w/ PD risk
- The greater the caffeine intake, the lower the risk of PD. The caffeine content in coffee was responsible for its effect.
- In contrast, BT consumption was associated w/ reduced risk, irrespective of the total caffeine intake or cigarette smoking.
- There was no assn betw/ GT consumption & PD Parkinson's disease risk.
- Subjects with high intake of both caffeine and BT had lowest risk of developing PD.
- None of the other macro- and micronutrients in any of the consumed foods or beverages had a strong dietary influence on development of PD.

Tan LC, Koh W-P, Yuan J-M, et al. Differential effects of black versus green tea on risk of Parkinson's disease in the Singapore Chinese Health Study. *Am J Epidemiol.* March 1, 2008;167(5):553–560.

Green Tea Shows Liver Protection in Systematic Review

- 10 qualified studies (8 from China, 1 Japan, 1 USA) w/ various outcomes, eg liver cancer, cirrhosis & fatty liver disease
- 1989–Dec 2007
- Study designs differed: 4 RCTs, 2 cohort, 1 case-control & 3 cross-sectional studies.
- The heterogeneity in study design, outcomes, cofounders & amount of tea consumption precluded further meta-analysis.
- 8 studies showed a significant protective role of GT against various liver diseases.

THE SOUL & SPIRIT OF TEA

- Also, the other 2 studies also showed the protective tendency of GT against liver disease.
- Conclusion: An increased consumption of GT may reduce the risk of liver disease.

Jin X, Zheng RH, Li YM. Green tea consumption and liver disease: a systematic review. *Liver Int.* 2008 May 14. Digestive Department, First Affiliated Hospital, Medical School, Zhejiang Univ, Zhejiang, China.

Association b/t Coffee & GT Consumption & Liver Cancer Risk by Hepatitis Virus Infection Status

- N = 68,975 persons, 40–69 yrs from 6 public health centers throughout Japan in 1993–1994.
- Analysis restricted to subjects completing questionnaire, providing blood sample, no history of LC = 18,815.
- Results suggest that, regardless of HBV or HCV infection status, coffee consumption may reduce the risk of liver cancer, & GT consumption may not reduce risk of LC.
- The mechanism responsible for this difference in risk is unclear.
- Small numbers means results may be due to chance.

Inoue M, Kurahashi N, Iwasaki M, et al. Effect of coffee and green tea consumption on the risk of liver cancer: cohort analysis by hepatitis virus infection status. *Cancer Epidemiol Biomarkers Prev.* 2009;18(6): 1746–1753.

GTE Does Not Adversely Affect Liver Function or CVD Risk

- PC parallel safety trial
- N = 33; 3 wks
- 6 capsules/d day (2 before each principal meal) containing GTE (= 714 mg/d polyphenols) or placebo.
- Biomarkers of liver function and CVD risk (including BP & plasma lipids) were unaffected by GT polyphenol consumption.

Frank J, George TW, Lodge JK, Rodriguez-Mateos AM, Spencer JP, Minihane AM, Rimbach G. Daily consumption of an aqueous green tea extract supplement does not impair liver function or alter cardiovascular disease risk biomarkers in healthy men. *J Nutr.* 2009 Jan;139(1):58–62.

USP Proposed Caution Green Tea Concentrated DS

- In June 2007 United States Pharmacopeia proposed a "caution" not a "warning" for labels & therapeutic monographs on USP grade concentrated GT Extracts sold as Dietary Supplements.
- USP was concerned about potential liver problems associated w/ concentrated levels of catechins, based on adverse reaction reports.
- This is despite data suggesting liver benefit for GT when consumed as traditional infusion or beverage.
- USP proposal did not apply to GT infusions or beverages.
- April 2009 USP withdraws proposal, due in part because most of science & clinical evidence supports liver safety of GT.

Review: Control of Obesity & Diabetes Among Health Benefits of Green Tea

- 105 English peer-reviewed articles reviewed:
- Re GT's health benefits in humans & animals, absorption of metal ions & drug-metabolizing enzymes, antioxidation & inhibition of oxidative stress, carbohydrate metabolism & diabetes mellitus, & AEs.
- Tea catechins, especially EGCG, appear to have antiobesity and antidiabetic effects. Recent data from human studies indicate that consumption of GT or GTEs may help reduce body wt, mainly body fat, by increasing postprandial thermogenesis & fat oxidation.
- 1 study of 6 overwt men given 300 mg EGCG daily for 2 d suggests that EGCG alone has potential to increase fat oxidation in men & may thereby contribute to antiobesity fx of GT.
- Harmful fx of too much tea are mainly due to its caffeine content, presence of aluminum, & fx of tea polyphenols on iron bioavailability.
- Conclusion: Long-term consumption of tea catechins could be beneficial to high-fat diet-induced obesity & type 2 diabetes & could reduce risk for CVD.

Chacko SM, Thambi PT, Kuttan R, Nishigaki I. Beneficial effects of green tea: a literature review. *Chinese Medicine*. 2010;5:13.

Green Tea Enhances Exercise-Induced Abdominal Fat Loss

- R, DB, PC, 2 centers
- 2–wk screening; 12wk tmt
- N = 128 men/women (avg. 48 yrs); waist circumference ≥87 cm, women; ≥90 cm, men; mean BMI = ~32

- Beverage containing ~625 mg catechins or a control (ca 5–10 cups) [ea. = 39 mg caffeine]
- Increased activity level, w/ goal of achieving ≥180 min/ wk of moderate-intensity physical activity, and to attend at least 3 supervised exercise sessions / wk
- Compliance w/ bev & exercise = same for both groups.
- At week 12, catechin grp tended to have greater loss of body wt than control grp (P=0.079).
- 2 groups did not differ in % changes in fat mass or intra-abdominal fat.
- However, both total abdominal fat area and abdominal subcutaneous fat area decreased more at wk 12 in catechin group.

Maki KC, Reeves MS. Farmer M, et al. Green tea catechin consumption enhances exercise-induced abdominal fat loss in overweight and obese adults. J Nutr. February 2009;139(2): 264–270.

Tea & Obesity Fat Oxidation

- Human studies investigating the metabolic effects EGCG alone are absent.
- R, DB,PC, CO
- N=6 overweight men
- Dose: 300 mg EGCG/d for 2d.
- Fasting & postprandial changes in energy expenditure (EE) & substrate oxidation were assessed.
- RESULTS: Resting EE did not differ significantly between EGCG & P treatments, although during 1st postprandial monitoring phase, respiratory quotient (RQ) values were significantly lower with EGCG compared to P.
- CONCLUSIONS: EGCG alone has the potential to increase fat oxidation in men & may thereby contribute to anti-obesity effects of GT.
- More studies with a greater sample size and a broader range of age & BMI are needed to define the optimum dose.

Boschmann M, Thielecke F. The effects of epigallocatechin-3–gallate on thermogenesis and fat oxidation in obese men: a pilot study. J Am Coll Nutr. 2007 Aug;26(4):389S-395S. Univ Medicine Berlin, Charité Campus Buch, Franz-Volhard-Center for Clinical Research, Berlin, Germany.

Green Tea Reduces Body Fat & Related Conditions in Japan Trial

- Japanese women & men with visceral fat-type obesity were recruited for the trial.

- After a 2–week diet run-in period, a 12–week DB MC trial was performed
- Subjects (n=240; catechin group, n = 123, control group n = 117).
- Dose: GT containing 583 mg of catechins (catechin group) or 96 mg of catechins (control group)/d.
- The subjects instructed to maintain their usual dietary intake & normal physical activity.
- RESULTS: Data were analyzed using per-protocol samples of decreases in body weight, BMI, body fat ratio, body fat mass, waist circumference, hip circumference, visceral fat area, & subcutaneous fat area were found to be greater in catechin group than control group.
- A greater decrease in systolic blood pressure (SBP) was found in catechin group vs control group for subjects whose initial SBP was 130 mm Hg or higher.
- LDL cholesterol was also decreased to a greater extent in the catechin group.
- No adverse effect.
- CONCLUSION: The continuous ingestion of GTE high in catechins led to a reduction in body fat, SBP, and LDL cholesterol, suggesting that the ingestion of high catechin GTE contributes to decrease in obesity & CVD risks.

Nagao T, Hase T, Tokimitsu I. A green tea extract high in catechins reduces body fat and cardiovascular risks in humans. *Obesity*. 2007 Jun;15(6):1473–83. Health Care Food Research Laboratories, Kao Corporation, Tokyo, Japan

Green Tea Combo in Weight Loss

- R, DB, PC clinical trial.
- N = 105 subjects (5 withdrawn consent, 2 drop-outs not related to study preparation).
- INTERVENTION: 2 tablets/meal concept supposed to generate a "psychological" therapy-like approach during 12 wks supported by measured physical activity. The tablets 1 (1 hr before meals, comprises extracts of Asparagus, Green tea, Black tea, Guarana, Mate and Kidney beans) and 2 (taken half hr after meals, comprises extracts of Kidney bean pods, Garcinia cambogia, and Chromium yeast) are taken 2x daily w/ 2 main meals.
- RESULTS: A significant change of the Body Composition Improvement Index (BCI) was observed in active extract group compared to P (p = 0.012). Weight, BMI, waist-to-hip ratio was not statistically different between groups. Body fat loss was greater in active group (p = 0.011)

compared to placebo. A wt loss parameter corrected for exercise was introduced & found to be higher in active group (p = 0.046) than in P, meaning that formula was more efficacious, due to a concurrently performed exercise program—a recommended strategy for lifestyle modification.

- CONCLUSIONS: A significant change of the BCI & decrease in body fat was statistically significant in active extract subjects compared to P.
- Some outcome measures, eg weight & BMI, failed to produce significant difference between groups.

Opala T, Rzymski P, Pischel I, Wilczak M, Wozniak J. Efficacy of 12 weeks supplementation of a botanical extract-based weight loss formula on body weight, body composition and blood chemistry in healthy, overweight subjects—a randomised double-blind placebo-controlled clinical trial. *Eur J Med Res.* 2006 Aug 30;11(8):343–50. Dept of Mother's and Child's Health, Poznan University of Medical Science, Poznan, Poland.

MonCam® Green Tea Extract (w/ GreenSelect® Phytosome) Shows Activity in Weight Loss & Obesity-related Risk Factors

- N=100 100 overwt subjects (20–40% over ideal wt; 44 women, 56 men, 25–60 yrs); MC, 90 d
- 150 mg/ d Monoselect Camellia® (MonCam; Velleja Research; Italy), oral preparation containing highly bioavailable standardized GTE complexed w/phospholipids (GreenSelect® Phytosome; Indena; Italy), plus a hypo-caloric diet, compared w/ hypo-caloric diet alone.
- Diet + MonCam resulted in statistically significant wt loss, positively influencing lipid profiles as demonstrated by plasma total cholesterol & triglycerides.
- Grp A (diet-only) had avg. body wt of 95.086 kg @ baseline & 90.49 kg @ 90 days. Group B (MonCam + diet) had avg wt of 96.142 kg @ baseline & 82.298 kg @ 90 days.

Di Pierro F, Borsetto Menghi AM, Barreca A, Lucarelli M, Calandrelli A. GreenSelect® Phytosome as an adjunct to a low-calorie diet for treatment of obesity: a clinical trial. *Altern Med Rev.* 2009;14(2): 154–160.

Systematic Review of Green Tea Catechins & Caffeine on Anthropometric Variables

- 15 trials (n = 1243) met the inclusion criteria.
- Of these, 7 trials (n = 600) evaluated GT catechins w/ caffeine.

- Conclusion: "ingestion of green tea catechins w/ caffeine may positively affect BMI, body weight, & waist circumference.
- However, the magnitude of effect over a median of 12 weeks is small and not likely clinically relevant."

Phung OJ, Baker WL, Matthews LJ, Lanosa M, Thorne A, Coleman CI. Effect of green tea catechins with or without caffeine on anthropometric measures: a systematic review and meta-analysis. *Am J Clin Nutr*. 2010 Jan;91(1): 73–81.

Herbs in Dermatology—Review

- Focus of review is on RCTs w/ botanicals in trtmt of acne, inflammatory skin diseases, skin infections, UV-induced skin damage, skin cancer, alopecia, vitiligo, & wounds.
- Studies w/ botanical cosmetics, bot drugs & bot food supplements.
- Nonclinical experimental research on botanicals was considered to ltd extent when it seemed promising for clinical use in near future.
- In acne therapy, Mahonia, tea tree oil, and Saccharomyces may have the potential to become standard treatments.
- Mahonia, SJW, licorice & some traditional Chinese medicines appear promising for atopic dermatitis.
- Some plant-derived substances like dithranol and methoxsalen (8–methoxypsoralen) [in comb w/ UVA] are already accepted as standard treatments in psoriasis; Mahonia and Capsicum (capsaicin) are next candidates suggested by present evidence.
- Oral administration & topical application of antioxidant plant extracts (green & black tea, carotenoids, coffee, & many flavonoids from fruits & vegetables) can protect skin from UV-induced erythema, early aging, & irradiation-induced cancer.
- Hair loss and vitiligo are also traditional fields of application for botanicals. According to the number and quality of clinical trials with botanicals, the best evidence exists for the treatment of inflammatory skin diseases, i.e. atopic dermatitis and psoriasis.
- Many more controlled clinical studies are needed to determine efficacy & risks of plant-derived products in dermatology. Safety aspects, especially related to sensitization & photodermatitis, have to be considered.
- Therefore, clinicians should not only be informed of beneficial effects but also specific adverse effects of botanicals used for dermatologic disorders & cosmetic purposes.

Reuter J, Merfort I, Schempp CM. Botanicals in dermatology: an evidence-based review. *Am J Clin Dermatol*. 2010;11(4):247–67. Competence Center Skintegral,

Department of Dermatology, University Medical Center Freiburg, Freiburg, Germany.

Oral Green Tea Polyphenols Not Found to Prevent Skin Photoaging

- R, DB, PC, 2yrs
- N = 56 women 25 to 75 yrs w/ moderate-to-advanced skin photoaging
- 2 GTE caps /d; 99.5% caffeine-free GT caps = 250 mg polyphenols, incl 175 mg catechins
- Drop-out rate = ca 37–38% in both groups
- Conclusion: 2 yrs of supplementation w/ GTPs did not result in statistically significant changes in clinical or histological parameters of skin photoaging.

Janjua R, Munoz C, Gorell E, et al. A two-year, double-blind, randomized placebo-controlled trial of oral green tea polyphenols on the long-term clinical and histologic appearance of photoaging skin. *Dermatol Surg*. Jul 2009;35(7): 1057–1065.

Green & White Tea etc. in Skin Rejuvenation

- Test efficacy & tolerability of investigational study cream in rejuvenating facial skin.
- 3 ingredients: green & white teas, mangosteen, and pomegranate extract [Vitaphenol Skin Cream. La Jolla Spa MD, La Jolla CA] vs. P cream.
- N = 20 healthy females (35—65 yrs) w/ demonstrable facial wrinkling, achieving a Rao-Goldman wrinkle scale score of 2 or above
- applied Vitaphenol or P cream to randomized half of face 2x/d for 60 d & returned for follow-up after 2 wks
- Twice as many subjects indicated enhancement of skin texture (eg, reduction in pore size, roughness, & touch) w/ usage of Vitaphenol vs P.
- 41% of subjects preferred half of face that had been receiving Vitaphenol, while only 0.06% of subjects favored P side.
- Tests demonstrated avg improvement in skin smoothness of 1 mm3, whereas skin treated w/ P showed an avg decrease in smoothness or an increase in skin roughness of 0.9 mm3.
- CONCLUSION: The addition of 3 antioxidants, green & white teas, mangosteen, and pomegranate, have an additive effect to enhanced improvement of age-related changes in skin.

Hsu J, Skover G, Goldman MP. Evaluating the efficacy in improving facial photodamage with a mixture of topical antioxidants. *J Drugs Dermatol*. 2007 Nov;6(11):1141–8. Univ of California, San Diego

Green Tea Extract & Genital Warts

- 3–arm, R, DB, PC, 12 wks w/12–week treatment-free follow-up.
- SETTING: 28 hospitals & practices in Germany & Russia.
- N = 242 outpatients (125 men, 117 women) w/ 2–30 warts
- INTERVENTION: Topical application of Polyphenon E 10% Cream, Polyphenon E 15% Ointment, or P to all external genital warts 3 x/ d.
- RESULTS: For 15% ointment, 75% to 100% clearance in both ITT & per-protocol populations.
- For 10% cream, 53.8% males & 39.5% females achieved complete clearance. AEs observed in only 7.9% of patients, w/ no serious AEs or deaths reported. Local skin reactions were generally mild to moderate & resolved w/ continued treatment w/out sequelae.
- CONCLUSIONS: Polyphenon E 15% ointment, composed of a de-fined GTE, proved to be efficacious & safe for both genders in treatment of external genital warts.

Gross G, Meyer K-G, Pres H, Thielert C, Tawfik H, Mescheder A. A random-ized, double-blind, four-arm parallel-group, placebo-controlled Phase II/III study to investigate the clinical efficacy of two galenic formulations of Polyphenon(R) E in the treatment of external genital warts. *J Eur Acad Dermatol Venereol.* December 2007;21:1404–1412. Department of Dermatology and Venereology, Univ of Ros-tock, Rostock, Germany

Veregen®

- The 1st FDA-approved chemically-complex botanical drug in over 50 years!
- Chinese green tea, Japanese extract (Mitsui Norin), German company (Medigene) to US (Bradley Pharma)
- Active ingredient: "Sinecatechins" 15%; oint.
- Indication: External genital and perianal warts (Condylomata acumi-nata) in immunocompetent patients ≥18yrs of age.

GT Mixture & External Genital Warts

- Observational trial:
- N = 1005 men & women > or = 18 years w/ 2–30 EGWs used Polyphe-non E ointment 10% or Polyphenon E ointment 15% 3x/d until com-plete clearance of all EGWs or for max. 16 wks.
- Results: Total of 1004 pts evaluable for safety & 986 for efficacy; 838 completed treatment after 16 wks.
- Complete clearance of all EGWs was obtained in 53.6% (G10%)) and 54.9% (G15%)) of patients with Polyphenon E vs. vehicle (35.4%).

- Statistically significant differences in clearance rates appeared after 6 wks of active treatment.
- 2–fold higher chance of complete clearance under active treatment.
- Time to complete clearance was shorter w/ active treatment
- Recurrence rates during follow-up were low & similar across groups.
- Conclusion: Polyphenon E ointment is effective & well tolerated in treatment of EGWs.

Tatti S, Stockfleth E, Beutner KR, Tawfik H, Elsasser U, Weyrauch P, Mescheder A. Polyphenon E: a new treatment for external anogenital warts. *Br J Dermatol.* 2010 Jan;162(1):176–84. Epub 2009 Jul 27. The Hospital Clinicas, Universidad de Buenos Aires, Buenos Aires, Argentina.

Review: Green Tea & Bone Density

- Epidemiological evidence shows association betw/ tea consumption & prevention of age-related bone loss in elderly women & men.
- Ingestion of GT & GTC may be beneficial in mitigating bone loss of this population & decreasing their risk of OP fractures.
- Review describes fx of GT or its bioactive components on bone health, w/ an emphasis on (1) prevalence & etiology of OP; (2) role of oxidative stress & antioxidants in OP; (3) GT composition & bioavailability; (4) fx of GT & its activ`e components on osteogenesis, osteoblastogenesis, &osteoclastogenesis from human epidemiological, animal, & cell culture studies; (5) possible mechanisms explaining the osteoprotective effects of GT bioactive compounds; (6) other bioactive components in GT that benefit bone health; (7) a summary & future direction of GT & bone health research & translational aspects.
- In general, tea & its bioactive components might decrease risk of fracture by improving bone mineral density & supporting osteoblastic activities while suppressing osteoclastic activities.

Shen CL, Yeh JK, Cao JJ, Wang JS. Green tea and bone metabolism. *Nutr Res.* 2009 Jul;29(7):437–56. Department of Pathology, Texas Tech University Health Sciences Center, Lubbock, TX 79430–9097, USA. leslie.shen@ttuhsc.edu

TEA'S BENEFITS—CONCLUSION AND SUMMARY

- Modern pharmacological & clinical research on Tea is being conducted all over the world.
- Most of the research is focusing on GT.
- Research based on both infused T beverage & GTE as DS, particularly catechins.

- CV benefits continually supported along w/anticancer fix, esp. GI cancers.

ACKNOWLEDGMENTS

The author gratefully acknowledges the following persons who have assisted the author and/or the American Botanical Council in ways that made it possible for the information in this chapter to be compiled and edited. Profound gratitude is expressed to Scott Hoyt of Tea Dragon Films and co-author/co-editor of the book in which this chapter has been published, for his generous support of the American Botanical Council's nonprofit educational mission through his firm's underwriting of the Tea record in ABC's HerbMedPro database. Also, to Lori Glenn, managing editor of ABC's HerbClip publications and database, and to Jenny Perez, ABC's Educational Coordinator who assisted with the preparation of this manuscript.

REFERENCES

Roan S. L-theanine comes into focus. *Los Angeles Times*, May 4, 2009.

Chacko SM, Thambi PT, Kuttan R, Nishigaki I. Beneficial effects of green tea: a literature review. *Chinese Medicine*. 2010;5:13.

Bolling BW, Chen CY, Blumberg JB. Tea and health: preventive and therapeutic usefulness in the elderly? *Curr Opin Clin Nutr Metab Care*. 2009 Jan;12(1):42–8.

Appendix B

THE NINETY-NINE PLUS NAMES FOR TEA

Phil Cousineau

In the venerable tradition of giving mythic numbers to revered qualities and things, such as the legendary 99 names for snow among the
Inuit and Yupik, the reputed 99 names for *genius* in Yiddish, the 99
Most Beautiful Names for Allah in Islam, and 99 Real Names for God
in Hebrew, and 99 names for potatoes among the Irish, comes this
modest sampling of names for *tea* around the world. As the tea ma-
vens, Victor H. Mair and Erling Hoh, reveal in *The History of Tea*, there
is a remarkable continuity in the etymological history of the word.

> "Just as we can analyze the distribution of words for tea
> derived from Southern Min *te* as having traveled by sea (ini-
> tially carried by Dutch ships, then later by English ships)
> to Europe and America, so can we discern a pattern in the
> spread of words derived from *cha*. Namely, either they went
> overland from north and southwest China to bordering
> regions such as Tibet, or they went by sea in primarily Por-
> tuguese ships from Cantonese-speaking ports to countries
> where the Dutch and the British were not yet engaged in
> extensive trade."

If we follow the trade routes of tea as it spread around the globe, we see that it found a home everywhere it went, and in a profound sense also made those places feel like home. The grand story of the worldwide distribution of tea also reveals that the Beatles were right as rain when they sang about their beloved "cuppa." Wherever you can find a cup of tea feels like home:

"Sail me on a silver sun
Where I know that I'm free
Show me that I'm everywhere
And get me home for tea."

Afrikaans: tee

Albanian (Tosk Southern dialect): çaj

Arabic: chai or shai

Armenian (Western dialect): tey

Amharic (Ethiopia): shai

Arabic: shāy

Aramaic: chai

Assamese (India): sah

Australian English: tea, Billy tea (bush tea boiled in a tin can)

Azerbaijani: caj

Basque: tea

Belarusian: harbatu

Bengali/Bangla: cha

Bulgarian: chai

Byelorussin: garbata

Cambodian: dteuk dtai g'dao

Cantonese: caa (tshaa)

Cassubian (North-Central Poland): arbata

Catalan: té

Cebuano (Philippines): tsa

Chechen: chay

Chinese (Cantonese and Mandarin): cha

Croatian: caj (pronounced chai)

Czech: caj (pronounced cha-i)

Danish: te

Dutch: thee

English: tea

Esperanto: teo

Finnish (dialects): tee, sai, tsaiju, saiju or saikka

French: thé, tasse, tisane

Frisian: tee

Galician: té

Georgian: chai

German: der Tee

Greek: téïon, tsai

Haitian Creole: té

Hausa (Niger and Nigeria): Shayi

Hawaiian: ki

Hebrew: teh

Hindi: chai

Hmong daw: tshuaj yej

Hungarian: tea (plural: teak)

Icelandic: te

Indonesian: teh

Inuit: ti

Irish: tae

Iroquois: assin, ye, o la (black tea from illex vomica)

Italian: tè, cia

Japanese: o-cha, and variants matcha, sencha, hojicha

Kalaallisut (Greenland): tii

Kannada: chahā

Kazakh (Kazakhstan): shai

Khasi: sha

Kinyarwanda (Rwanda): icyayi

Konkaki (India): chya

Korean: ta, cha

Kurdish: çay

Kyrgyz: chai

Latin: thea

Latvian: teja

Lithuanian: arbata

Laotian: saa

Low Saxon: tei

Luxembourgish: Téi

Macedonian: chaj

Malay: teh

Malayam (India): Thēyila

Maltese: te

Maori: tī, tī raurau (tea leaves)

Marathi: chacha

Miwok Indian (Central Sierra): tij-y

Mongolian: cai

Mohawk: Kahentanawenhton (pronounced Gah-hehn'-da-nah-wenh'-don)

Moroccan (colloquial Arabic): ashay (green tea), atay (green tea)

Navajo: dei

Nepali: chiyā

Norwegian: te

Occitan (Old Provençal): tì

Oneida: athnekut

Pashto (Afghanistan, Iran): chay

Pawnee: kskiikaraaku', (green leaf)

Persian: chay, cha-i (colloquial)

Plautdietsch: (Mennonite German): tee, teebrat (tea tray)

Polish: herbata

Portuguese: cha (pronounced shah)

Punjabi: chah

Rapa Nui (Easter Island): ti, tetera (teapot)

Romanian: ceai

Romani (English gypsy): chao

Russian: chai

Sami (Scandanavian Arctic) deačča,

Scottish Gaelic: tì

Serbian: caj (pronounced chai)

Sindi: chahen

Sinhalese (Sri Lanka): thé, theepot (teapot)

Slovak and Slovenian: caj

Somali: shaah

Spanish: té

Swahili: chai

Swedish: te

Sylheti: sa

Tagalog/Filipino: tsaa

Tajik: choy

Tamil (Sri Lanka): theneer

Taiwanese Mandarin: tsha

Tatar: çäy

Telugu (India): theneeru

Thai: chah, chah yen (Thai iced tea)

Tibetan: cha, ja, pö-cha (butter tea), cha-nga-mo (sweet tea)

Timuca (Southeast American Indian): cassene ("black drink")

Tlingit (Northwest American Indian): cháayu

Turkish: çay

Ukrainian: chaj (pronounced chay)

Urdu (Pakestan): chai

Uzbek (Uzbekistan): choy

Vietnamese (North): che, Vietnamese (South): tra

Wolof (Senegal): achai (pronounced uh-chuy)

Welsh: te

Tok Pisin (Papua New Guinea): tea (liquid), lipti (leaves), kap bilong ti (tea-cup)

Xhhosa (South Africa): na

Yiddish: tey

Yoruba (West Africa): tee

Zulu (Southern Africa): itiye

List compiled by Phil Cousineau

Appendix C

THE WISDOM OF TEA[1]

James Norwood Pratt and Roy Fong

ROY FONG: Chinese people prize tea. But to us, tea is not just about how it tastes; tea is about how it feels. A perfect cup of tea leads to perfect timing. A perfect cup is a fusion of self and tea. Once you reach that point, you reach a perfect cup of tea.

JAMES NORWOOD PRATT: Yes, tea is timing and the interludes that are required. It is the result of someone who makes tea well, Roy. You can make that tea so it would have more or less aroma. It is your gongfu tea ritual style that brings out the depth, the quality of your Tie Guan Yin tea.

ROY: The art of gongfu style tea means working further, or practicing more. It is a simple term that people use for martial arts, but in this case, the work is always different. You never finish your gongfu training; there is always further work to do. You get to know the tea better as you get to know yourself better, and you continue to progress. Your practice gets to a point where you don't think about how

---

1. Excerpted from *The Meaning of Tea: A Tea Inspired Journey*, by Phil Cousineau and Scott Chamberlin Hoyt, New York, Talking Leaves Press, 2009. pp. 135–156.

to make the tea. You just make this personal connection with the tea, and then everything just happens. I never really think about measuring tea or deciding what to do next. I just make tea.

NORWOOD: Yes, after thirty years constantly making tea in this fashion, you can do it perfectly just about every time.

ROY: Well, you know perfection is an illusion and an elusive term. What is perfect today I am sure is not going to be perfect tomorrow. I don't really think of it that way. I don't think about making perfect tea, I just make tea and it happens. I suppose I could make it better, and obviously time does help. I've been doing this for thirty years because tea attracted me and it continues to allow me to grow. Somebody who has been doing it all their life may have it in their blood, but sometimes somebody from out of nowhere can see the flaws or other ideas or other avenues that just do not come to those who are actually doing this everyday. Somebody like me comes in with fresh ideas, and sometimes it does help. I don't know why I know these things, but to me it makes sense that I just approach the experts and speak to them.

THE IMPERIAL TEA COURT

Traditionally, you call your best tea the "monkey-picked," because it is supposed to flag your own personality, your outlook on life, your personality in tea, and your philosophy. Somebody who drinks monkey-picked tea is supposed to be able to tell, "Ah! this is monkey-picked!"

NORWOOD: There is a signature to tea. It is someone's calligraphy and allows you to recognize a person's particular tea.

ROY: Absolutely. That's what it is supposed to be, so you don't lightly call tea the "monkey-pick" because it is your name card. If you don't do it well, people will remember you for bad "monkey-picked" tea.

THE WISDOM OF TEA

ROY: If you want to think about *the wisdom of tea* or the *perfection* of tea, you can think of it this way. The Chinese believe that the universe is comprised of five elements: metal, wood, water, fire, and earth. Making perfect tea is an attempt to combine the five elements. If you combine them *eloquently and completely*, you create harmony, and, you may come very close to perfection. Metal is the mineral content in the soil that allows the plant to be molded and allows the plant to grow properly. The earth grows the plant and the earth makes the teapot, which makes the tea possible. Fire is the sun that makes everything grow; you heat the water with the fire on the pot. So the questions are: how much tea leaf? How much heat? How much water? How do you make the pot and what *kind* of pot? In this case, we are asking the water to revive the tea in the pot and bring it back to life. All of these things create an attempt to reach a kind of perfection each time that I make tea. Philosophically, I try to think this way so I can attempt to try to balance the five elements. Sometimes it all works out and you didn't even think about it. To me, it achieves such inner peace that I can't even describe it except to say that it is like a long bout of meditating.

NORWOOD: It creates harmony.

ROY: Yes. I remember when I first started to make gongfu style tea. It seemed like an hour flashed by in just a few moments. Thirty years later, I still have these moments of harmony. I am not a scholar or a philosopher. It doesn't happen often, but when it does, I think I've come close to a kind of harmony.

NORWOOD: Perhaps if we prepare ourselves as carefully as we prepare our tea, it would happen more often.

ROY: Perhaps—but the whole idea is to prepare tea without having to prepare tea. You don't measure your tea by measuring your tea; you don't measure your water by measuring your water. You do it all in such harmony that everything happens properly.

NORWOOD: You quoted your Chinese forefathers. Allow me to quote mine—Dr. Samuel Johnson, my Anglo-Saxon forefather—on this question. In his great English dictionary he defines tea time in a very Chinese way. "Tea time," he says, "is anytime tea is served." The English had not yet settled on a set hour, and for Johnson, in the 1700s, it was anytime that tea was served. Dr. Johnson was prepared to drink tea in quantities, and he had such a clear conscience and such a keen mind that I am convinced that it's the tea that helped bring us that dictionary.

ROY: There is a level of tea for everyone. If you want to be artistic, there is tea for you; if you want to be philosophical, there is tea for you—even for small children.

TEA AND THE SCHOLARS

NORWOOD: There was a young artist from Hong Zhu who visited me soon after you had made a tea gift to me. After he walked into the room, I was preparing it and he's smelled the *Longjing* (Dragon Well), and said, "Ah, for me that is an aroma that is always mingled with the smell of ink." That was because as his father and all of those scholars in Hong Zhu were practicing their calligraphy, they were also drinking their Dragon Well tea.

ROY: Hong Zhu is a magical place; it's always been the basket of civilization for China. Hong Zhu was the center for a lot of scholars, calligraphers, and painters; even a lot of the most famous court officials are from there. Fortunately, with tea it's easier. You can definitely take the approach, but you don't really have to go back there. In my experience with tea and Taoism, fortunately, it's rather easy. You have to directly experience it; you have to touch it, you have to feel it to experience it. But you also need to quietly allow it to happen and not be so conscious of form. When people have asked me about learning about tea, I must tell them that I feel like I am more the messenger than the teacher. The messenger shows you the door and you have to decide to open it or not. Nobody else can do that for you. Tea is that messenger. You don't have to say much. When you have opened the door enough times, you have experienced the Tao.

THE POWER OF METAPHOR

NORWOOD: The experience of tea itself is in a realm that no word has even entered. Therefore, you can only imply metaphor to speak of tea, as in poetry. To describe tea requires a poet of the appetites. First and alone, a poet can talk about the tea in the cup, but it's still talk— and talk is cheap. Tea is an experience and an experience is dear.

ROY: *It's as if the tea actually communicates with you.* The better you learn how to deal with tea, the better it rewards you. It tastes better. I am not aware of any teabag that has this kind of quality. With a well-made tea that really connects with you, you can almost feel the hard work and the care that went into the making. The more you drink and understand it, the more you appreciate it. This is a depth of value that cannot be purchased.

NORWOOD: What you are weighing is not just one pound of pedigree tea, which has been carefully nourished in Ang Shi county in Fujian, and very carefully manufactured to your specifications, but the care of that particular leaf. When it is handled respectfully, you have exactly that sense of harmony.

ROY: If you are a painter, you don't want to paint something that nobody wants. You want to paint something that is sought-after, because you are good at it. You want people to feel good looking at your work. To me, tea is like that. I can't draw a straight line. So tea is as close as I can get to the feeling of the painter. There are paintings that have been looked at for centuries, and you can try to figure out what the original intent of the artist was. Perhaps tea is easier because you can touch it and you can feel it. So you can sense the way tea talks to you. Whatever you do to tea, it will react in a particular way. For the Chinese, it is more important how tea feels in your emotions.

NORWOOD: Tea does enter you. In that sense, we do become one with the tea and the tea becomes a part of us.

ROY: That's because you are able to do something about it. You could either make it stronger by brewing it differently or by altering the temperature to make it more suitable for the moment, your state of mind. I don't think any sort of art can react in this way. You certainly cannot change how a painting is talking to you, but you can certainly change the way that tea talks to you.

ALERTNESS

ROY: As far as having an alert mind for preparing tea, I think that's precisely what you *don't* want to have. If you are totally worried about it and you are completely focused, you are too nervous, and good tea is not going to happen. It's only when you are now communicating directly with tea that you can be making adjustments without thinking about it. If everything you do with tea is from the heart, it is moving deep into your being and you don't have to worry about measuring it. When somebody is very good at making tea, he or she *wills* the tea to be this way or that way. In some way you do it without thinking.

Regarding the process of having to be completely alert and focused, *you really just need to pay attention.* You need to give the tea this moment out of the cycle of life, this one moment, and the rest of it will happen itself. The more you worry about it, the more you want to do something, the more you take away from the moment. I never really bother about it. Sometimes your best doesn't turn out to be the best. That's life. I don't allow it to bother me. I preach to everybody who will listen to me to just relax, just listen to yourself, just listen to what the tea wants. Sometimes, when I make tea for other people, I ask them to smell the aroma. I explain that the aroma tells you everything about the tea. In that regard, when you smell the tea, or taste the aromatics, it can transport you to that eighteen-hundred-meter altitude where the mist and the clouds congregate and the tea just blossoms. You know the lushness itself. It definitely tells you all this. When I drink the tea, I try to imagine the whole cycle of this tea's life—it shows you that. It's difficult to explain. Sometimes words just don't do it. But it is like the clouds and mists in Chinese paintings that made them wonder, "How could any place be like this?"

NORWOOD: My teacup is one of my principle teachers on how to be happy. If my teacup could talk it would say the same thing from one day to the next: "Happy, happy, happy. Have you forgotten you are here to be happy?" When I do forget how to be happy, it is time for another cup of tea. I was taught by my tea master how to say thank you for tea. It is by tapping the table. This was the way some wise soul said thank you to the emperor centuries ago, and the Chinese are people who have long memories.

THE TEA JOURNEY

ROY: Tea can be a messenger. Tea can take you on a journey. Tea is an intricate part of life itself. When people say they want to learn about tea, I tell them that they can't just learn about tea by drinking it. That's not enough. Eventually, you are going to find what you are going to want to learn about the poetry from that area where the tea come from, and you'll want to visit there and step on that soil where the tea comes from and get your shoes dirty. You'll want to sit in the marketplace and watch the people go by, and you'll want to eat in a local diner and get really infused with the local energy. Only after these experiences will you understand how intricate tea is. You can't just take the tea out and say to them, "This is Dragon Well tea." But you can say that it's Dragon Well tea and tell them where it came from and what that means.

NORWOOD: The Western world has had a romance with tea ever since we had our first sip. Your ancestors had tea four thousand years before my ancestors ever had their first sip, which was only four hundred years ago. Even then, they didn't just take to the tea itself. They also adopted the tea wares, the architecture, poetry, and furniture. All over Europe there was a fascination with Chinese fashion, for using beautiful things to make the tea in. That's the nature of tea. When you think of any culture that has adopted tea you are also thinking of the artworks that tea inspired there.

TEA CULTURE TODAY

ROY: There is a revival of tea culture in a positive and a negative way, especially in China, but really worldwide. Everybody thinks they know about tea, but they don't *really* know about tea. There is a new urge to learn about tea, and in China, there is a revival of tea. Everybody was drinking tea because this is the thing you do and it's a cheap beverage. Now people drink tea because they can. So people are fighting, clamoring for more expensive tea just because they can. The challenge people like me or people who really care about tea have is, Where do you maintain this balance to produce good tea? Chemicals have been a blessing, but also have brought a hell of a lot of difficulty because once farmers discover chemicals, they tend to use it and overuse them. I feel that the teas of yesteryears are probably gone; they might not ever happen again. Teas that you and I drank when we first met may never be as available again.

NORWOOD: That's right. Now you can get Tie Guan Yin only every third year.

ROY: That is because you have to do ten times the amount of work that you did fifteen years ago to get maybe twenty percent of the tea you used to get. I know a lot more about tea than I did fifteen or twenty years ago, but I feel like it's almost a losing battle. This new urge to acquire the best tea makes it less of an incentive to make better tea, because you can sell it for whatever. The tea doesn't have to be that good, because there is a new group of people who are willing to pay *anything* for it. With pollution and smog at the lower altitudes, around six hundred meters, you can't see the sky. If smog is blocking out the sun, how is the plant going to produce food? How will tea taste any good?

NORWOOD: Those air problems are a factor at the agricultural level of the countryside in today's world. It has its parallel with the cultural attitude of the people who are living in cities. I feel very strongly that urban stress has everything to do with the importance of tea in today's world. Roy, you have often said that you and I are apostles of this tea plant and that we are just its messengers. You've said the reason that anybody has shared our pleasure in tea is because in a society that is demanding more and more of people and delivering less and less, tea becomes one of those rare links to nature. That's what tea is a product of and that's what it leads us back to, and that's why we desperately need it. It doesn't make any changes in the tea drinker, perhaps, but it gives him an adjustment. He can see more clearly for a little while.

ROY: We have been saying that for about a decade, because we have been steadily getting worse, quality-wise. But the number of people who are willing to accept less for more is steadily increasing, so it's a sad stage if you have never had tea like *this* before, the way it should be.

NORWOOD: We have never equaled the Longjing.

ROY: This year's Longjing is probably the best in four or five years, and it's a shadow of what it used to be. The greatness that was achieved effortlessly not so long ago I don't think can even be achieved anymore. When the weather does not cooperate, there is very little you can do. The seasons are out of order—when it's supposed to be warm it isn't; when its supposed to rain it doesn't. Scientists can measure all they want, but the farmers know what's happening here. This is where they live and this is what they do; all good farmers are feng shui masters. They just cannot help but know where the plant is, where the sun is at the correct position, where the best air is moving through, where the best energies are. This comes from many, many generations working the land and being in tune with nature. Feng Shui teaches how to position yourself correctly, and farmers are feng shui masters. Farmers know more than anybody else when the sky is not right, heavens are not right. So people can deny all they want. They can sit in their comfortable air conditioned office and say there is no global warming; they can claim that the proof is not in yet. Everybody who is involved with tea will tell you that in the last ten years, the harvest has been worse every year. Perhaps tea is paying the price. I think farming and tea transcend national and cultural boundaries.

NORWOOD: You don't have to believe in the existence of Shen Nung, the Divine Cultivator or Immortal Farmer, who is reputed to have discovered tea. Of course, he was one of the first four emperors of China, supposedly legendary. Nobody can say for sure.

ROY: Back then, there were no written records. But you know that this is how farmers are. People who live closer to the earth just know. Now we are talking about tea as an antidote to modern excesses and how tea is not what is used to be. I think tea is not even a shadow of what it used to be.

NORWOOD: We may remember a certain Tie Guan Yin that we believe would rank higher than the one we are drinking now. But that does not detract from our enjoyment from the Tie Guan Yin that is in the cup before us.

ROY: It's not just how it tastes; it's like wine. Tea is a matter of who you are with and how the day is going. But overall, the quality of tea by any standard is certainly not what is used to be not so long ago.

NORWOOD: But it's still the closest thing we have to an antidote to an antidote to civilization and its discontents.

THE SWING OF RECOGNITION

ROY: I don't think that I am a teacher. I have certain information that may be helpful, and again, we are only the messengers.

NORWOOD: The audience wasn't there twelve years ago, it just didn't exist. In 1996, the entire tea market in the United States was less than one billion dollars. By now, in 2006, it is well over seven billion dollars. We have seen an explosion, a renaissance of tea.

Roy: And these numbers do not include sales in restaurants, because you can't really track sales in Chinese restaurants, since they don't serve coffee. They only serve tea. I challenge you to find a Chinese restaurant—no matter how bad it is—that doesn't sell some kind of tea. This is precisely what tea is—it is so much into your daily life and such a part of you that you don't even think about it. It's like your skin. You don't think about a patch of your skin, because it's a part of you. Tea is like that.

Norwood: Even Eskimos drink tea. It would be indispensable to any group in any country that I could think of. I was reading about Pygmies of the Congo not so long ago, and they were pictured drinking tea. This was an exotic novelty for them. It had come from who knows where? They would have been amazed as to where it came from! The article said they had a myth as to where it came from, but they had already learned to prepare and enjoy it, and I'll bet you would have trouble with Pygmies if you cut off their tea supply!

Roy: Yes, there has been a big swing of recognition of tea. People are no longer willing to settle for just any sort of tea. When I was a child a teabag was fine. I thought the best thing to do to tea was to add sugar and water. But until you have a chance to compare a high-quality Oolong to teabag tea with milk and sugar, you'll never know the difference. Teabags are made entirely for convenience. There is no artistry. It's a nice beverage, but you would never think about it as an art form. The complexity of the fine tea is one story, and the preparation is another story, and the multilevels of flavor and feelings is another story. No, I don't think you can get a good story from your everyday teabag.

Norwood: You just put your finger on it. Half of the pleasure of tea is in the preparation, and so you are denied that part of the pleasure if you resort to the convenience of a teabag. The pleasure of the tea doesn't end when you sip it; there is still the aftertaste. There is the sensation throughout your body. But the pleasure of the tea doesn't really end there. As a matter of fact, I believe that it's only when you have finished washing your tea equipment and put it all back in place, ready to be used again, that you have completed your tea ceremony.

ROY: Let me put it to you this way. Drinking out of a teabag is something like someone saying to a painter that from now on, you can only paint on a two-by-two-inch canvas, and you can only do ninety strokes, never more, never less. What kind of art would that be? While it could be precise and it could even be enjoyable to some people, it would certainly be no art form. The whole thing about creating art is that you are allowed to go beyond any boundary that you could ever imagine. Similarly, if you try to tell a tea maker that he must exactly measure his tea, and he must exactly measure its temperature, and he must exactly measure the steeping time, all this instruction would not allow him to feed and grow his ability to serve tea, because everything had been prearranged. There would be no meaning. In contrast, when you make tea, you should allow it to decide how it wants to go along with you.

NORWOOD: Spoken like a true Taoist.

THE MOST ENJOYABLE ASPECT OF TEA

ROY: My friendship with you has not been something that you could have looked for or found. It just had to happen. Actually, I don't think we could have stopped it from happening, despite ourselves. We've been friends in the way that tea takes its own course.

NORWOOD: That's right. When the student is ready, the teacher appears. This is a clear example of how we are taught. You needed a student, and I showed up on the spot.

ROY: Tea can be enjoyed with music and poetry and flowers, fine paintings and other works of art, but most of all, tea can be enjoyed with friends.

THE SOUL & SPIRIT OF TEA

NORWOOD: Music is supposed to be the universal language, so it must be accompanied by tea.

ROY: In the end, the most enjoyable part of having tea is when you share it with friends, especially when we make gongfu style tea. It's a perfect time to share time together without infringing on each other. We communicate without having to speak too much or trying to entertain each other, or trying to lengthen a meeting together. The tea takes its course and you follow. To me, it's perhaps more important than tasty treats or other elements like music. Tea is music without having anything played.

NORWOOD: However, when your friend shares a certain taste for luxury, it does make the tea taste better. I will never forget drinking Dragon Well tea with you on the dragon boats in Ghiangzhou to the accompaniment of classical Chinese music, with the scenery of West Lake all around us. I thought your company and that tea were unusually enjoyable. Of course, the earth is the mother of all things. The earth brings forth all things, which includes tea. So tea is one of her chthonic messages. What the earth's truths are and what the earth teaches through you is renewal. This is our earthbound way of learning. Tea not only expresses these truths, but refines them. Imagine this leaf and its tenderness just at the beginning of its youth, with all of its promise still inside plucked from that leaf and preserved. To preserve the nectar of the leaf in its natural state and to be renewed and reawakened thousands of miles away in a strange country where someone brings it together again with life giving water and nectar—this is to free something that you and I can imbibe. That is the renewal at a remove in time, and at a remove in space, which is even further symbolized here in our beloved tea plant, isn't it? That is what the leaf is teaching us. Tea is renewal.

ROY: For me, the future of tea is very clear. I know exactly where I want to go and I know exactly what I need to do. I feel like the last thirteen or fourteen years have flown by. But I am not doing what I think I am good at. I never had a chance really to spend one hundred percent of my energy devoted to the one thing that I really enjoy, which is to learn the way of tea. I want to learn many more different aspects of tea, how to make tea better, or maybe read some tea poetry, or how to grow tea better. During the Tang dynasty, tea was powdered and whipped in the bowl like they do in the Japanese tea ceremony now, and you drank the whole thing. The tea at that time was referred to as *tea congi*, because it was white-colored. I want to make that tea. In those days, you would take freshly harvested tips of the tea, soak them in water until they soften, and then strip the outer skin off until white inside. You would steam them, press and grind them. This is one of my ambitions. The future to me means going back to learn more about tea. Before I am gone from this earth, I need to buy or lease land close to a tea field. I want to feel the seasonal changes with the tea so that I can make the adjustments based on how the tea should be feeling. I am a very basic person, so I don't have any grand plans, but I do have a clear set of goals. In the Chinese thinking, you feel that the clouds and the mist are in high places, which is where the immortals live. How can the tea be bad there if that is where the immortals dwell?

NORWOOD: My own ambition is also simple. I want to go to heaven in a teacup. I found that you fill the cup with the teas to take me to heaven. One of the highest honors I have ever received was when you made me Honorary Director of your own Imperial Tea Court, here in San Francisco. I should simply not let you out of my sight. As you continue to do these things, I want to be close by and to shout encouragement, but also to drink the products and talk about it with you. It's been a wonderful ride.

ROY: The journey is so long with so much to do. No matter how bad things are, or how good things are, there is more in tea than you can ever do. So for me, there is so much more to learn. I have spent thirty years of my life pretty seriously trying to learn about tea, and I feel I can finally answer a good question once in a while.

THE SOUL & SPIRIT OF TEA

TOP 20 TEA DEFINITIONS

A Selection of Essential Terms from *The Tea Dictionary*
by James Norwood Pratt

The nomenclature and verbiage of tea is complex, colorful, and important for any serious tea aficionado, connoisseur, or entrepreneur. While it's tempting to use casual slang or personal variation on centuries-old terms, standardization of terminology includes: cupping descriptives, leaf styles, origins, and much more. Although it's all but impossible to pick the absolute most relevant or important tea definitions for a given individual or company, there are a few that must be reserved for the prime "top spot," or Top Twenty, in this case.

The World of Tea is as rich and various as that of wine, but vastly more subtle and mysterious. As our sleepy old tea trade begins to wake up in the United States, we are realizing the need for a dictionary of the worldwide language spoken in the World of Tea. Just as any devotee of fine dining must understand "Menu French," American tea lovers increasingly need to know "Tea Chinese" as well as a host of other terms variously derived from Hindi or Japanese.

Preeminent tea sage Pratt declares, "None of us knows all there is to know about tea, but to benefit the age-old Tea Society to which we all belong, let our knowledge, like our tea, be shared and our ignorance, like our thirst, overcome."

ANTIOXIDANTS: Antioxidants are any substances that prevent or slow oxidation in the body. They neutralize the damaging effects of free radicals, which are byproducts of cell metabolism. Free radicals may be likened to rust; they travel through the cells, disrupting normal cellular functioning. Such damage, it is thought, assists the body to age and causes many other ailments. Like a rust preventive and remover, antioxidants are free radical scavengers that mop up and counteract the damaging effect of these free radicals within the cells of the body.

BERGAMOT: Literally, "Prince's pear" (Turkish), bergamot is a four-meter-high citrus tree (*Citrus bergamia*) that is the source of oil of bergamot, the key aromatic ingredient of Earl Grey scented tea. Grown in Turkey, Greece, Corfu, southern Italy, and principally, today, in Sicily, bergamot produces a bitter, orangelike fruit that is not eaten fresh, but can be made into marmalades and liqueurs, although it is principally raised for the oil its rind yields for use in perfume and scenting tea.

CAFFEINE: 1, 3, 7-trimethyl-xanthine, or caffeine ($C_8H_{10}N_4O_2$), occurs in some sixty plants, including coffee, tea, mate, guarana, chocolate, and kola nuts. It is a feeble, basic, colorless compound with a slightly bitter taste, which acts as a central nervous system stimulant and a diuretic. In tea, caffeine has an important function in performing the "cream," or precipitate, which appears on the surface when a tea infusion cools. Caffeine does not play an active part in the changes taking place during manufacture. In a tea infusion, its bitter taste might possibly make up part of the briskness of the liquor. Caffeine in tea has a different effect than caffeine in coffee.

CAMELLIA SINENSIS: Literally, "Chinese camellia"—the botanical name for tea—is an evergreen shrub that grows to tree heights in some cases. There are eighty-two different species of *Camellia sinensis*, of which tea is the most complex, with three major varieties numbering almost four hundred recognized cultivars. The varieties are *Camellia sinensis var. sinensis,* known as China bush; *Camellia sinensis var. assamica*, known as Assam bush; and the commercially unimportant *Camellia irrawadiensis*, called Cambodia tea. Most cultivars fall under China bush; among many others, for instnace, Shuixian, Dahongpao, Rongui, and some several dozen others best known for producing Oolong.

CATECHINS: The primary polyphenol found in tea, catechins account for 30–40 percent of dry leaf weight. The four main catechins in green tea leaf are; Gallocatechin (GC), Epigallocatechin (EGC), Epicatechin (EC), and Epigallocatechine Gallate (EGCG). The EGCG type also gives green tea antimicrobial properties that defend the body against various food-poisoning microbes.

CHAI: A Western term for sweet spiced tea from India, where chai is known as *masala chai: masala* is Hindi for spice; *chai* is Hindi for tea. Chai is incredibly popular in India, and since the early 1990s, increasingly popular in the United States. There is no fixed recipe or preparation method for masala chai. All chai has four basic components: tea, sweetener, milk, and spices. As a secondary meaning, chai is the word for tea in Russian and many other languages. It no doubt derives from cha yeh, the Chinese words meaning tea leaf.

CTC: The crush-tear-curl method of processing black teas; with this process the leaf is made into the stronger tasting, higher-caffeine dark teas typically found in teab'ags. Not all CTC is necessarily low-grade tea, but it does provide a much more intensely flavored cup than the more delicate whole-leaf teas.

CULTIVAR: Literally, "cultivated variety," cultivar refers to any plant subvariety within a particular cultivated species that is distinguished by one or more characteristics. Thus, wine-grape cultivars include Chardonnay, Pinot Noir, Cabernet Sauvingnon, and others, while cultivars of tea include Ti Quan Yin, Shuixian, Yunnan Dayeh, Quimen, to name a few. By definition, every clone—the CR-6017 developed for Nilgiri Estates or the AV-2 widespread in Darjeeling—is a cultivar. More famous black-tea cultivars are China's Keemun and Da-Yeh, or "big leaf," from which Yunnan Black is made. Longjing and numerous other green teas are also made from specific cultivars, just as Fujian's white tea Yinzhen is made exclusively from the Da Bai, or "big white," cultivar. China's widely propagated "wild" tea strain called Jiu Keng is a recently discovered cultivar, though numerous Oolong cultivars have been known for centuries: Da Hong Pao, Ti Quan Yin, Shuixian, Rongui, Fenghuang, Dancong, Maoxie, Ti Lohan, White Rooster Crest, Qilan, Taoren, and many others.

GOLDEN TIP: Buds, and sometimes the first leaves that have picked up tea juices during the rolling process and show "hair" gummed into a mat, are called "golden tip." After fermentation and firing, these buds and first leaves, being practically devoid of chlorophyll, turn golden in color and are most desirable.

GUYWAN: Alternatively Gaiwan; in Cantonese, a method called Cha zhong, literally, "covered cup." Another Chinese invention, this simple, elegant way to prepare tea is older than the teapot. It consists of a porcelain cup that has a saucer and a lid but no handle, and the three elements are always used together. The guywan can serve as both a steeping vessel and a drinking cup. After steeping tea, it can be decanted into other cups or one can drink directly from the guywan, using the lid to restrain the leaf and keep the tea warm.

"HIGH" TEA: Decidely not the same as "Afternoon Tea," High Tea is served at the end of the day as a workingman's meal, usually of leftovers. Unlike afternoon tea, high tea consists of heavy savories such as meat and cheese as well as various kinds of desserts. In England, it is sometimes also called Yorkshire tea.

MUSCATEL: Tasting term derived from the flavor and aroma peculiar to grapes of the Muscat family, muscatel is named for the captial city and port of Oman on the Persian Gulf, and source of historic wines mentioned in the Bible and throughout the Middle East, as in Omar Khayyam and friends. Though of many subvarieties, muscat grapes have a character all their own and usually are used for sweet dessert wines. Resembling musk, *musky* is the usual dictionary definition of this term traceable well over a thousand years back in Western languages to Old Provencal as *muscadelle*. In tea, it denotes a unique muscatlike fruitiness in aroma and flavor found exclusively in the most highly prized Darleelings—usually Second Flush—when it is found at all. So rare is this taste characteristic that many American colleagues say they've never encountered it, and a Darjeeling tea estate owner said that his father congratulated him in 2003 for producing teas with the most pronounced "muscatel" flavor the father remembered since the days of the British Raj. As rare as it is unmistakable, muscatel remains a mystery even for those who have experienced its charm. One Darjeeling estate manager suggested to me it is somehow related to infestations of green fly in the gardens. Howsoever explained, muscatel is greatly to be wished for all concerned.

THE SOUL & SPIRIT OF TEA

ORANGE PEKOE (OP): This manufacturing term applies to a long, largely unbroken leaf grade that sometimes contains leaf buds that fall between Pekoe grade, the only larger unbroken grade, and Broken Orange Pekoe, the next smaller. The OP classification is often confused by consumers who mistakenly believe it refers to tea flavor, as opposed to leaf size. The name conjures up a vision of a flavory and exotic variety. Early Dutch traders seem to have used "orange" to imply Holland's ruling House of Orange.

ORTHODOX MANUFACTURE: Traditional method of tea manufacture that uses machines to mimic manual methods employed in old China. In this process, each batch of leaf is withered and then put into rollers, which bruise and shape it prior to oxidation. Following oxidation, that is, "fermentation," the leaf is fired to arrest further chemical change and preserve it free of moisture, and then is graded by leaf size. All of the world's great black teas are produced by Orthodox Manufacture, which preserves the integrity and full flavor of the leaf. It is expensive and time-consuming compared to CTC manufacture.

OXIDATION: This stage follows rolling in orthodox manufacture of black tea, when the leaf is left to oxidize. The time required for oxidation varies widely, depending on the nature of the leaf, the rolling method used, the temperature of the leaf, and the ambient atmosphere's warmth and humidity. Various chemical changes that take place during oxidation are responsible for the briskness, strength, and color of the resulting tea. The aroma of the leaf develops markedly as oxidation proceeds. The term *oxidation* has replaced the old misnomer *fermentation* to describe this process, in which, after all, nothing ferments—that is, produces alcohol.

PLUCKING TABLE: For uniform growth and ease of plucking, tea bushes on estates outside China and Japan are kept pruned to provide a waist-high flat "table." From this plucking table, in season, the tea "flushes," that is, sprouts young shoots consisting of two leaves and a bud, at predicatable intervals called "plucking rounds" so that this fresh growth may be harvested.

SHRIMP EYE: The Chinese term for the stage during boiling of water when the first tiny bubbles appear on the bottom of the kettle. After *shrimp eye* comes the *crab eye* and then the *fish eye* stage before *string of pearls* and finally, *raging torrent*.

TANNINS: "Tannins" is the now obsolete term for the polyphenol content of tea, principally catechins. The color of the infusion, its pungency, strength, color, and tartness of liquor depend largely on these "tannins" and their combination with other constituents. The term was adopted in the 1800s before it was understood that tea pholyphenols have nothing in common with tannins found in tannic acid.

TISANES: Herbal infusions, tisanes are often mistakenly referred to as herbal "teas," although containing no *Camellia sinensis* leaf. Tisanes use a variety of flowers, berries, seeds, peels, leaves, and roots of different plants, such as chamomile, ginseng, rose petals, hibiscus, peppermint, valerian, lavender, and jasmine, to name a few. Tisanes are typically caffeine-free.

WATER TEMPERATURE: Different teas require different temperatures of water: Black and Pu-Er tea need boiling water, but this will "burn" or "cook" green and white teas. For these, water should be considerably cooler at around 165–185°F (73–85°C), depending on the tea. Oolongs are best steeped in water just below boiling point, at 185-200°F (85-93°C), always depending on the particular tea. The darker the Oolong, the higher the temperature.

ALSO FROM TEA DRAGON FILMS

The Meaning of Tea

The book, *The Meaning of Tea: A Tea Inspired Journey*, explores the calm and purposeful nature of tea through the words of tea growers, tasters, entrepreneurs, shopkeepers, and scholars from eight countries. Through more than 50 interviews, these engaging characters reveal a reverence for the plant, the ceremony, the production and the distribution of tea, as well as its ability to bring peace, calm, health, friendship, and often wisdom, into their lives.

Music of Tea CD

Original world music inspired and played by the instruments of India, China, Japan, Morocco, and Europe, as well as the American folk tradition. This collection formed the original soundtrack by Joel Douek and Eric Czar for the documentary film The Meaning of Tea directed by Scott Chamberlin Hoyt. Besides sixteen soothing instrumentals with hints of natural sounds, this CD offers two additional bonus tracks: Marco Polo by Loreena McKennitt on CD, as well as an original song, "Tea, SD—Living Easy" with lyrics by Danna Rosenthal and sung by Hillary Fortin. 18 Tracks with 51 minutes of music.

Making of Tea

A short silent film that captures the art and beauty of making a "white filament" Oolong tea called Oriental Beauty. 11 minutes with original tea music.

The Meaning of Tea on DVD

Director Scott Chamberlin Hoyt travels through India, Japan, Taiwan, Morocco, England, France, Ireland, and even Tea, South Dakota. Unveiling tea's mysterious appeal, the film considers the question of whether there is any inherent "meaning" to be found in tea, particularly in an amped-up, high-tech era increasingly dominated by mass-marketing and fast food. The DVD offers Special Features including a director interview on the making of the film. Experience the Japanese Tea Ceremony; enjoy additional interviews with "Tea People"; meet the "Tea Contrarian"; and see an alternate opening and ending to the film. By visiting places where tea is still revered and by investigating its role in these societies, the film suggests the profoundly positive role tea may play in the renewal of our world. 74 minutes with 45 minutes of Special Features. Available in Multi-Language Edition.

In the Magic of the Green Mountains— on DVD

Vermont herbalists Jeff and Melanie Carpenter sold their natural products business to buy raw land and start an organic farm to grow medicinal herbs—rather than source them from half-way around the world. It is a story that is beautifully portrayed, entirely on 16mm film, and provides a glimpse into the scenic beauty of Vermont, with its gently rolling green hills. This heart-warming and uplifting lyrical documentary, reveals the unfolding journey behind the emergence of Zack Woods Herb Farm—today a reliable partner to a local community seeking sustainable, healthy living. The farmers themselves, exemplify a relationship of living wholistically with nature, that requires giving, as much as receiving. We see into their lives, the healing dimension, the changes. The unforeseen hardships, are met, with commitment, unwavering purpose, and with a touch of magic. The film is about love and partnership—about how embracing the green world, will inspire us to roll-up our sleeves, and dig our hands into the soil, to grow our own. When the mind slows down, the heart opens. 71 minutes.

In the Magic of the Green Mountains— music CD

All original music from the film, and more—23 tracks altogether. Great listening whether you're in the garden pulling weeds, or on the road traveling somewhere.

For more information please visit
TEABLOG.THEMEANINGOFTEA.COM